HOSPITALITY SECURITY

PROCEDURES, POLICIES, AND TRAINING

Bassim Hamadeh, CEO and Publisher
Mary Jane Peluso, Senior Acquisitions Editor
Alisa Munoz, Project Editor
Alia Bales, Production Editor
Jess Estrella, Senior Graphic Designer
Alexa Lucido, Licensing Manager
Natalie Piccotti, Director of Marketing
Kassie Graves, Vice President of Editorial
Jamie Giganti, Director of Academic Publishing

ISBN: 9781-79351-254-3

cognella® ACADEMIC PUBLISHING
3970 Sorrento Valley Blvd., Ste. 500, San Diego, CA 92121

HOSPITALITY SECURITY

PROCEDURES, POLICIES, AND TRAINING

FIRST EDITION

Anthony V. DiSalvatore
CPP, PSP, PCI, CFE, CLSD

cognella
SAN DIEGO

CONTENTS

I dedicate this book to those who provide inspiration and hope to all that are in need or despair. Who unselfishly give from their soul and demonstrate the fundamental basic of life, to love one another.

ACKNOWLEDGMENTS

> *"We shall never know all the good that a simple smile can do."*
>
> —Mother Teresa
> *A nun and missionary who devoted her life to caring for the sick and poor in Calcutta*

I dedicate this book to those whom I hold close to my heart—to those I carry with me wherever I go. My wonderful wife, Beth. My great children, Andriana and Remo, who have always been and always will be the driving force that inspires me to make the world a better place as they make their mark in life by enjoying the adventure and doing great things. My brother Remo—a Franciscan—who makes this world and the next better by saving one soul at a time. My brothers Joe and Fred who have raised great families. My mother, Beverly, and my father, Remo, who unselfishly devoted all they had to provide a better life to the next generation. In fact, it was my Mom who got me started in hospitality. And to where I am today.

> I recall my first experience in the hospitality world was when I was little, and my Mom would bring me with her to work. I would walk with her from hotel room to hotel room as she would perform her housekeeping duties of cleaning the room, making the bed, etc. I can remember my Mom letting me search for any tips left behind. On occasion, I would find one—although, looking back on it now, I think she may have placed a dollar bill here and there for me to find.

And to all those who have gone onto the next step of the journey. May we one day be reunited.

I also dedicate this book to the many who have influenced my life in a positive manner by their actions, words, or example when I was growing up on Lake Avenue or on the dirt road called Mohawk Avenue in the town of Clementon in the great state of New Jersey. The lessons learned and the values taught laid the foundation for the man I am today. I was raised poor—but raised right, not realizing that fact until years later, in a one bedroom/one bathroom house with my parents, three brothers, and a dog, all helping me to develop the "can do" attitude I have today.

Unfortunately, through the years, I have lost touch with many of those who were very important in my life. Some simply placed the next step of this journey of life over the last; some moved on to pursue other endeavors—like myself—leaving their roots behind. As the years have passed by at mind-numbing speed—I realize that it has been decades since I have had any contact with those who have unknowingly molded and shaped me. Hopefully, somewhere out there, they are reading this and know how special those days were to me—of living on a dirt road; running through the woods; swimming in the ponds and streams; playing pickup games of football, baseball, and soccer.

It seems like only yesterday that I left the Clementon Police Department to pursue a career with the New Jersey State Police when my former lieutenant—James Gaw of the Clementon Police Department—gave me a money clip that had the following inscribed on it, "Tony Remember Your Roots." If I can provide you with a key life lesson and words to live by—this would be in the top ten.

ABOUT THE AUTHOR

"And those who were seen dancing were thought to be insane by those who could not hear the music."

—Friedrich Nietzsche
A German philosopher, cultural critic, composer, poet, and Latin and Greek scholar

Rather than select the typical, "formal-looking" photo that is usually placed in this section of a book, I have chosen to select this photo that was taken on the hustling and bustling streets of Hoboken, New Jersey, by my brother Padre Remo, while enjoying two of my most favorite things in life—family and food! In the one square mile city of Hoboken—among other things—is the home of Frank Sinatra, the site of the first baseball game at Elysian Fields, and delicious Hoboken bread. Hoboken has the same unique feeling that I experienced in Rome, Italy, decades ago, a city maintaining a small-town feeling. When dealing with others, I try to translate this into conversations and interactions so that there is a personal connection and bond that remains long after, similar to the feeling I have when reminiscing about my previously described experience with my brother. I may not recall exactly what was discussed but remember the feeling of bonding, friendship, and love.

More importantly, this photo illustrates to me the significance of maintaining a balance between work life and family. Too many times in my past, work was all consuming and with that, came the unfortunate side effect of the inability to spend time with my family and loved ones. My heart ached being away from my children, Andriana and Remo, I missed many important milestones in their lives and, at times, was unable to be there with them during their hour of need. For example, my daughter broke her arm while on a neighbor's trampoline and due to work commitments—being thousands of miles away—I was unable to be with her at the hospital. Another example involves my son, Remo, when I was not able to attend his soccer games or be there during times that he needed his DAD. Work took up all my time as I was committed to providing for the financial needs of my family.

Over the years, I have finally been able to achieve somewhat of a semblance of balancing the two—now that my children are adults. I only wish that I was able to achieve this sooner in my career and in life. Please do me a favor and learn lessons from my experiences by remembering to spend as much time as possible with your family. Because, as I have discovered too late, you will never be able to recapture those precious years again. If there is one thing that I could do over or change, it would be to achieve a work-life balance and spend much, much more time with my children.

Anthony V. DiSalvatore, CPP, PSP, PCI, CFE, CLSD, possesses over 30 years of experience in security-related positions. He has been involved in the opening of numerous casinos, hotels, and entertainment complexes. He has been involved from the ground up on the design, implementation, and operation of various properties across the country. These properties had a total value ranging from several million dollars to billions of dollars. DiSalvatore served as a state trooper for the New Jersey State Police and received a Distinguished Service Award for actions taken.

Anthony has also been recognized for actions taken while working at large properties in South Florida, New Jersey, and New York City. DiSalvatore performed an integral role during Hurricanes Francis and Wilma in South Florida, Hurricane Sandy in New Jersey, and the largest power outage in US history in New York City by ensuring that business continuity and disaster recovery plans were executed.

He holds an associate degree in arts and science from Gloucester County College, a bachelor's degree in law justice from Glassboro State College, and master's degrees in education administration from Seton Hall University and criminal justice from Rutgers University. DiSalvatore is a member of the American Society for Industrial Security (ASIS) International; is a former vice chair of the Gaming and Wagering Protection Council; has previously held memberships in the Crime and Loss Prevention Council and Business Management and Business Continuity Council; and has been recognized by ASIS as a triple crown recipient for being a Certified Protection Professional (CPP), Physical Security Professional (PSP), and Professional Certified Investigator (PCI).

Anthony is also a Certified Fraud Examiner and Certified Lodging Security Director and has presented at numerous venues across the country. He has also been treasurer of the Las Vegas Security Chiefs' Association, the gaming subsector lead in the Department of Homeland Security Commercial Facilities Coordinating Council, and possesses a secret level clearance.

Throughout his career, DiSalvatore has always done his best and has left lasting impressions on others. The following letter received from a former general manager of a property reinforces this:

> "Hi Anthony, I know we'll see each other before you leave; however, I would like to thank you very, very much for all your hard work and particularly for the professionalism and sense of hospitality you brought to the security department. I was very sorry to hear that you've decided to leave us. Selfishly, you always hope that the best people stay with you forever; however, I am

> very happy for the great opportunity you have ahead of you ... your promotion is certainly well deserved! Please don't forget about us and know that you can always come back to us in case things don't work out, in case you have a change of heart, or in case life brings you back to AC. Thank you!"

Anthony enjoys mentoring and educating those entering the realm of the security world. He finds it rewarding to mold and guide the next generation of security officers toward their potential and provide guidance toward their career path. He finds it very rewarding to teach others to believe in themselves, their abilities, to always do the right thing, and make good life choices. He also believes that being able to impact others in a positive way and playing a part in making better lives for others, organizations, and society is instrumental in reaching the goal of making the world a better place. Doing these things is good for the soul.

Finally, Anthony believes that it is important to have positive interactions with others, wherever one is guided in life, and that it is important to leave an indelible footprint imprinted on others of the good things that were achieved. This footprint and the enduring memory of being treated with dignity and respect should remain long after one has physically moved on to the next adventure. This sense of making a difference and, more importantly, of people remembering how they were treated and how they felt their voices were heard when interacting with you is a sure sign that the needle has been moved closer towards peace and unity between individuals, groups, teams, organizations, and nations.

CHAPTER

1

OVERVIEW OF A HOSPITALITY SECURITY DEPARTMENT

"Simplicity is the ultimate sophistication."

—Leonardo da Vinci
Italian Renaissance inventor, painter, sculptor, mathematician, scientist, and writer

The concept of hospitality security has been around for a long time. The safe refuge and protection of persons and their effects goes hand in hand. *Merriam-Webster* defines hospitality as "generous and friendly treatment of visitors and guests." *Merriam-Webster* also defines hospice as "a lodging for travelers, young persons, or the underprivileged; especially when maintained by a religious order." These both exhibit the essential ingredients of the hotelier of today. The concept of hotels and hospitality was exhibited by the Greek and Roman empires when they were the dominant societies of civilization by providing travelers a place to rest, by providing accommodations, by providing thermal baths. Places for travelers to rest and find refuge continued to develop through the Middle Ages where monasteries and abbeys were among the first to regularly offer refuge. The concepts of the hospitality industry and hospitality security continued to develop through the ages to where it is today and will continue to develop and morph to keep pace with the ever-changing rules and **norms** of society.

Personally, I have always thoroughly enjoyed my role and experiences working in various hospitality security settings. A key role of a hospitality security professional is to offer superior guest service while also providing a safe and secure environment for all. Interjecting these concepts into the hospitality security realm, where guests visit properties for a variety of reasons, including rest and relaxation, can, now and again, be daunting. At times, the hospitality security professional may wrestle with the concept of providing superior guest service and, under certain circumstances, making a decision and taking action involving a guest. For example, this may happen when a guest exhibits unacceptable behavior which impacts the safety and security of others in a negative manner, requiring action to be taken by the hospitality security professional. Proper training and selection of staff aid in recognizing these types occurrences and in making correct decisions.

Goals and Purpose

The following is a result of my many years dedicated to developing and establishing Hospitality Security Departments in the United States. Hospitality Security Departments have historically been viewed as nonrevenue generating cost centers that were necessary to provide for the safety and security of patrons, guests, employees, and assets of the company. Over the years, there has been a paradigm shift from hospitality security being one dimensional—mainly providing protection—to being multidimensional—taking on additional roles and responsibilities. Besides providing for the safety and security of the guests, employees, and company assets, the goals and purpose of the Hospitality Security Department also include the following:

- **Superior customer service**: This has become an integral part of the functions of a professional Hospitality Security Department. So much so, that when selecting hospitality security personnel, persons who have the aptitude and ability to perform their duties in this manner is essential. The focus on blending the two has made customer service synonymous with hospitality security. At times, top-level executives have tried to reinvent the wheel and focus on changing the name of the Hospitality Security Department and representatives to something relating to guest service, i.e., guest relations agent, guest service officer, etc. Sometimes, the uniform worn is not clearly identifiable as belonging to a security representative, which can have a negative result and impact on the patrons of a property who may become confused and agitated when a Hospitality Security Department representative is needed. Remember—security by any other name is still security.
- **Safety committee**: Many times, the leader of the Hospitality Security Department will be responsible for being the champion of the safety committee. These duties include conducting monthly meetings, tracking accidents and incidents, documenting safety inspections, implementing safety programs, etc. An effective and robust safety program will have a positive impact on the education of employees on how to safely perform their job duties—which should result in a reduction in employee accidents and associated costs.
- **Risk management**: When responsible for this area, the Hospitality Security Department leader will address calls from guests and patrons who have claims of illness, injury, or some other mishap that has occurred. The importance of a fact-written hospitality security incident report that answers who, what, when, where, why, and how, in conjunction with CCTV coverage, are most useful when addressing matters in this area.
- **Valet**: Responsibility for this area involves setting the tone for the guest experience by greeting the guest, providing a fond farewell, and acquiring and returning guest vehicle keys and the vehicles associated with them. Generally, this involves a three-part valet

parking ticket with one part being issued to the guest, one kept with the vehicle keys, and one kept with the vehicle. The vehicle is parked in a numbered parking spot that is under the care and control of the property. The parking spot should be recorded on the ticket attached to the vehicle key and placed in a secured area on a key holder associated with the parking spot number. The valet parking ticket should display words to the effect that "the customer agrees to inspect the vehicle prior to leaving the property. The property is not responsible for any items left in the vehicle and will not accept possession of any items. Claims of damage or loss must be reported to the Hospitality Security Department prior to the vehicle being taken from the property."

- **Transportation**: In the past, as a leader in hospitality security, I have been responsible for this area and regulating the traffic flow into and out of the property roadways, parking garages, and overflow parking areas. This involved detailed planning, the hiring of additional personnel, working with police officers, and opening and closing of parking areas and garages. If you are ever in this position, it is a good practice to color and number code the parking areas and the vehicles that provide service to them. This information should be given to patrons who utilize the property transportation system via a ticket that contains the corresponding information.
- **Manager on duty**: To be effective in this position, the skills a person possess should include the following: the ability to be an active listener, an excellent communicator, and an analytical thinker, as well as provide superior guest service. The effective and professional hospitality security leader has all of these attributes and many more, which are applied routinely in the performance of the duties involved in leading the Hospitality Security Department.

As you can see, to be an effective leader in the hospitality security environment of today, a person must be able to multitask, be a diplomat, be part father confessor (similar to my brother, a Catholic priest in Hoboken, New Jersey), be part policeman, etc. Having a capable, detail-oriented, and responsible person as the leader of the hospitality security team—who encompasses the previously mentioned roles—should have a positive impact on the bottom line of any property. By being proactive and taking a hands-on approach, the hospitality security leader should realize a significant monetary savings to the property which has the same impact of generating revenue. The hospitality security leader must also constantly make good decisions and provide a safe and secure environment. These are but a few of the many things that a leader of the Hospitality Security Department should do to provide patrons with a sense of safety and security. This, in turn, will encourage everyone to come back and visit the property, ensuring the longevity, success, and livelihood of the property and its employees.

Communication and Etiquette

Some of the most important areas to patrons and guests of a property include the feeling of safety and security. Many times, surveys are sent out to the guests and patrons of a property that include a question pertaining to safety and security. I have been told, in the past, that this is one of the key drivers that determines if people will visit or return to a property. That is one reason why it is of paramount importance that the leader of the Hospitality Security Department does everything possible to ensure that the security team is well trained to provide a safe and secure environment to all patrons, guests, employees, and assets. This is demonstrated by providing protection from situations that could jeopardize the welfare and security of the patrons, guests, and employees of a property. Remember that even though hospitality security representatives are not members of law enforcement, they do have the authority and right to protect the property and its occupants.

To provide for this feeling of safety and security, hospitality security representatives need be vigilant in their observations, accurate in their reporting, and respond accordingly to situations in a professional, courteous manner while abiding by all policies, procedures, rules, regulations, ordinances, and the law. Members of the hospitality security team demonstrate this by being available at all times—even when on break. This especially holds true in the event of emergencies, such as fire, power outages, etc. When an emergency arises while a hospitality security representative is on break, and the emergency is broadcast over the two-way radio, the hospitality security representative should return to duty as soon as possible. This is one reason why it is so important that hospitality security representatives listen to their two-way radios at all times. A member of the hospitality security leadership team will make the decision when such orders should be given.

Another key component that is essential for the positive perception of any Hospitality Security Department is the ability of members of the hospitality security team to be able to effectively communicate with patrons, guests, and employees in a professional, courteous manner while exhibiting good manners and following the rules of etiquette. This may be difficult, at times, when a hospitality security representative has numerous contacts with the public and is asked the same question over and over again, for example, "Where is the nearest restroom?" Each time any question is asked it should be responded to with enthusiasm while being mindful of body language and tone of voice. The response should include a smile, eye contact, an upbeat inflection of speech spoken in a clear audible manner. The response should not include eye rolling, sighing, mumbling, looking down at the ground, ignoring the person asking the question, etc. When discourteous treatment of patrons, guests, and employees occurs, it automatically lowers the perception of professionalism of the Hospitality Security Department.

It is important that the hospitality security team is trained and remembers to practice basic courteousness at all times. This can be especially effective when handling or addressing situations involving patrons, guests, or employees. Handling and addressing situations may be a major difficulty or it can be routine. This is determined by how effectively a hospitality security representative evaluates a situation, addresses the people involved, anticipates potential situations that may arise from any action taken—or not taken—and has a plan to address them should they develop.

One of the essential steps that must be adhered to is to give the patron, guest, or employee the opportunity to comply voluntarily with any direction from a hospitality security representative. Regardless of how minor or routine a situation may seem to someone handling them in the role of a hospitality security representative, to the person involved, it may seem like a major ordeal. One way of increasing the chances of a positive outcome in any situation is to suggest the desired course of action to be taken by the person involved without providing an ultimatum. For example, suggest that someone get some fresh air and then come back to the property rather than stating that he or she should get out now or be evicted. When situations are addressed in this manner, the odds are that the desired outcome will have a greater chance of occurring more easily.

If it becomes necessary to remove a patron from a property, it is best to do so with as little disruption as possible. The other guests at the property should not be disrupted any more so by the removal than by the behavior exhibited by the person who is being removed. A simple suggestion that the person go outside and get some air may suffice. If all other options have been exhausted, and it becomes necessary to physically remove someone, only the minimum amount of assistance from hospitality security representatives that is necessary to remove the person is permitted. Remember that this is a last resort and that it is always better to give people options instead of backing them into a corner. Any time a person perceives that he or she is backed into a corner, bad behavior may result.

Innovative Ideas and Methods

As a Hospitality Security Department leader, I have always sought out innovative ideas and methods to improve the overall performance, morale, and effectiveness of the team. For example, when extended hospitality security services were requested to safeguard an area, room, etc., I proposed to charge the individual or group for every hour the services were used and that the revenue be accounted for in the hospitality security budget. This helped to move the needle from hospitality security as a nonrevenue generating source to one that could demonstrate and produce flow-through dollars to the bottom line for the property.

Other areas to be on the lookout for include the latest technology and innovative advances in the security field that could prove useful to the hospitality security team. One such example is electronic key management systems. Electronic key management systems increase the effectiveness of conforming to rules and regulations and act as a workforce multiplier by providing the ability to do more with less hospitality security personnel. This, in turn, has a positive impact on the Hospitality Security Department's budgetary bottom line.

The way an electronic key management system works is that keys are assigned to users, and the number of users needed to access a key is programmed into the system. Keys are accessed and returned at the key storage unit by providing any or all or the following: access code; identification card; or a biometric measure, such as a fingerprint. Since hospitality security personnel do not need to be involved in the issuance and return of keys, electronic key management systems provide the opportunity to reduce staffing levels and enable hospitality security personnel to focus on other duties.

A neat bit of technology that I had uncovered and utilized over the years was a rechargeable flashlight that could recharge in only 90 seconds. These flashlights recharged without the use of batteries of any kind due to a fancy ultracapacitor energy storage system. This flashlight could also be set to strobe and high beam and could have a cone placed over the light so that it could be used to direct traffic.

Two other examples of technology that proved to be useful to Hospitality Security Departments that I have had the pleasure to lead were handheld electronic devices used to verify identification and guard tour systems. The electronic handheld device is useful to verify identification to ensure that it is authentic and that the person is of the legal age to enter an area that has age restrictions and also to consume alcohol. My preference in regard to this type of device has always been to keep it simple. Basically, it should be programmed to display a large red "X" if the identification is invalid or the age on the identification swiped through the machine is under the acceptable age. A large green check mark should appear if the identification swiped through the machine is valid and the person is of the acceptable age.

The electronic guard tour system has proved to be useful to track dates, times, and who inspected a location. This system is designed to record and track this information when it makes contact with a physical preprogrammed checkpoint. When tours are completed, the information can be downloaded as a report and reviewed to ensure that all critical and assigned areas were inspected. This is useful when conducting investigations that involve damage to property incidental to a break-in, vandalism, etc., because it helps to determine a window of opportunity of when the incident occurred. This allows the investigation of the incident to focus on a specific timeframe by determining when the area of interest was last patrolled by a hospitality security representative and when the event was reported or discovered. When selecting this type of product, I have always found that selecting one that is very durable to be the best choice. Otherwise, the device can be susceptible to damage if dropped, gets wet, or is driven over by a golf cart—which, believe or not, has actually happened.

Technology can greatly assist any Hospitality Security Department, but it cannot replace its greatest and most essential component, the personnel who comprise the hospitality security team. Proper training, having the tools and equipment to perform at an optimum level, being treated with dignity and respect are the essential ingredients needed for the morale, effectiveness, and retention of hospitality security personnel.

Throughout my career, I have been involved in the design, installation, and operation of Hospitality Security Departments at various venues across the country. My goal has always been to do my best and to demonstrate the value of any security department that I was responsible for in the field, driven by the economy, safety concerns, and the protection of others. At brand-new properties that are built from scratch, it is important to remember that everything that is needed for the Hospitality Security Department needs to be ordered, built, designed, etc.—even paper clips. In the event that operational equipment is needed or a project must be undertaken, it increases the chances of having it approved if the following is outlined, explained, and discussed with leadership.

Return on investment—ROI—of the implementation of a project or equipment should be clearly explained to leadership. Return on investment is used to explain the benefit and profit that a project or equipment will bring to the property. It answers the question, "What are we getting for our money?" Be careful not to exaggerate or embellish the ROI; you may be held accountable for your projected savings in the hospitality security budget.

Other items to discuss and explain to leadership are the possible deterrent and displacement effects a project or piece of equipment may have on those who have bad intentions—such as criminal activity. Deterrence can be explained in the following manner, people will not commit an act, such as criminal activity, because they are afraid of being caught and of the punishment associated with the act. Whereas, displacement will relocate, or displace, undesirable acts—such as criminal acts—to another location away from the property.

Other areas of importance that should be reviewed with members of the leadership team include any ongoing operational costs, staffing, training, maintenance, life cycle of system, replacement costs, etc. These should be thoroughly discussed so that the leadership team can make an informed decision regarding the request for security equipment or projects. Remember that one of the first questions that will probably be asked is, "Is this a want or a need?" Be sure to answer honestly and to have facts to support your response. Usually, if the answer to the question is that it is a "want,"the request will not be approved. However, if the answer to the question is that it is a “need,” there will generally be additional discussions during which you will have the opportunity to present the facts and explain why it is needed.

When addressing whether equipment or a project is a want or a need, it should be tied into the safeguarding, protection, security, and safety of the patrons, guests, employees, and assets of the property. Many times, projects and equipment go hand in hand during the construction of new properties. For example, various types of equipment are available that provide layers of protection. The scope of the project involving the installation of this equipment should also be included in the communications, meetings, and discussions with members of the leadership team. Prior to meeting with leadership and the decision-makers, the following information regarding the equipment or system should be obtained and available in a manner that is easy to understand. This includes the specifications, life cycle, maintenance cycle, and life expectancy of the equipment or system. This will aid in determining the ROI and enable budgetary planning of maintenance and replacement costs.

It should be explained to members of the leadership team that there is no one particular process or method that is one-hundred-percent effective in the protection of any asset. The best approach is to implement layers of protection that become increasingly more difficult to defeat as one gets closer to an asset. For example, when protecting an area containing a valuable asset, there should be protocol and procedures in place in addition to CCTV, access control on the doors leading into and out of the area, utilization of mantraps, etc. These protective measures should increase in difficulty to bypass as one gets closer to the valuable asset. The methods and processes of protection should be reviewed and discussed with members of the leadership team pertaining to exactly what the needs are and what the expectations are so that there are not any surprises when the equipment is installed, processes are implemented, and systems are activated.

It is important to establish good communications with vendors who work on any of your security equipment, systems, etc. Whenever possible, it is best to have only one vendor responsible for a particular piece of equipment or system, the reason being that when a vendor other than the vendor who installed a piece of equipment or a system is contacted to work on the system, the vendor will generally have no idea what the previous concerns or issues were and will have to do a general diagnosis instead of a specific one—which will take time and cost money. Then, worst-case scenario, over the course of time, if multiple vendors are used and multiple repairs or adjustments are made, vendors may point fingers at each other for any issues that may arise. This is why, whenever possible, make one vendor responsible for any improvements, upgrades, or repairs on any equipment or systems. It allows you to develop a good rapport with the vendor, is cost effective, and makes it easier to address and resolve any issues that are encountered with equipment or systems.

A Security Operations Center is Critical

The following is a brief overview of one of the most critical areas in the Hospitality Security Department. The Hospitality Security Operations Center is the nerve center of the Hospitality Security Department. The role of the Hospitality Security Operations Center is similar to that of a conductor of an orchestra. Hospitality security representatives who operate in this area are the maestros of the security operation in relation to the tempo at which personnel are dispatched to scenes and incidents are addressed. The Hospitality Security Operations Center is usually informed of incidents by the telephone or two-way radio. Many times, the Fire Command Center and other life-safety systems are maintained in the Hospitality Security Operations Center. It is important that a hospitality security representative ensures that all are in working order at all times. Any time that any part of this area is not operating properly, a member of the hospitality security leadership team should be notified immediately.

Many times, alarms and CCTV cameras are viewable by the Hospitality Security Operations Center. When this is the case, areas such as elevators, parking garages, exit doors of the property, etc., can be viewed which aids in the protection and safety of patrons, guests, and employees. This is also beneficial when it comes to monitoring and responding to the activation of intrusion devices, such as door sensors. When programmed accordingly and activated, the CCTV camera at the location of the intrusion device or door sensor will automatically provide coverage of the area. This enables the area to be viewed and decisions to be made instantly, resulting in the appropriate **response** without jeopardizing the safety of the hospitality security team.

Another area that unites technology with the Hospitality Security Operations Center is combining emergency call box alerts with a CCTV system. Often, emergency call boxes are placed in garages or other areas of a property. When the push button is activated on the emergency call box, an immediate voice communication is established with the Hospitality Security Operations Center. When this occurs, it specifies the location of the emergency call box in conjunction with a view of the person at the emergency call box; this enables the Hospitality Security Operations Center to quickly evaluate the situation and swiftly take appropriate action.

For those properties that have elevators, the following system should be implemented to provide the utmost care and safety for those who operate and use the elevator. An emergency call button should be clearly marked inside of the elevator that, when activated, provides the user with immediate voice communication with the Hospitality Security Operations Center. A fixed CCTV camera should be installed between the ceiling and the wall in the back corner of the elevator facing toward the elevator doors. When the emergency button is activated, the Hospitality Security Operations Center is able to immediately speak with and view the person in the elevator and take appropriate action.

The previous examples of the use of technology demonstrate the synergy created that enables the Hospitality Security Operations Center to quickly evaluate a situation and swiftly take the appropriate action without the delay of dispatching security personnel to the location of the event to gather information and facts. This force multiplier effect allows the roles of many to be completed by a few and provides for a safer environment for patrons, guests, employees, and the company assets. This is one of those situations where it is a win-win for everyone. By providing a safe and secure environment, security financial resources that would have been needed for staffing can be utilized in other areas like training.

Guidelines for Team Development

The next chapters will provide the nuts and bolts needed for the operation of a Hospitality Security Department. However, the following are guidelines and suggestions that can be utilized to provide an environment that is conducive to developing an "us" and "we" mindset instead of a "they and "them" mindset between those who are on the front lines of the Hospitality Security Department and hospitality security leaders.

- It is important that everyone be treated with dignity and respect.
- There should be a free flow of ideas and suggestions without the fear of reprisals or being criticized.
- Communication should be encouraged between all levels of the Hospitality Security Department, and credit should be given where credit is due.
- When someone does a great job, has a tremendous idea, or has a new, innovative way of improving the **effectiveness** or efficiency of the Hospitality Security Department, it should be embraced, implemented, and not hidden away.
- There should not be selective enforcement of rules, regulations, policies, guidelines, and procedures. They should be applied and enforced in a consistent manner throughout the property and within the Hospitality Security Department at every level—from the leader of the department to the newest member who may have been hired 24-hours ago.

A strict adherence to an open-door policy should occur—in fact, at one Hospitality Security Department of which I had the honor to be the leader—I moved my office, desk, and file cabinets outside of the entrance of the Roll Call Room and gave my large office to my investigators. This is the only exception when I did not completely abide by having an open-door policy, the reason being that I did not actually have a door. My "office" was located in the general hospitality security administrative area at the entrance of the Hospitality Security Department's Roll Call Room.

Take the time to experience the life of the security personnel who are on the front lines of the department. Stand side-by-side with those posted on stationary posts, and walk the property with those performing roving duties. Dress in the same uniform that is worn by those whom you are working side-by-side with; this will provide a real flavor of a day-in-the-life of those who are the first line of protection of the property. Only in this way, will you understand the hospitality security positions through their eyes. The amount of useful information gathered by performing this exercise and the comradery it develops can be the building blocks used to provide great reinforcement for developing a team instead of an operating department. This is also helpful in determining and identifying upcoming training topics and areas that need more attention to detail, tools, and equipment.

Afterwards, you may take into consideration some ergonomic measures that could be helpful to the hospitality security team. For example, posts that are on a hard surface like stone, slate, concrete, etc., could be moved to a carpeted area, or an antifatigue mat could be provided. Perhaps, posts that are out of the public view or in areas where there is no impact on whether the hospitality security representative on the post is sitting or standing could be provided with a padded chair, affording security personnel the option of sitting or standing at the post.

Likewise, it is important as the leader of the Hospitality Security Department to work side-by-side with the leaders of the department and ascertain what is the motivational force that produces excellence. Are there any ideas or processes that could be developed or improved? Ask if there is anything that you could do better though you may not get an accurate response. Probably a better way to phrase that question would be, "What would you do if you were the leader of the Hospitality Security Department?" Remember to really, really listen to the responses and comments while observing the body language of those who share these things with you. Respond by providing encouragement, being honest, and taking action on getting things done. In this way, all will know that you talk the talk but, more importantly, walk the walk.

If I could provide words of advice for those making the transition into the realm of hospitality security, it would be to not focus on what you were and what you did. Rather, the focus should be on who you are, what you are doing, and what you are planning to do. We all know of someone one who recalls his or her greatest high school sports achievements as if they were yesterday when, in actuality, they occurred many, many years ago.

This holds true for everyone whether it is in regard to one's personal or professional life. Always set goals to improve and be better in your passion and in your life. Only in this way, will you be able to live in the present and not get caught in the trap of living in the past or the other entanglement of "someday" x, y, or z will happen. If timelines and timetables are not established, the plans of the future usually never become a reality. For example, this reminds me of the person who buys a car that he or she is going to "fix up one day," and before you know it, ten years have gone by, and weeds are growing out of the engine compartment. By living in the present and establishing timetables and dates of when projects and goals are to be completed and achieved, you and the hospitality security team will flourish and exceed all expectations.

In my opinion, by embracing these actions, your team will make the leap from being a Hospitality Security Department to being a hospitality security team which will genuinely enjoy its work environment and take pride in its performance, the team, and themselves. In conclusion of this chapter, I would like you to keep the following in mind. First, hospitality security personnel are your most valuable asset. Hospitality security equipment can be changed and replaced without having an impact on the dynamics of the Hospitality Security Department and the esprit de corps of the team. The way hospitality security personnel interact, support, and energize one another is a major factor in establishing—and sustaining—a great hospitality security team. Second, as the leader, it is your duty to always bring your "A" game, constantly have your finger on the pulse of the department, be approachable, and always treat others with dignity and respect. And last but not least remember that the most important elements in the successful operation of any Hospitality Security Department include the selection of the best qualified candidates, training, having the tools and equipment needed to perform its duties, developing a sense of trust among the team, and performing the basics with brilliance.

Discussion Questions

1. Explain how technology can act as a workforce multiplier in a hospitality security arena.
2. Explain the meaning of the acronym ROI.
3. What is deterrence?
4. What are the most valuable assets of a Hospitality Security Department?
5. What is displacement?
6. What are the goals and purpose of the Hospitality Security Department?
7. Explain what you believe to be the most import aspects of the Hospitality Security Department.

CHAPTER

2

THE IMPORTANCE OF HOSPITALITY SECURITY STANDARD OPERATIONAL PROCEDURES, POLICIES, AND TRAINING

"There's one thing stronger than all the armies in the world, and that is an idea whose time has come."

—Victor Hugo
A French poet, novelist (Les Misérables), *and statesman of the Romantic Movement*

Hospitality security standard operational procedures, policies, and training are the foundation of any Hospitality Security Department. These procedures and policies are the equivalent of a playbook for the hospitality security team. Training translates into the reviewing, learning, and the embodiment of these essential documents to the extent that they are embraced, demonstrated, and performed during interactions with patrons, guests, and employees. Only when these crucial areas are ingrained into the DNA of all members of the Hospitality Security Department will the team be capable of performing all tasks, duties, and assignments with a high degree of confidence and consistency. The execution of the hospitality security standard operational procedures and policies is paramount in providing a safe and secure environment for the patrons, guests, employees, and assets of the property.

Keep the Team Informed

There are various methods that I have used in the past to keep security teams abreast of the standard operational procedures and policies of the department. They include the following:

- When possible, every preshift briefing should include a standard operational procedure or policy to be reviewed and discussed. This helps to generate discussion and communication between all members of the team, which can be further reviewed with security team members by the security leadership team while making its rounds to the various posts. This also provides reinforcement of the current procedures, policies, and practices of the security team.
- Posting of the key elements of the standard operational procedure or policy on the security assignment sheet that is distributed to all members of the hospitality security team at the preshift briefing. This communication should coincide with the procedure or policy that is reviewed during the preshift briefing for that day and contain other pertinent information regarding activities and events that are scheduled or that the team needs to be aware of.
- Hospitality security leadership meetings should be conducted on a periodic basis. During these meetings, events, incidents, policies, and procedures should be reviewed and discussed. A determination should be made regarding the revision of any standard operational procedure or policy based upon the incidents and events under review. Also, topics for training should be discussed and approved based upon recent property incidents, hospitality national incidents, and areas in which the hospitality security leadership team determines that training is needed.
- Hospitality Security Department meetings should be conducted on a periodic basis. When possible, I always liked to have monthly departmental meetings with each shift one hour prior to the start of the shift. Items on the agenda included standard operational procedures, policies, training, open discussions, and the recording of questions, concerns, or suggestions from the hospitality security team. These items were gathered from each shift departmental meeting and compiled into a list. At the next meeting, all of the items on the list were reviewed with answers and responses to all of the shifts.
- At various times, which included leadership meetings, departmental meetings, and preshift briefings, calibrating the Hospitality Security Department's thinking was always an essential element in ensuring the consistency of the performance of the security team regarding procedures and policies. Calibrated thinking basically gets everyone on the same page. For example, if there was a dress code policy or procedure that needed clarification, photos would be exhibited, and the questions would be presented after each photo, "Acceptable or unacceptable?" After which, the answer would be provided with an explanation. These practices worked well and should aid in clarifying many types of standard operational procedures and policies.

Why are standard operational procedures important? Let me ask another question, "If you were going to have a dental or medical procedure, would you have it performed by someone who 'kind of' knew what he or she was doing, was told by someone a couple of years ago how to do it, or did not have a clear procedure in mind before the actual dental or medical procedure was to be performed?" I know I would look for someone else.

The following is a true story that involved a friend of mine, which kind of demonstrates this point. My friend was going to have an elective medical procedure performed and discovered that it could be done for a lot less money in another country. When I found out about it, my response was words to the effect, "What are you kidding me? Get it done in this country (the United States)." My reasoning was that in another country there were no certainties on the person's background, training, who would perform the procedure, etc. Thank goodness, my friend had the procedure performed in the United States where all of the answers to these questions were known, and the medical procedure was a tremendous success. This story helps to illustrate that the hospitality security standard operational procedures must be known and understood by all members of the Hospitality Security Department. Having a general idea or "kind of" knowing what to do, is not good enough.

Demonstrate and Reinforce the Importance of Procedures, Policies, and Training

To demonstrate and reinforce the importance of hospitality security standard operational procedures, policies, and training, the highest-ranking members of the property and the Hospitality Security Department should place emphasis on them and their importance and significance to the successful operation of the property and department. When this is done, the importance and significance of these documents trickles down and is absorbed by the members of the property and the Hospitality Security Department. On the other hand, if the importance and significance of the standard operational procedures, policies, and training are not stressed by the leaders of the property and Hospitality Security Department, they will less likely be adhered to. This could result in chaos in the form of inconsistent enforcement, training, and the abandonment of specific procedures. This could have a negative impact on the perception of or the actual protection and safety of the property's guests, employees, and assets. This could also result in civil or legal action against the property for failure to safeguard, protect, etc., the occupants, guest valuables, and assets of the property.

Standard operational procedures are important for many more reasons. They provide instructions on how to perform a certain operation within the Hospitality Security Department while applying a consistent standard. These should include detailed, specific information and, if necessary, step-by-step instructions and checklists that are easy for members of the Hospitality Security Department to follow. If the procedures are formatted in this manner, they also provide the possible advantage of reducing mistakes. This is helpful for retraining or disciplinary purposes when addressing situations if a mistake does occur. In these circumstances, the person who made the mistake must have the information about where the error occurred reinforced by a member of the hospitality leadership security team. The team member explains the proper way to perform a specific function or duty and ensures that it is clearly spelled out in black and white in the hospitality security standard operational procedures while stressing its adherence for the safety and security of patrons, guests, employees, and company assets.

Hospitality security standard operational procedures should be approved, authorized, and written by the leader of the Hospitality Security Department because of his or her in-depth knowledge of the procedures, policies, and the structure of the department. They should be kept as simple as possible, written in a manner that is clear and easy to understand. To ensure that the hospitality security standard operational procedures are written in this manner, it is best to have other members of the hospitality security leadership team, who are knowledgeable in the area, review the procedures pertaining to their area of expertise. Another benefit of having the hospitality security standard operational procedures reviewed in this manner is that the hospitality security team will be actively involved in the process. This will result in the likelihood that the hospitality security team will be more likely to buy-in, support, and enliven the procedures since all will have been given the opportunity to be part of the process and know that their voices and ideas have been heard and acted upon.

After the previous steps in the development or review of the hospitality security standard operational procedures have been completed, I always like to have someone who is unfamiliar with the areas and topics read and review them to see if they understand them. Many times, after the review, the hospitality security standard operational procedures will have items added or removed to make them easier to understand.

Remember that when creating, updating, or reviewing the hospitality security standard operational procedures to ask the question, "Why are we doing this; is it necessary?" Sometimes, you will come to the realization that, perhaps, parts of, or an entire procedure, may not be necessary. One of the final steps that I like to do prior to finalizing a new procedure or revision is to have someone who is unfamiliar with the area that is being addressed actually go out in the field and perform the procedure. This should be performed exactly as it is written in the drafted version. In the past, when I have accompanied someone who was performing this task, if he or she gave me funny looks or asked a lot of questions, I knew there was more work to be done, and I would take copious notes for the next revision.

When the updated version was completed, the previous process would be implemented and, once again, I encouraged feedback and any suggestions that would make the hospitality security standard operational procedure easier to use and understand. After the final review of the procedure has been completed, tested for ease of use, and verification has been completed to ensure that mandatory, regulatory, and any other requirements have been fulfilled should the hospitality security standard operational procedure move onto the next step of the process. The final review of the hospitality security standard operational procedures, policies, self-imposed standards, and training should be conducted by the property's legal department and executive team. Only after this review has been completed and approved by the property's legal department and executive team should these procedures be implemented.

One of the main goals when implementing the hospitality security standard operational procedures is that members of the hospitality security team should have a solid grasp and understanding of every step that is contained in them and why they must be performed consistently in the correct manner. The rationale for performing the procedures correctly include regulatory, mandatory, and legal reasons. The standard operational procedures provide for the safety and well-being of the occupants of the property and provide protection of the company assets. It is always a good practice to include an explanation of the "whys" when explaining and presenting the procedures or any time something needs to be done. Personally, I have found that when an explanation is provided to myself, or others, on the "why" something is done or needs to be performed, it is easier to get behind and support an idea, concept, or procedure. This simple communication allows for any idea, concept, or procedure to gain traction and momentum, which usually leads to its successful development, implementation, and execution.

Create, Review, and Update

The hospitality security standard operational procedures should be created, reviewed, and updated as needed. For example, there may be circumstances that arise that call for the immediate creation and implementation of a hospitality security standard operational procedure for the Hospitality Security Department. If this type of situation is encountered, it is recommended that the previous steps listed be adhered to. There is nothing worse than a procedure that is poorly written, confusing, is frequently reissued due to revisions, or does not adequately address a situation, process, etc., because it was hastily written and implemented.

Hospitality security standard operational procedures are living documents; they need to remain current to be useful, especially where technology is involved. The procedures should be reviewed systematically at least every twelve months to ensure that they meet the needs of the Hospitality Security Department or if a procedure(s) is even needed at all. When revised, it is important to put in the date of revision on the procedure(s) and to keep the old copy of the procedure(s) that was revised. This is useful for legal and performance issues to determine what procedure(s) was in effect at the time that an incident, event, emergency, or crisis occurred.

Remember that the standard operational procedures, policies, self-imposed standards, industry standards, and training will probably be examined during a civil, criminal, or legal action. The legal standard of care is established based upon a variety of factors, including statutory requirements, industry standards, and self-imposed standards. Self-imposed standards are policies, procedures, rules, and regulations that a property determines should be followed during the normal operation of the property. If these self-imposed standards are not followed and someone is injured as a result, your property could have exposure to liability.

This is one reason why all standard operational procedures, polices, self-imposed standards, and training should be reviewed and approved by the Legal Department and executive team of the property. Additionally, hospitality security leaders should keep abreast of the latest technologies, best practices, industry trends, court cases, and laws to ensure that the hospitality security standard operational procedures, policies, self-imposed standards, and training provide sufficient direction, guidance, and protection to those who use them.

Discussion Questions

1. How often should hospitality security standard operational procedures and policies be reviewed and/or updated, and why is it important to do so?
2. Why are standard operational procedures and policies important?
3. What is calibrated thinking, why is it important, and provide an example.

4. In what manner should hospitality security standard operational procedures and policies be written?
5. Explain the possible implications if best practices, procedures, and training are not established and/or adhered to.
6. Explain why the highest-ranking members of the property and the Hospitality Security Department should stress the importance of policies, procedures, and training.

CHAPTER

3

STANDARD OPERATIONAL PROCEDURES

"Before beginning, plan carefully."

—Marcus Tullius Cicero
An Ancient Roman statesman, orator, lawyer, and philosopher

When developing this chapter, I was torn between providing general guidelines on security procedures or providing detailed procedures that simulate the real thing. As you will see, I have elected to take the approach of providing procedures that simulate real situations rather than provide generalities. My reasoning is that when I think back to when I first started in this field decades ago—procedures were basically vague, general, nonspecific, generic guidelines that required lots of energy and effort to ensure that what was being said, was being heard and that what was being heard, was being said.

Another reason why I have elected to take this approach is that I have been involved in numerous openings over the past couple of decades, ranging in value from hundreds of millions of dollars to billions of dollars. From the knowledge learned through these experiences, I wanted to compose a resource tool that is useful to those who are in the process of developing and opening a property and for those that are looking to "tweak," review, or revise their current standard operational procedures. I have learned a great many things over the years regarding the importance of standard operational procedures and hope that you may be able to benefit from these experiences.

One of the key elements that I have learned is that strict adherence to policy and procedures are the foundation which a successful Hospitality Security Department relies upon to be effective and efficient in any organization. The following procedures should provide a good pathway to the road for success and address many areas of those associated with the operation of hospitality security programs. Remember that procedures are living documents and should be reviewed and updated at least every twelve months. When revised, it is important to put in the date of revision on the procedure and to keep the old copy of procedure that was revised.

This is useful for legal, criminal, civil, and performance issues to determine what procedure was in effect at the time that an incident, event, emergency, or crisis occurred.

You may wonder how a standard operational procedure comes into existence. Usually, the spark that begins the life of a standard operational procedure is an event or incident that occurs in the industry. These incidents or events can range from being a single isolated incident or event at one location or could involve many incidents or events at many different locations. Another way that a standard operational procedure is born is as a result of a risk assessment. Risks that are identified may have standard operational procedures developed to reduce the risk level. The bottom line is that someone, somewhere decides that a procedure needs to be in place to proactively patrol, respond, and address the situation.

The development and adherence to policy and procedures is yet another method to document and exhibit professionalism to those in the organization and to the rest of the industry. For many reasons, it is important for all security personnel to review and be familiar with each and every procedure. As I like to tell my security teams, "How we do things today may not be how we do things a year from now. Hopefully, we should learn how to do things better. Who knows what technology is waiting in the wings to help us be more effective and efficient?" This is a reason why I recommend that security leaders actively engage their teams and encourage ideas and open discussions regarding the operational procedures.

There is a direct correlation between the quality, thoroughness, and absorption of the standard operational procedures and how effectively and efficiently the Hospitality Security Department should operate and respond to situations. The standard operational procedures should specify the Hospitality Security Department's mission, objectives, and the processes that should be utilized to attain them. Hospitality security personnel need to know what is expected so that their performance can reflect meeting or exceeding the expected outcome of any incident, event, emergency, or crisis. The life, safety, and security of the organization and the internal and external guests depend upon the knowledge that is exhibited by security personnel in the handling of ordinary day-to-day situations and emergency situations. A well trained Hospitality Security Department that has a good understanding of the policies and standard operational procedures are key elements for results of the best possible outcome being produced in any situation.

Formatting Standard Operational Procedures

The following is a format that can be used for presenting the standard operational procedures for a Hospitality Security Department. The information listed below should be included in the top portion or header of the document.

- Subject of standard operational procedure
- Standard operational procedure number
- Implementation date
- Revision date
- Approval—usually the leader of the Hospitality Security Department
- Page number

The standard operational procedures should be sequentially numbered, and the format should consist of an index at the beginning listing the subject and number corresponding with each standard operational procedure. Each procedure should consist of a header—which states the subject, procedure number, implementation date, revision date, approval, and page number. The person-in-charge of the Hospitality Security Department should review every standard operational procedure and is usually the person whose name is placed in the approval section of the procedure. Although the format is important, remember, the content is more critical than the format, and the absorption of the knowledge contained in standard operational procedures is key to the successful operation of any Hospitality Security Department.

An important area of the header in the standard operational procedure is the revision date. This is very important when it comes to the operation of the team because it indicates what policy and procedure was in place on a given date and time. This can be critical when responding to guest complaints; performance issues; lawsuits; and the proper protection of guests, employees, and company assets.

Remember that the standard operational procedures will likely be examined during criminal, civil, and legal actions. The legal standard of care is established based upon a variety of factors including statutory requirements, community standards, and self-imposed standards. Self-imposed standards are policies, procedures, rules, and regulations that a property owner determines should be followed during the normal operation of the property. If these self-imposed standards are not followed and someone is injured as a result, your property could be liable. Remember that the protection of people is always paramount over the protection of property assets. Standard operational procedures should keep abreast of the laws, trends, and best practices in the industry. Standard operational procedures should be crafted to meet the specific needs of your operation as issues and concerns dictate and should be reviewed by the executive committee, general manager, and the legal branch of your organization. Below is a list of some standard operational procedures that should serve as a guide to spark discussion and assist in developing property-specific departmental procedures that are standardized and assist in facilitating the professional operation of any hospitality security organization:

- Guest room inspections
- Bomb threat
- Fire
- Robbery
- Elevator emergencies
- Suspicious substances
- Deceased persons
- Counterfeit currency
- Threat alerts
- Active shooter

Case-by-Case Examples

These examples of standard operational procedures should provide a good backbone for your hospitality security team. The following are examples of some of these standard operational procedures.

Standard Operational Procedure: 000	**Effective Date:**
GENERAL RESPONSIBILITIES	**Revision Date:**
Approval:	**Page 1 of 1**

The Hospitality Security Department is responsible for the overall security of the property. It is important that all duties are performed in a professional and courteous manner. If, at any time, there are any questions or concerns pertaining to the general responsibilities, a member of the hospitality security leadership team should be contacted immediately. The Hospitality Security Department's general responsibilities should include the following:

- The physical safety of patrons, guests, and employees.
- The physical safeguarding of the company assets.
- The control and maintenance of the issuance of temporary visitor credentials and vendor access credentials.
- The documentation of all unusual occurrences.
- Incidents should be recorded and should contain the following:
    - Assignment number
    - Date
    - Time
    - Nature of the incident
    - Person(s) involved in the incident
    - Hospitality Security Department personnel assigned

Standard Operational Procedure: 000	**Effective Date:**
Guest Room Inspections	**Revision Date:**
Approval:	**Page 1 of 3**

Over the decades, I have had been part of discussions pertaining to the entering of guest rooms and the protections afforded by the Fourth Amendment of the US Constitution: "The right of the people to be secure in their persons, houses, papers, and effects, against unreasonable searches and seizures, shall not be violated, and no Warrants shall issue, but upon probable cause, supported by Oath or affirmation, and particularly describing the place to be searched, and the persons or things to be seized." It is a delicate balance when it comes to maintaining guest privacy, creating a positive guest experience, and providing for a safe and secure environment for guests, employees, and patrons.

Properties cannot obstruct justice and should comply with police investigations. However, keep in mind that properties that comply with an unreasonable search or seizure that results in harm to the guest could be exposed to civil liability. Guests can bar governmental agents from entering, as in their own home, but these restrictions do not extend to property personnel. Courts have recognized that the Fourth Amendment protection from unreasonable searches and seizures applies to searches and seizures in guest rooms. Consent exceptions allow for warrantless searches and seizures. Basically, the consent exception means that a party's agreement, actual or implied, to a search and/or seizure renders a warrant unnecessary. The courts have upheld that properties do have a right to get into the guest rooms on a regular basis. The expectation and right to privacy in a guest room is less than it is in a person's home, private residence, or personal vehicle.

In general, part of every contract to rent a room has a waiver that is signed, allowing property staff and employees to enter a room for a variety of reasons. These waivers or contracts usually communicate that the property reserves the right to conduct a visual inspection of all guest rooms every twenty-four hours to ensure the well-being of the guest and the condition of the room. If service is refused during this time period, a member of the property leadership team should check the guest room.

Generally, a Do Not Disturb (DND) door hanger does not have any value between the guest and the property unless the signed contract states so. Guests may be able to negotiate alternative arrangements. Many properties that have used DND signs in the past are using signs that indicate that the room is occupied with language that indicates that the property reserves the right to enter guest rooms, even when this sign is displayed, for maintenance, safety of guests, security, sanitation, or any other purposes.

Many properties have been considering the use of DND signs and when to enter guest rooms due to concerns pertaining to drugs, prostitution, human trafficking, methamphetamine labs where customers were making meth in guest rooms, etc., Relatively recent horrific events have likely expedited properties and their Hospitality Security Departments to take proactive measures to add additional layers of protection to provide for the safety of guests staying at their property. There has been a trend for guest rooms to be inspected on a daily basis by representatives of the property to check on the well-being of the guests and to determine if there are any items that could be involved in the planning of causing harm to others. These items include firearms, explosive devices, detailed maps of the property, etc. The guest room inspection program may have a deterrent effect on those who wish to cause harm or injury

Standard Operational Procedure: 000	**Effective Date:**
Guest Room Inspections	**Revision Date:**
Approval:	**Page 2 of 3**

to others. Unfortunately, the behavior may still occur, but the chance of it occurring at a property that implements a well designed guest room inspection program in conjunction with a well trained Hospitality Security Department increases the possibility of detecting unwanted behavior by those with bad intentions of harming others.

The implementation of a guest room inspection program should include the following:

- Informing guests of the guest room inspection program prior to confirmation of a reservation.
- Acknowledgement of the guest room inspection program by guests prior to the confirmation of reservation.
- Upon arrival to the property, guests should be informed of the guest room inspection program.
- Guest acknowledgement of the guest room inspection program should occur during the check-in process.
- Verbiage should be posted in the guest room regarding the guest room inspection program.
- Verbiage should be posted at the property regarding the guest room inspection program.
- The normal protocol should be followed—property personnel should knock on the guest room door and announce their presence prior to entering any guest room.
- Staff should be trained accordingly in regard to the guest room inspection program, which should include the implementation of "See something/Say something."
- Upon observing weapons, unusual items, drugs, suspicious behavior, etc., the Security Operations Center should be immediately notified.
- Upon receipt of any reports of weapons, unusual items, drugs, suspicious behavior, etc., the Security Operations Center should immediately contact a member of the hospitality security leadership team.

Under normal circumstances, the Hospitality Security Department should not allow law enforcement to enter a guest's room without a warrant. However, if a guest's tenancy expires, for example, when the check-out time has passed, or the guest has been evicted, Fourth Amendment protections do not apply, and consent may be given for a search by law enforcement. When this occurs, those with proper **authorization**, generally members of the hospitality security leadership team, may aid the police and consent to a search of the room. Properties should clearly and consistently communicate the check-out times to guests. In the event that check-out times are extended beyond the posted check-out time, it should provide a process to record these extensions so that team members know if a guest is protected by the Fourth Amendment. The following should be included regarding some of the ways to protect the property and ensure that violations of the Fourth Amendment do not occur:

Standard Operational Procedure: 000	**Effective Date:**
Guest Room Inspections	**Revision Date:**
Approval:	**Page 3 of 3**

- Have a clear check-out policy.
- Notify guests at check-in of the check-out time.
- Post the check-out time in the guest room.
- Ensure procedures are consistent.
- Be consistent in communicating the check-out policy.
- Be consistent in enforcing the check-out policy.
- Document extensions provided to guests regarding the check-out policy.
- Communicate extensions to the appropriate team members.

Remember, that if a guest is given permission for a later check-out time or a property practices allowing guests to stay past the posted check-out time, the Fourth Amendment protections should last until the later check-out time.

Standard Operational Procedure: 000	**Effective Date:**
BOMB THREAT	**Revision Date:**
Approval:	**Page 1 of 6**

During my career, I have encountered situations that involved bomb threats and the detection of packages deemed to be suspicious in nature. When these types of situations are encountered, it is best to immediately activate the bomb threat emergency plan and bomb threat procedures. In addition to the normal means of advising employees and departments, notification should include a word, name, etc., that should be communicated. Training and instruction of responsibilities during a bomb threat should be received by employees as part of the on-boarding process, which includes the word, name, etc., that is associated with implementing the bomb threat plan. The purpose of this procedure is to provide protection for all employees and guests in the event that a bomb threat is received and to provide guidelines for the safeguarding of the company assets. This procedure should be put into effect when bomb threat information is received by the Hospitality Security Department. All hospitality security personnel should familiarize themselves with these instructions and adhere to them in the event of a bomb threat or explosion.

Bomb threat prevention and training are the best ways to prepare, prevent, and respond to situations of this nature. Careful and full compliance with preventative techniques should not only help diminish the bomber's chances of success but also facilitate the revealing of a hoax. This also helps to minimize the use of manpower, time, and effort. The following are proactive preventative measures that should be implemented in order to quickly identify situations of this nature:

- Be vigilant. When an abandoned package is observed, hospitality security personnel should make inquiries to nearby guests to determine if the owner of the package is nearby.
- If no one claims the abandoned package, security personnel should immediately review CCTV coverage; check with employees assigned to the area; and inquire how long the abandoned package has been there, how it got there, description and location of person who abandoned the package, etc.
- If there is no reason to be suspicious of the package, and it has remained in the same location for an extended period of time, it should be taken to the appropriate preapproved area.

The following is a guideline designed to obtain as much information as possible from a subject who calls in a bomb threat. The techniques used to obtain information from a caller in a minimal amount of time include the following:

- Remain calm.
- Note the time.
- If possible—refer to the bomb threat checklist form—the appearance of this form should alert co-workers that you are in receipt of a bomb threat. This form should be in a bright color—like neon yellow, neon green, etc. The use and appearance of this easily identifiable form should be quite obvious to other employees and should be the signal to implement the bomb threat procedure.

Standard Operational Procedure: 000	**Effective Date:**
BOMB THREAT	**Revision Date:**
Approval:	**Page 2 of 6**

- Note the number displayed on the caller ID window of the phone—write it down.
- Immediately, while keeping the caller on the phone line, inform a co-worker by predetermined code or method that a bomb threat is occurring.
- Keep the caller on the line as long as possible. Encourage the caller to talk, obtaining as much information as possible.
- Record accurately and thoroughly the caller's words, accent, slang, background noises, etc.
- If the caller does not indicate the location of the bomb, or the time of the possible detonation, tactfully inquire about this information.
- Inform the caller that the building is occupied and the explosion of a bomb could result in death or serious injury to many innocent people.
- Report immediately to the highest-ranking member of the security leadership team.
- The general manager, or designee, should authorize any news releases.
- The Hospitality Security Department should immediately notify law enforcement of the bomb threat.

The steps to be followed when a bomb threat is received include the following:

- Establish a Command Center.
- A sweeping, systematic, methodical, and thorough search is to be conducted by leaders who are familiar with the area with the assistance of the hospitality security team. Those familiar with the area should know when something is out of place more easily than those unfamiliar with the area.
- Those participating in the search should have the telephone number of the command center and should not discuss their actions with guests or other nonparticipating employees.
- Providing that it is safe to do so, security personnel not directed to be part of the search should continue their duties as if a search were not being conducted.
- Those participating in the search should not touch, move, or place anything over an object that is deemed suspicious.
- If any unusual or suspicious object is located, a member of the hospitality security leadership team is to be contacted immediately.

The following are some of the areas that should be included in the search of a suspicious device:

- Perimeter wall areas
- The underside of tables
- Behind all curtains

Standard Operational Procedure: 000	**Effective Date:**
BOMB THREAT	**Revision Date:**
Approval:	**Page 3 of 6**

- Trash cans
- Under and behind furniture
- Ceiling tiles
- Crawl spaces
- Electrical and plumbing fixtures
- Drainage systems
- Perimeter walls
- Trash cans
- Mailboxes
- Utility and other closet areas
- Flammable storage areas
- HVAC ducts
- Fire hose or extinguisher racks
- Rugs
- Damaged surfaces

When discretion is not necessary, searches for explosive devices should include the following:

- Conduct a visual search from the floor, and then work your way up to the ceiling.
- Initiate the visual search at the wall area, and then work toward the center of the room.
- Divide each area to be searched into vertical zones, the first being from the floor to table height—then the next zone should be from table height to ceiling.
- Coordinate the search to ensure that all are using the same uniform searching method.
- If the bomb threat states a time of detonation—make sure that there are not any searches being conducted during the window of the detonation time. For the safety of all—make sure an adequate amount of safe time is allotted on either side of the detonation time

---

Standard Operational Procedure: 000	**Effective Date:**
BOMB THREAT	**Revision Date:**
Approval:	**Page 4 of 6**

The decision whether and when to evacuate should be the sole responsibility of the upper leadership of the property. The first consideration should be the safety of the occupants, guests, and employees. It is very difficult to determine the validity of a bomb threat. There are no specific universal criteria that can ensure the correct decision. Remember, safety first; protection of life and injury is of paramount concern when addressing this type of situation. Many times, to help determine the likelihood of a bomb threat being authentic, a scale of one to ten is used regarding the probability that it is an actual event. For example, if a call is received and the caller states, "There is a bomb on your property," and hangs up, it may be rated at the lower end of the scale. If a call is received and the caller states, "I have placed a beige briefcase in the men's bathroom located on the ground level next to the restaurant. The briefcase is next to the trash can by the sink, and it is set to go off in thirty minutes." If a briefcase is discovered at the location matching the description provided by the caller, it may be rated at the higher end of the scale.

At times, a suspicious package may be discovered while a security representative is conducting a proactive patrol. This happened to me when I was a leader of a security team. Hanging from a rafter in the ceiling of a parking garage was a threaded pipe with caps on each end resembling a pipe bomb. Proper protocol and procedure were adhered to, and the investigation revealed that the suspicious device was left there by a construction worker who placed his medicine in the container and hung it from a rafter and forgot to take it with him when he went on lunch break. Needless to say, the construction worker was advised not to place his medicine in any device that resembles a pipe bomb or any other suspicious container.

Evacuation guidelines should include the following:

- To avoid panic, the word "bomb" should not be used when communicating to guests or people unfamiliar with the situation.
- To evacuate or not evacuate, that is the question. The appropriate response should be implemented with the number one focus and consideration being the safety of all.
- When a decision is made to evacuate—evacuees are to be treated with dignity and respect.
- Personnel should speak politely to evacuees and insist on complete compliance. An attitude of total assurance should be displayed by security personnel.
- No one is permitted to return to the evacuated area until the "All Clear" has been given.
- Each threat is unique and should be addressed with the utmost care to protect the patrons, guests, and employees of the property.

Standard Operational Procedure: 000 **Effective Date:**

BOMB THREAT **Revision Date:**

Approval: **Page 5 of 6**

When an explosive device detonates, hospitality security personnel should respond to the scene to ensure maximum protection to life and property and to protect the crime scene for law enforcement. The Security Operations Center should maintain a log of all pertinent activities including the following:

- Time and person receiving bomb threat call
- Areas assigned to be searched
- Time law enforcement and bomb technicians were notified
- Time and type of emergency responding agencies notified
- Time and arrival of law enforcement officials and bomb technicians
- Time, name, and arrival of emergency responding agencies
- Time evacuation ordered
- Areas evacuated
- Time explosive device detected
- Place explosive device detected
- Time explosive device deactivated or detonated
- Place explosive device deactivated or detonated

The role of security personnel after the activation of an explosive device includes the following:

- To provide for the personal safety of all and to protect the integrity of the crime scene.
- Only emergency responding agencies and law enforcement should be permitted into the area surrounding the postblast scene.
- The first responding member of the hospitality security team arriving on the scene should protect the scene and make notification regarding the situation. The response of security personnel should include the following:
    - Render first aid to the injured.
    - In the event of a dying declaration, a member of the Hospitality Security Department should include the following regarding the information obtained:
        - Name of victim
        - Date and time
        - Location

Standard Operational Procedure: 000	**Effective Date:**
BOMB THREAT	**Revision Date:**
Approval:	**Page 6 of 6**

  - Statement of victim
  - Names of all other witnesses to the statement
- Keep witnesses and suspects separated.
- Prevent conversation among witnesses and participants; be alert to document any spontaneous admissions or accusations.
- All statements should be accurately recorded.
- Do not touch or move any objects.
- All nonessential personnel are to return to normal duties.

Standard Operational Procedure: 000	**Effective Date:**
FIRE	**Revision Date:**
Approval:	**Page 1 of 2**

The purpose of this procedure is to save lives and protect the company assets. The fire department is the governing body whenever its services are needed. Its directives are to be followed. Hospitality security personnel are not to ignore requests or contradict instructions issued by the fire department. Upon the discovery of a fire, hospitality security personnel should include the following in their response:

- Immediately broadcast a coded signal over the radio.
- Provide the exact location of fire.
- Provide the nature of fire.
- Immediately locate the nearest pull station and activate.
- If the fire is small enough to be put out by a fire extinguisher, make sure there is a safe means of egress and perform **PASS** only if it is safe to do so:
    - **P**ull—Stand back from the fire about eight feet, and remove the lock pin of the fire extinguisher.
    - **A**im—the nozzle of the fire extinguisher at the base of the fire.
    - **S**queeze—the handles of the fire extinguisher together.
    - **S**weep—from side to side.
- Advise if fire is controlled or not under control.
- Request additional personnel if needed—never use the word "fire" on the radio.
- Available security personnel should immediately respond and proceed to location of alarm—providing it is safe to do so.
- Only necessary radio communications should be communicated until the emergency is over.

Upon the receipt of a report of a fire—hospitality security personnel should include the following in their response:

- Hospitality security personnel should be dispatched to the location to report the fire condition—providing it is safe to do so.
- Hospitality security personnel should respond to the Fire Command Center **(FCC)** with emergency keys to escort the fire department to the location of the fire.
- Hospitality security personnel should be stationed at the exits of the property.

Standard Operational Procedure: 000	**Effective Date:**
FIRE	**Revision Date:**
Approval:	**Page 2 of 2**

If there is a fire in a multiple floor structure, the response from hospitality security personnel should include the following:

- Providing it is safe to do so—hospitality security personnel should respond to the fire floor in General Alarm to investigate. All nonemergency-related responders investigating the event should go to the nearest fire stair and proceed to at least three (3) floors below the fire floor. Remember that when the fire stairs doors are closed, it is a suitable shelter from a fire. The immediate danger is the fire floor in alarm, one floor above the fire floor, and one floor below the fire floor.
- The responding firefighters should exit on the floor below the fire floor. Firefighters should use the stairs to climb to the fire floor.
- Hospitality security personnel should direct all nonemergency-related responders to go at least three floors below the fire floor.
- If the fire department determines that further evacuation is needed, occupants, employees, and guests should be instructed to exit in a quick, safe, and orderly manner. Hospitality security personnel should use all available resources to assist in the evacuation.

Standard Operational Procedure: 000	**Effective Date:**
ROBBERY	**Revision Date:**
Approval:	**Page 1 of 2**

Remember that cash handling areas are usually very heavily covered with CCTV cameras and that there should be excellent descriptive proof of who committed any **robbery** which should lead to the identification and apprehension of those involved in such acts. The Hospitality Security Department and security personnel should include the following procedures when responding to robbery and robbery attempts.

In the event of a robbery or attempted robbery, hospitality security personnel should report the incident and location immediately to the Security Operations Center for possible camera coverage and identification. The information to be gathered regarding the observations of the robbery or attempted robbery should include the following:

- Number of people involved
- Race, sex, and approximate ages of those involved
- Body type, approximate height and weight of those involved
- Description of clothing
- Facial features, scars, or speech characteristics
- Description of any weapons used
- Unusual physical characteristics
- Last known location or direction of travel of those involved

A robbery occurs when force is used to obtain anything of value. The force may be direct or implied. A weapon may be shown, or the person may indicate that he or she has a weapon. All employees should assume that a weapon is being used. If a robbery or robbery attempt is made, the perpetrator should not be confronted. Any employee who is confronted by anyone attempting a robbery should cooperate with the request made by the subject. Employees should not make any attempt to stop or apprehend those involved. If a robbery attempt is made at an area that has "**hold up buttons**" or **duress alarms,** the alarm should be activated only when it is safe to do so. Employees should not do anything that would jeopardize the safety of patrons, guests, employees, or themselves. Each robbery or robbery attempt is unique and should be addressed with caution. The best thing to do is to be a good witness. The safety of patrons, guests, and employees is paramount. Information regarding the robbery should be gathered quickly and passed along to law enforcement.

PROTECTION OF THE CRIME SCENE

- The area should be secured by removing all nonemployees and securing the area from the public by the use of stanchions and security personnel.
- Any witnesses should be separated and not permitted to speak with each other.

Standard Operational Procedure: 000	**Effective Date:**
ROBBERY	**Revision Date:**
Approval:	**Page 2 of 2**

- A review of CCTV coverage of the incident should be prepared and ready for review and distribution to law enforcement.
- Upon arrival of law enforcement, a member of the hospitality security leadership team should meet with the law enforcement agent in charge and comply with any reasonable instructions.

Standard Operational Procedure: 000	**Effective Date:**
ELEVATOR EMERGENCIES	**Revision Date:**
Approval:	**Page 1 of 2**

If anyone has ever been "trapped" in an elevator, even for a couple of minutes, you know that it can be a harrowing experience. During my career, I have seen people respond in a variety of ways while being entrapped and when extricated; some become very emotional, angry, sad, quiet, visibly shaken, combative, threatening, sobbing, laughing, crying, etc. The point is that there is no way to predict how someone will react. One time a person who was entrapped for a relatively short period of time—about three minutes—kicked and damaged the elevator and then, when extricated from the elevator, became very abusive and threatening to security representatives and other personnel who helped him. Perhaps you would have thought that he might have been a little thankful—wrong. The elevator emergency procedure is to be employed in the event of an elevator emergency or failure. Safety to patrons, guests, and employees is paramount. The procedures implemented by the hospitality security team should include the following:

- Voice contact with the occupants of the elevator via the elevator telephone should be maintained until the occupants are safely released. It is important that the occupants be reassured, in a calm and professional manner, that they are safe.
- Hospitality security personnel should be dispatched to the scene, and notifications are to be made to the fire department and the Facilities Department advising them of the incident and giving the exact location of the disabled elevator car.
- If there is an immediate life-safety issue, a trained member of the Facilities Department may attempt to extricate those trapped in the elevator, otherwise all should await the arrival of the fire department.
    - If there is an immediate life-safety issue, only a trained member of the Facilities Department may access the doors at the upper landing for occupant removal. After the doors are opened, they should be wedged or blocked open to eliminate the possibility of the elevator car moving.
    - If there is an immediate life-safety issue, and the elevator car is at the proper floor level with inoperable doors, only a trained member of the Facilities Department may attempt to open the doors from the exterior of the car by using the elevator emergency door key. This can be tricky since the emergency stop button, inside the elevator, should be engaged whenever the emergency door key is utilized.
- The intervention of a trained member of the Facilities Department to extricate those from an elevator is only to occur if there is a life-safety issue, otherwise await the arrival of the fire department.

Standard Operational Procedure: 000 | **Effective Date:**

ELEVATOR EMERGENCIES | **Revision Date:**

Approval: | **Page 2 of 2**

- Any elevator that has suffered a malfunction should be taken out of service until a representative from the elevator service company responds, identifies, and fixes the issue. Only after the cause of the elevator malfunction has been identified and fixed should the elevator be placed back into normal service.

Hospitality security personnel involved in an elevator emergency call should include the following in their response:

- Identify occupants of elevator and render first aid if needed.
- Prepare reports including the documentation of the following:
    - Witness information
    - Preservation of CCTV-video evidence
    - Name of person who contacted the elevator company
    - Time the elevator service company was contacted and notified
    - Name of the service elevator representative who responded
    - Time the elevator service representative arrived
    - Time the elevator service representative departed
    - List the specific elevator that was out of service
    - Time and date the elevator was placed back into service
    - Name, department, and company of person who placed the elevator back into service or kept elevator out of service

Standard Operational Procedure: 000	**Effective Date:**
SUSPICIOUS SUBSTANCES	**Revision Date:**
Approval:	**Page 1 of 3**

When suspicious substances are encountered by members of the Hospitality Security Department, it usually involves a letter, parcel, liquid, powder, or any other material or item with suspicious material on it. When suspicious substances are discovered, hospitality security representatives should include the following in their response:

- Hospitality Security Department personnel should educate employees in an ongoing manner. Training should include how to respond in the event that an employee encounters a suspicious substance, letter, package, parcel, etc. He or she should not:
    - Touch it
    - Smell it
    - Clean it up
    - Open it
- The Hospitality Security Department should be contacted immediately.
- Others are not to be permitted near the item or substance.
- The item or substance should be isolated.
- Those who discovered the item should remain in the area until the arrival of a representative of the Hospitality Security Department.
- The directions provided by security personnel should be followed.
- If the area is within an office environment, all doors and window should be closed in the immediate vicinity of the suspicious item.

The following are some indications that a letter, package, or parcel may involve a suspicious substance:

- There is not a return address on the letter, package, or parcel.
- There is an inordinate amount of postage on the letter, package, or parcel.
- There are stains and signs of discoloration on the letter, package, or parcel.
- The letter, package, or parcel is labeled personal or confidential.
- The letter, package, or parcel is mislabeled or is addressed in different colored ink.
- Unusual odors are detected emanating from the letter, package, or parcel.
- Powder residue is observed on the letter, package, or parcel.

Standard Operational Procedure: 000	**Effective Date:**
SUSPICIOUS SUBSTANCES	**Revision Date:**
Approval:	**Page 2 of 3**

All reasonable efforts to determine the origin of the suspicious letter, package, parcel, or item should be undertaken by persons in the affected area. All information should be relayed to a member of the hospitality security leadership team.

When the Hospitality Security Department receives a report of a suspicious substance, the response should include the following:

- Adequate personnel should be dispatched to safely establish a perimeter of at least 50 feet around the suspicious letter, package, parcel, item, or substance.
- All persons associated with the suspicious letter, package, parcel, item, or substance are to be confined to the immediate area.
- Ensure that additional people do not enter the area or have contact with the suspicious letter, package, parcel, item, or substance.
- The security response team should be equipped with the proper protective equipment, including biowipes, disposable gloves, masks, etc.
- The general manager should be notified and kept abreast of the situation and developments.
- Law enforcement and the fire department should be alerted.
- Persons who had initial contact with the suspicious letter, package, parcel, item, or substance should be asked to cover the item with the appropriate device.
- Facilities should be contacted to shut off air handlers and the **HVAC** system in the affected area.
- The area should be considered a crime scene until cleared by law enforcement.
- Adequate parking areas should be secured by security personnel for fire trucks and other emergency vehicles.
- Security personnel should not discuss any specifics regarding the incident with employees, guests, media, etc.

Standard Operational Procedure: 000	**Effective Date:**
SUSPICIOUS SUBSTANCES	**Revision Date:**
Approval:	**Page 3 of 3**

- Security personnel should be prepared to respond to employee and guests regarding this type of situation as directed by the Public Relations Department or general manager. An example of the verbiage that may be used includes the following:
  - "The safety of our patrons, guests, and employees is of paramount importance. The area should reopen as soon as possible. Thank you."

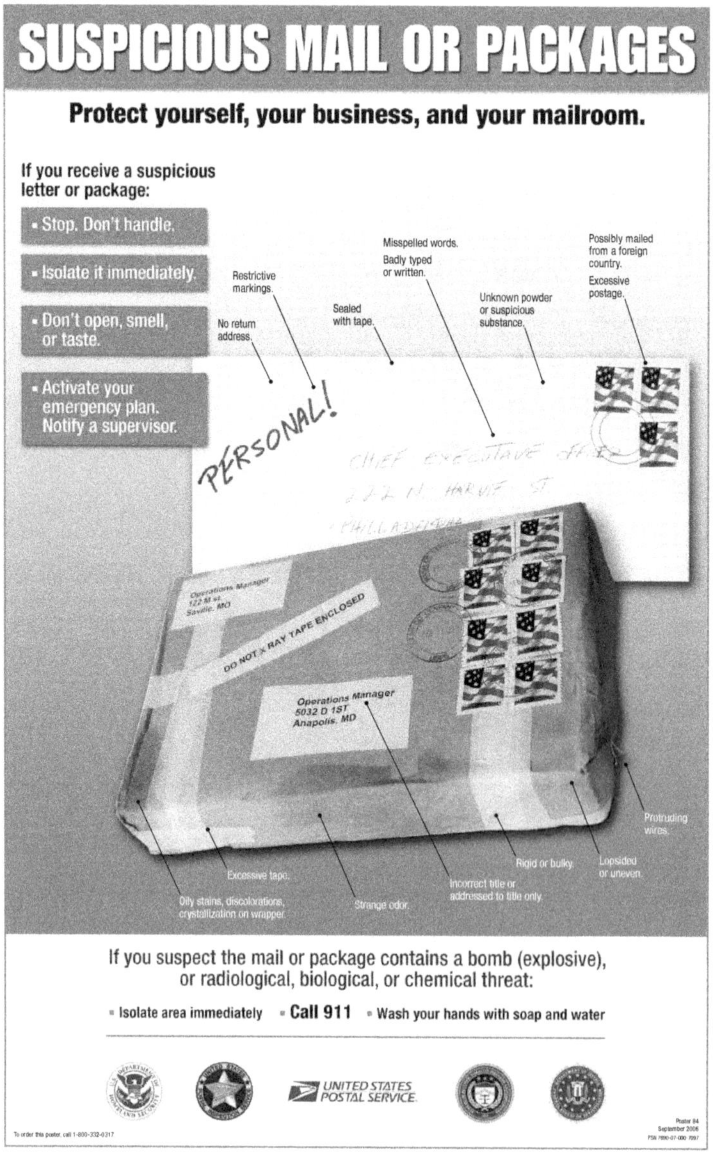

Fig. 3.1: United States Postal Service, "Suspicious Mail or Packages," usps.com, 2006.

Standard Operational Procedure: 000	**Effective Date:**
DECEASED PERSONS	**Revision Date:**
Approval:	**Page 1 of 3**

During my career, I have had the unfortunate circumstance to address situations that pertained to deceased persons. Many times, the circumstances were of natural causes. However, on other occasions, the death of an individual was the result of an accident, suicide, or possible criminal activity. Unfortunately, when these incidents occur in a guest room, they are usually discovered by housekeepers going to clean a room or provide a turn-down service. When discovered in this manner, and if CCTV is available, the person who discovered the deceased is usually observed exiting the room, running down the hall with his or her arms waving in the air over his or her head, calling for help.

Some other ways that unattended deaths are discovered in a guest room include the following:

- Hospitality security responds to a room for a wake-up call because the guest is not answering the guest room phone.
- The guest did not check-out of the guest room as scheduled.
- A loud noise emanates from the guest room, and hospitality security personnel investigate.

The purpose of this policy is to ensure that the following protocol and procedures are included in the response to the discovery of an unattended death that occurs at the property.

Sadly, I have been involved when deaths have occurred that were of suspicious origin or someone tragically took his or her own life. One such incident occurred during the holiday season when a young adult checked into a guest room and invited two close friends to the guest room. It was later discovered that the young adult apparently had a habit of twirling a gun on his or her finger, would place the gun to his or her temple, and pull the trigger without the gun being loaded.

On the evening of this incident, the same scenario played itself out, and this time, you guessed it, there was a bullet in the gun, which instantly killed the young adult. The added twist is that one of the people invited to the room had ended a relationship with the person who killed him- or herself a short time ago to be with the other person who was invited to the guest room. All had been friends prior to this tragic incident and were friends up until the time the incident occurred. The Hospitality Security Department was immediately notified by one of the guests in the room, and the response was immediate. The hospitality security personnel responded so quickly that they discovered the horrific scene with blood still flowing from the head of the unfortunate young adult along with the sobs and cries of those who witnessed this tragedy.

Personnel responding to a report of an unattended death should include the following in their response:

- If trained to do so, immediately determine if CPR or automated external defibrillator (AED) is needed.
- Immediately notify the Hospitality Security Operations Center upon the discovery and have emergency first responder services contacted.

Standard Operational Procedure: 000	**Effective Date:**
DECEASED PERSONS	**Revision Date:**
Approval:	**Page 2 of 3**

- In the event that it is determined that the person is deceased, the area should be treated as a crime scene until determined otherwise.
- If the deceased person is discovered in a room, a telephone other than the one in the room should be used.
- Do not remove, touch, or alter anything at or around the scene. It is best to remain out of the immediate area of the deceased so as not to disturb or destroy any possible evidence.
- Note time of day, and visually survey the scene. Make note of anything that appears out of the ordinary or seems odd.
- Remain at the scene until released by a member of the hospitality security leadership team or law enforcement.
- Discuss only with the proper authorities involved with the incident.

When notified of an unattended death, the Hospitality Security Operations Center should:

- Dispatch the highest-ranking member of the hospitality security leadership team.
- Notify law enforcement.
- Notify the leader of the hospitality security leadership team—who should notify the appropriate property leaders.
- Note time of notification and arrival of all agencies involved.
- Post a member of the hospitality security team outside of the scene with a pen and notepad.
- Any person who wishes to enter the area should have his or her name and contact information recorded.
- Hospitality security personnel should remain at the scene until the arrival of law enforcement.
- Hospitality security personnel should turn over the crime scene to law enforcement along with the names and information of any individuals who entered the crime scene prior to their arrival.

A member of the hospitality security leadership team should ensure that the following is completed:

- All witnesses are interviewed.
- Have the area secured until completion of the formal investigation.
- Assist law enforcement as needed.

Standard Operational Procedure: 000	**Effective Date:**
DECEASED PERSONS	**Revision Date:**
Approval:	**Page 3 of 3**

- Photographs are taken of the scene.
- Ambulance personnel and/or the medical examiner is escorted through the back-of-house areas, and the removal of the body is out of the public view.
- Assist law enforcement, as requested, regarding notification of next-of-kin and the safeguarding of valuables and the deceased personal belongings.
- Prepare all necessary reports.

Standard Operational Procedure: 000	**Effective Date:**
COUNTERFEIT CURRENCY	**Revision Date:**
Approval:	**Page 1 of 7**

It is important to remember that the passing of a counterfeit bill can occur by those who are knowingly committing a crime and by others who may have been given the counterfeit bill as change from a legitimate purchase or transaction. The totality of circumstances involving the discovery of a counterfeit bill should be taken into consideration and addressed accordingly. For example, patrons who have a counterfeit bill that was given to them as change from a legitimate transaction should not be made to feel like they are being treated like a criminal when information is being gathered by a representative of the Hospitality Security Department.

Some telltale signs that a person passing counterfeit bills may have criminal intent include having multiple counterfeit bills in his or her possession, purchasing an inexpensive item with a large denomination counterfeit bill, giving the change of the purchase to another person—known as a "bag man"—who reissues counterfeit bills in exchange for the change received from purchaser of an item with a counterfeit bill. If any of these activities are observed, they should be scrutinized and investigated to determine if law enforcement should be contacted. The following procedures should be implemented by the Hospitality Security Department when addressing suspected US counterfeit currency.

- A hospitality security representative should respond to the location and speak with the patron.
- Examination of the suspect bill should include the following:
  - Watermark
  - Color-shifting ink
  - Microprinting
  - Security thread

- When placed under an ultra violet light, authentic bills should exhibit the following properties:
  - $5 bill glows blue
  - $10 bill glows orange
  - $20 bill glows green
  - $50 bill glows yellow
  - $100 bill glows red

- If the bill is confirmed as counterfeit, the following personal identification should be requested from the subject:
  - Name
  - Address
  - Date of Birth
  - Phone Number

Standard Operational Procedure: 000	**Effective Date:**
COUNTERFEIT CURRENCY	**Revision Date:**
Approval:	**Page 2 of 7**

A patron should only be detained if law enforcement requests security to do so or if members of the hospitality security leadership team have reason to believe that the patron is involved in passing multiple counterfeit bills or is involved in a counterfeiting scam.

The steps involved regarding the processing of counterfeit bills should include the following:

- The bill should be logged and assigned a case number. The counterfeit bill log should contain the following information:
    - Date
    - Date of incident
    - Location of incident
    - Case number
    - Hospitality security representative name and identification number
    - Disposition of case

- A hospitality security representative should complete a US Secret Service counterfeit note report.
- The report should be completed as described in the instructions listed on the US Secret Service counterfeit note report.
- The "Remarks" section should contain a brief narrative stating who, how, and at what location the bill was discovered.
- The suspected counterfeit bill should be attached to the completed US Secret Service counterfeit note report and delivered to the US Secret Service, mailed to the US Secret Service, or turned over to law enforcement for processing with the subject who presented the counterfeit note.

Standard Operational Procedure: 000	**Effective Date:**
COUNTERFEIT CURRENCY	**Revision Date:**
Approval:	**Page 3 of 7**

DEPARTMENT OF HOMELAND SECURITY
United States Secret Service

COUNTERFEIT NOTE REPORT

INSTRUCTIONS TO BANK:

1. Prepare and submit one copy of this completed form **with each suspected counterfeit note** to your local **SECRET SERVICE OFFICE.**
2. If desired, an additional copy of this form should be prepared and retained for your records.
3. Unless advised otherwise, the suspect note submitted to the Secret Service should be considered counterfeit.
4. The Secret Service **WILL NOT** return a copy of this form.

NAME OF BANK: ____________________
BANK ROUTING NUMBER: ____________________
POINT-OF-CONTACT: ____________________
POINT-OF-CONTACT'S E-MAIL: *(if different from above)* ____________________
POINT-OF-CONTACT'S TELEPHONE NUMBER: *(include area code)* ____________________
POINT-OF-CONTACT'S FAX NUMBER: *(include area code)* ____________________
MAILING ADDRESS OF BANK: *(include ZIP Code)*

____

DO NOT WRITE IN THIS SPACE

Classification Number ____________________

IMPORTANT NOTICE

Bank tellers and persons surrendering the note should date and initial each counterfeit note one time with pen and ink in the border area of the note for identification. If the person surrendering the note knows from whom he/she received it, or has a description of the passer, or his/her auto, or any other information, **TELEPHONE the local police department or Secret Service office IMMEDIATELY** and hold the note. (The telephone number of the nearest Secret Service office may be found at www.secretservice.gov.) Otherwise, if no information is available, please mail the note to the Secret Service local office on the day it is received. The submitting bank agrees to abandon any property interest in counterfeit notes it surrenders to the Secret Service.

DESCRIPTION OF COUNTERFEIT NOTE OR RAISED NOTE (for raised note give serial number only)

DENOMINATION	FEDERAL RESERVE BANK *(Series 1996 - Letter/Number)*	NOTE POSITION LETTER/NOTE POSITION NUMBER

NOTE POSITION LETTER/FACE PLATE NO.	BACK PLATE NO.	SERIES	SERIAL NUMBER

COUNTERFEIT NOTE RECEIVED FROM

NAME OF INDIVIDUAL / BUSINESS	DATE OF ACTIVITY OR DEPOSIT
HOME ADDRESS *(OR BUSINESS LOCATION WHERE COUNTERFEIT WAS PASSED)*	HOME PHONE *(with Area Code)*
	BUSINESS PHONE *(with Area Code)*

NAME OF PERSON SURRENDERING AND INITIALING NOTE	NAME OF TELLER RECEIVING AND INITIALING NOTE

INFORMATION ABOUT COUNTERFEIT NOTE

DOES THE CUSTOMER HAVE ANY INFORMATION AS TO THE SOURCE OF THE COUNTERFEIT?	☐ Yes	☐ No
WAS THERE ANY SUSPICIOUS ACTIVITY?	☐ Yes	☐ No
IS THIS A NON - CUSTOMER?	☐ Yes	☐ No

REMARKS:

DISPOSITION (For Secret Service Use Only)

☐ Genuine note and SSF 1604 returned to bank (Receipt No.____________________)

This form is not subject to the requirements of Pub. L. 96-511 "Paperwork Reduction Act of 1980." 44 U.S.C., Chapter 35, Section 3518 (c)(1)(A) states that, "...this chapter [Chapter 35] does not apply to the collection of information ... during the conduct of a Federal criminal investigation..."

PLEASE SUBMIT TO THE LOCAL SECRET SERVICE JURISDICTIONAL FIELD OFFICE

SSF 1604 (Rev. 09/2015)

Page 1 of 1

Department of Homeland Security, "Counterfeit Note Report," secretservice.gov, 2015.

Standard Operational Procedure: 000	**Effective Date:**
COUNTERFEIT CURRENCY	**Revision Date:**
Approval:	**Page 4 of 7**

Know Your Money

2004 style Federal Reserve notes (FRNs) incorporate background colors and large, borderless portrait images.

Paper U.S. currency paper consists of 25% linen and 75% cotton and contains small randomly disbursed red and blue security fibers embedded throughout the paper.

Portrait The 2004 style FRNs have an enlarged and off-center portrait without a frame.

❶ **Watermark** The 2004 style FRNs have a watermark that is visible from either side when held to light.

❷ **Color-Shifting** Ink The 2004 style $10, $20, $50 and $100 FRNs have color-shifting ink that shifts from copper to green as the note is tilted 45 degrees. The 2004 style $100 FRN has a color-shifting "Bell in the Inkwell". The $5 FRN does not have color-shifting ink.

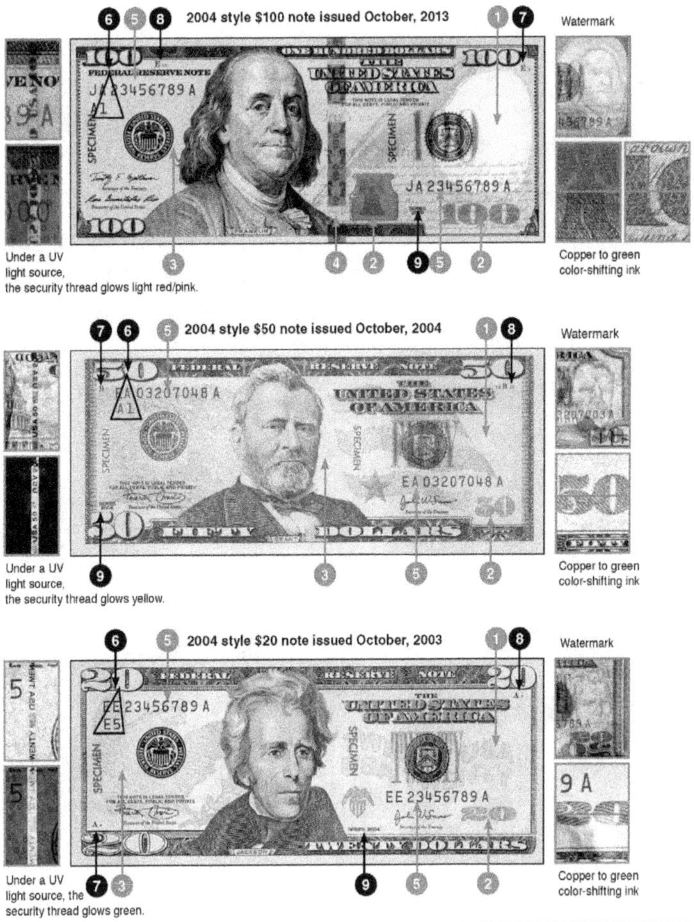

U.S. Secret Service, "Know Your Money," secretservice.gov, 2016.

❸ **Security Thread** All genuine FRNs, except the $1 and $2, have a clear thread embedded vertically in the paper. The thread is inscribed with the denomination of the note and is visible only when held to light. Each denomination has a unique thread position and glows a different color when held to ultraviolet (UV) light.

❹ **3-D Security Ribbon** The 2004 style $100 FRN features a blue ribbon woven into the paper. When you tilt the note back and forth, the bells and "100"s move side to side. If you tilt the note side to side, they move up and down.

Standard Operational Procedure: 000	**Effective Date:**
COUNTERFEIT CURRENCY	**Revision Date:**
Approval:	**Page 5 of 7**

❺ **Serial Numbers** The first letter of the serial number on FRNs of series year 1996 or later corresponds to the series year.

E = 2004	I = 2006	L = 2009A
G = 2004A	J = 2009	

Bank Indicators

❻ **Federal Reserve Indicators** The 2004 style FRNs have a letter and number designation, which identifies one of the 12 distributing Federal Reserve Banks. This letter and number designation appears beneath the serial number on the left. The number corresponds to the position of the letter in the alphabet, e.g.: A1, B2, C3, etc. The letter matches the second prefix letter in the serial number.

❼ **Note Position Letter and Number**

❽ **Face Plate Number**

❾ **Series Year**

❿ **Back Plate Number** (Not shown) Found on the bottom right-hand corner of the back of the note.

2004 style $10 note issued March, 2006

2004 style $5 note issued March, 2008

United States Secret Service

Standard Operational Procedure: 000 **Effective Date:**

COUNTERFEIT CURRENCY **Revision Date:**

Approval: **Page 6 of 7**

Know Your Money

	Portrait	Watermark	Security Thread	Microprinting	Other Microprinting	Color-Shifting Ink in Front Lower Right Numeral
2004 Style						
100	Franklin	Franklin	Left of portrait	"THE UNITED STATES OF AMERICA" along Franklin's collar; small "100" in the note's vertical borders; "USA" along bottom of Franklin's portrait	"ONE HUNDRED USA" along the golden quill; "USA 100" around the blank space containing the portrait watermark	Copper to Green Also appears in the bell in the inkwell
50	Grant	Grant	Right of portrait	"THE UNITED STATES OF AMERICA" along Grant's collar	"50"; "USA" and "FIFTY" in two blue stars to the left of the portrait; "FIFTY" along side borders	Copper to Green
20	Jackson	Jackson	Left of portrait	"THE UNITED STATES OF AMERICA 20 USA" in the border below Treasurer's signature	"USA20" borders beginning part of text ribbon "USA TWENTY", right of portrait	Copper to Green
10	Hamilton	Hamilton	Right of portrait	"THE UNITED STATES OF AMERICA" below portrait	"USA10" beneath torch to the left of the portrait; "TEN DOLLARS" along side borders	Copper to Green
5	Lincoln	Left: vertical "5 5 5"; Right: large "5"	Right of portrait	"E Pluribus Unum" at top of eagle's shield to the right of the portrait; "USA" between columns of eagle's shield; "FIVE DOLLARS" along side borders.	On back, "USA FIVE" on edge of purple 5.	None

Standard Operational Procedure: 000	**Effective Date:**
COUNTERFEIT CURRENCY	**Revision Date:**
Approval:	**Page 7 of 7**

	Portrait	Watermark	Security Thread	Microprinting	Other Microprinting	Color-Shifting Ink in Front Lower Right Numeral
1996 Style						
100	Franklin	Franklin	Left of portrait	"THE UNITED STATES OF AMERICA" along Franklin's collar	"USA100" in lower left numeral	Green to Black
50	Grant	Grant	Right of portrait	"THE UNITED STATES OF AMERICA" along Grant's collar	"FIFTY" along side borders	Green to Black
20	Jackson	Jackson	Left of portrait	"THE UNITED STATES OF AMERICA" in the lower oval framing of portrait	"USA20" in lower left numeral	Green to Black
10	Hamilton	Hamilton	Right of portrait	"THE UNITED STATES OF AMERICA" below portrait above Hamilton's name	"TEN" in lower left numeral	Green to Black
5	Lincoln	Lincoln	Left of portrait	"THE UNITED STATES OF AMERICA" in the lower oval framing of portrait	"FIVE DOLLARS" along side borders	None

Standard Operational Procedure: 000	**Effective Date:**
THREAT ALERTS	**Revision Date:**
Approval:	**Page 1 of 3**

The purpose of this policy is to establish specific levels of alert readiness and operational response based on the threat level reported by Department of Homeland Security's (DHS) National Terrorism Advisory System (NTAS).

Threat alerts should include a clear statement on the nature of the threat, which should be defined one of two ways:

- Elevated Threat—warns of a credible terrorist threat against the United States.
- Imminent Threat—warns of a credible, specific, and impending terrorist threat against the United States.

Threat alerts should be issued for a specific time period and should automatically expire. Alerts may be extended if new information becomes available or as a specific threat evolves.

GENERAL ALERT STATUS with no discernible threat activity:

- Conduct normal security patrols/assignments.
- Security personnel are to be alert for suspicious or unusual conditions and report such activity immediately to a member of the security leadership team to analyze the condition and report information to the appropriate law enforcement agencies as needed.
- Keep lines of communication open with local, state, and federal law enforcement agencies.
- Ensure two-way radio equipment is operational.
- Conduct training and develop plans as needed.

ELEVATED THREAT—Warns of credible terrorist threat against the United States.

Upon receipt of this notification, the Hospitality Security Department response should include the following:

- Dissemination of specific information to the appropriate security personnel regarding any specific information received concerning the possible threat.
- The Hospitality Security Department's focus should include the following areas: entry/exit points and other areas deemed susceptible.
- Any suspicious activity or unusual conditions are to be immediately reported to a member of the security leadership team.

Standard Operational Procedure: 000	**Effective Date:**
THREAT ALERTS	**Revision Date:**
Approval:	**Page 2 of 3**

The security leadership team should immediately report any suspicious activity or unusual conditions to law enforcement and ensure that the following occurs:

- Maintain close communications with law enforcement for updated information and alert status.
- Perimeter patrols are conducted and documented.
- Storage areas are locked and secure.
- All loading dock areas are to be locked and secured during periods of inactivity.
- Physical checks of the building perimeter and mechanical rooms are conducted and documented.
- Any anomalies, suspicious activity, or security breaches that are uncovered should immediately be reported to the leader of the Hospitality Security Department.
- Emergency plans and procedures are reviewed with the security team.
- Inspect and check security emergency response supplies to ensure that all are in good condition and working order.
- All security vehicles and other essential vehicles are inspected to ensure that all have a full tank of gas and are operational.
- Check on status of receiving additional fuel deliveries for vehicles and back-up emergency power generators.
- Prepare the Hospitality Security Command Center and place on standby status for activation.
- Members of the security leadership team should communicate alert status to the appropriate executive leaders of the property.
- Maintain communications with law enforcement for alert bulletins.

IMMINENT THREAT—Warns of a credible, specific, and impending terrorist threat against the United States.

The Hospitality Security Department's response should include the following when an imminent threat notification is received:

- Activation of a Hospitality Security Command Center.
- Assignment of security personnel to the perimeter roadways that provide access to the property.
- A member of the security leadership team should notify executive leaders of alert status.
- Deployment of vehicles to perimeter positions as needed.
- Implement the checking of identification in the back-of-house areas.
- Monitor vehicles located in area near the perimeter of the property.

Standard Operational Procedure: 000	**Effective Date:**
THREAT ALERTS	**Revision Date:**
Approval:	**Page 3 of 3**

- Verify and check deliveries to the loading dock areas.
- Establish regular communication with law enforcement.
- Be on high alert for any anomalies, suspicious activity, or security breaches that are uncovered. This information should immediately be reported to a member of the security leadership team and law enforcement.
- Implement emergency procedures as needed or deemed appropriate by law enforcement or members of the security leadership team.
- Implement vehicle checkpoints and visual inspections of vehicles.
- Implement access control at perimeter.
- Await updates from the appropriate government agencies.

Upon notification of a pending or actual critical incident, hazardous event, or emergency, a staff recall process should be implemented, which should include the following:

- Hospitality security personnel should be made aware of the impending condition and that it may be necessary to stay and work additional hours and possibly stay overnight. Any exceptions should be approved and authorized by the leader of the Hospitality Security Department.

Standard Operational Procedure: 000	**Effective Date:**
ACTIVE SHOOTER	**Revision Date:**
Approval:	**Page 1 of 3**

Having been shot six times during a motor vehicle stop as a New Jersey State Trooper, the topic of active shooter is one that holds a special place in my heart. First and foremost, in today's society, where terrorism has the possibility of occurring at any time, all employees should have knowledge and training of what to do in the event of an active shooter. To arm or not to arm hospitality security personnel, that is the question. Many factors should be taken into consideration and should be decided on a case-by-case basis. If to arm is chosen, continuous training is paramount, and working together with law enforcement is essential for the safety and protection of all. The purpose of this procedure is to provide guidelines and procedures that can best provide for the survival of members of the Hospitality Security Department, patrons, guests, and employees should they become involved in an active shooter event.

An active shooter is a person or persons actively engaged in killing or attempting to kill others with the use of firearms. The following active shooter information is provided by US Department of Homeland Security.

CHARACTERISTICS—ACTIVE SHOOTER SITUATION

- Victims are normally selected at random.
- The event is unpredictable and evolves quickly.
- Police response is usually required to end an active shooter situation.

COPING—ACTIVE SHOOTER SITUATION

- Be aware of your environment and any possible dangers.
- Take note of the two nearest exits in any area or facility you work or visit.
- Set your cell phone to silent mode.
- If you are in an office, stay in the office.
- Lock and secure the doors of the office.
- Only when facing immediate danger, and as a last resort, take action against the active shooter.

HOW TO RESPOND—WHEN AN ACTIVE SHOOTER IS IN THE VICINITY

- Contact hospitality security and 911 when it is safe to do so.
- Determine the most reasonable way to protect your life and the lives of other persons.

EVACUATE

- Plan an escape route.
- Leave belongings behind.
- Keep your hands visible.

Standard Operational Procedure: 000	**Effective Date:**
ACTIVE SHOOTER	**Revision Date:**
Approval:	**Page 2 of 3**

HIDE OUT

- Hide in an area out of view of active shooter.
- Block entry to your hiding place and lock doors.

TAKE ACTION

- Only as a last resort, and only when life safety is in imminent danger, should an attempt be made to incapacitate an active shooter. Act with physical aggression, and throw items at the active shooter.

HOW TO RESPOND—WHEN POLICE ARRIVE ON THE SCENE

- Remain calm and follow police instructions.
- Immediately raise your hands with fingers spread. Keep hands visible at all times.
- Avoid making quick movements toward police.
- Avoid screaming, yelling, or pointing.
- Do not stop to ask police for help or direction when evacuating. Proceed in the direction and area from where the police have entered.

INFORMATION TO PROVIDE POLICE OFFICERS, SECURITY, AND 911

- Location of the active shooter
- Number of active shooters, if more than one shooter
- Physical description of shooter(s)
- Number and type of weapons being used by the shooter(s), such as hand gun, rifle, and automatic weapon
- Number of possible victims at the location

RECOGNIZING SIGNS OF POSSIBLE WORKPLACE VIOLENCE

An active shooter can be a current or former employee. Alert a member of your departmental leadership team, Hospitality Security Department, and Human Resources if an employee exhibits potentially violent behavior. Indicators of potentially violent behavior may include one or more of the following:

- Increased use of alcoholic beverages, use of illegal drugs, or excessive use of prescription drugs
- Unexplained absenteeism, tardiness, or vague physical complaints
- Depression or acting withdrawn
- Increased severe mood swings

Standard Operational Procedure: 000	**Effective Date:**
ACTIVE SHOOTER	**Revision Date:**
Approval:	**Page 3 of 3**

- Noticeably unstable or emotional
- Increasingly talks about problems at home or work
- Increase in unsolicited comments about violence, firearms, or other weapons and violent crimes

PROCEDURE—PERSON WITH A WEAPON—NOT IN ACTION

This procedure should be followed when hospitality security personnel receive a report or personally witnesses a person with a concealed or other weapon, such as a knife or gun, in which the weapon is not in action.

- Do not approach the suspected person.
- Give a description of suspected person, weapon, and his or her location to the Hospitality Security Department.
- The Hospitality Security Department should contact law enforcement.
- The Hospitality Security Department should keep the suspected person under observation by the use of CCTV while awaiting the arrival of law enforcement.
- Hospitality security personnel should form a safety perimeter in the area to limit public access without alerting the suspected person(s).
- Security personnel should assist law enforcement and follow its directions and instructions.

The previous standard operational procedures should serve as a guideline and should be modified to meet the specific needs of your property. The standard operational procedures should be crafted in accordance to, and within the boundaries of, the laws and ordinances that are in effect in the jurisdiction in which the property is located. Remember that the protection and safety of people should always be of primary importance; objects and things should be secondary. Additional examples of emergency procedures and response plans are located in the Appendix at the end of this book.

Discussion Questions

1. Which property entities should review and approve standard operational procedures prior to implementation?
2. When a procedure is revised, what two important things should be done with the revised procedure?
3. What are the elements that should be included in the header of a standard operational procedure?
4. What should be taken into consideration when crafting standard operational procedures?
5. Why is it useful to put the revision date on a revised procedure and to keep the old copy of a procedure that was revised?
6. Explain the frequency of, and how and why it is important, for the standard operational procedures to be reviewed.
7. Explain why standard operational procedures are important to the operation of the Hospitality Security Department.

CHAPTER

4

EMERGENCY PROCEDURES AND RESPONSE PLANS

> *"First ask yourself: What is the worst that can happen? Then prepare to accept it. Then proceed to improve on the worst."*
>
> —Dale Carnegie
> *An American writer, lecturer, and developer of famous courses in self-improvement and public speaking*

Throughout my career, I have been involved in various situations which required the implementation of emergency plans, standard operational procedures, policies, training, and best practices. Some of the critical situations that I played a leading role in the security industry include the following: Hurricane Frances, Hurricane Wilma, Hurricane Sandy, power outages—including the largest power blackout in history of the United States that occurred in August of 2003, unattended deaths, and suicides, to name a few. At times, things occur where there is not a specific written plan or procedure that outlines exactly what should be done. In these cases, best judgement should be used while ensuring that no actions are taken that could be deemed as being illegal, unethical, or immoral.

For example, during a crisis that lasted for an extended period of time at an older property that had guests staying in it, a situation arose that needed to be addressed regarding the disposal of waste from the public restrooms. To recap in a nutshell, the property was involved in the largest power outage in US history, and, as a result, one of the many situations that a had to be addressed was that the waste in the toilets was unable to be flushed. After thinking about this for a while, a request was made of the fire department to connect a fire hose and direct the nozzle into each toilet. This action resulted in the waste being flushed into the system and the cleaning of the area.

Prepare for Emergency Situations

It is always advisable to make preparations regarding responses to emergency-related situations with all internal and external departments that may be involved. These procedures and responses should be reviewed with fire, law enforcement, and other agencies that would respond to your property regarding these events. It is always a good practice to have periodic meetings and conduct tabletop exercises to walk through the procedures and plans. If possible, it is always beneficial for everyone to conduct training on-site where emergency responders, firefighters, law enforcement, etc., can practice scenarios with the Hospitality Security Department.

These practice sessions aid in the communication, execution, and confirmation that all responding agencies and departments are on the same page or can provide an opportunity to resolve any discrepancies prior to an actual event. Areas to review include emergency situations, triage areas, communications, and "what if" scenarios. Reviewing the hospitality security emergency procedures with all agencies that will be responding to the property when emergency situations occur should result in the optimum performance, communication, and execution of these emergency procedures by all involved in regard to providing for the safety of guests, employees, and occupants of the property.

In preparation for an emergency event, it is a good idea to gather nonperishable supplies that would be needed and store them in a sealed and appropriately labeled portable triage container. For example, items that would be needed for triage stations should be secured in a sealed plastic barrel with wheels for mobility. This portable triage station should be identifiable by having a large pole with a red banner with white lettering affixed to the top with "triage" written on the banner. By sealing the container in a manner that it would be easily recognized if it were tampered with, the need to conduct weekly inventories of the contents would be prevented. Similarly, other emergency containers should be developed for other events like hurricanes, earthquakes, etc. These emergency event containers should be stored in a secured area and kept under the view of the CCTV system.

Conduct a Postcrisis/Emergency Meeting

If possible, it is a good practice to conduct a meeting to solicit information during an emergency to provide updates and modify or continue the course of action, taking into consideration the information gathered during the meeting. These meetings should be conducted in or near the Operations Command Center and should be short, direct, and to the point. The purpose of the meeting during a crisis or emergency is to be able to react and respond immediately to any urgent or possible life-threatening situations.

The postcrisis/emergency meeting should be conducted as soon as possible after the crisis. The meeting should be timely so that everyone can clearly remember the facts regarding the emergency. The purposes of the postcrisis/emergency incident meeting should include the following:

- Review how and why it happened.
- What measures have been implemented to discourage or prevent this from happening again?

- If the preventive measures have been put into place or if the measures have not been instituted, a timeline should be established with clear lines of responsibility and a definitive timetable of when each phase and project is to be completed.
- What worked well.
- What could have been done better.
- How the emergency should be addressed in the future should it occur again.

The information gathered from the meetings should result in the emergency procedures and response plans being updated with the revised methods on how to address situations that occurred. This information should be distributed to appropriate personnel throughout the property. It is important that the top leader of the property—usually the general manager—gets behind and supports the emergency procedures and any revisions to ensure that everyone understands the importance of these documents as they relate to the safety and well-being of all of the occupants of the property.

Frequently, when an emergency crisis occurs, it usually involves more than one type of emergency. For example, an evacuation may be ordered as a result of another type of emergency event such as a fire, bomb threat, etc.

I can remember seeing newscasts on television of the first bombing of the World Trade Center on February 26, 1993. The images of people who were in the building being asked questions by reporters and responding in a dazed, vague manner, commenting that they did not know what to do—we never thought this would happen—left an indelible impression on me that remains to this day. The importance of emergency procedures and response plans cannot be stressed enough and should be part or the DNA of the property requiring mandatory training and refresher courses to ensure that everyone knows exactly what to do should an emergency arise. It is imperative that all department leaders be familiar with the specific duties and responsibilities required of them and their respective departmental team members during a crisis or emergency situation. The importance of these emergency procedures should be emphasized from the very top of the organization by the general manager and the executive leadership of the property. Only in this way, will this document come to life and assist in the protection and safety of all guests, visitors, patrons, and employees of the property.

It is also important to address the uniqueness of your property when drafting and implementing emergency procedures. Every property is different in design, location, and needs. Emergency procedures should be specific and address the uniqueness and the nuances of your property. When emergency situations arise, the procedures below should be applied to address the emergency situation or situations.

Case-by-Case Examples

Emergency Procedures & Response Plans: 000	**Effective Date:**
HEIGHTENED PROPERTY SECURITY ALERT PROCEDURES	**Revision Date:**
Approval:	**Page 1 of 2**

The purpose of this heightened security procedure is to increase security awareness in the event the National Terrorism Advisory System (NTAS) issues an Imminent Threat Alert or Elevated Threat Alert. The heightened property security alert procedure should also be used based on world conditions or information received by actual law enforcement intelligence of terrorist activities or other types of activities that could jeopardize the safety of employees, guests, visitors, and the property. Prior to implementing this procedure, a meeting should be conducted with the key leaders and decision-makers of the property—usually the executive team. The nature and type of alert or threat should be discussed, and the actions taken should be agreed upon and implemented. There should also be predetermined follow-up meetings to discuss any updates pertaining to the threat or alert. This procedure is designed to phase in as the perceived level of risk assessment increases. The heightened security procedures are as follows:

I. EXTERIOR PERIMETER OF THE PROPERTY

- Hospitality security will maintain a constant patrol of the perimeter of the property.
- Vehicles should not be permitted to stop and/or park along the curb line adjacent to buildings, in fire lanes, or in front of fire hydrants.
- Delivery trucks should be stopped, the delivery bill of lading should be examined, and the delivery area should be contacted to confirm information prior to entry into the property or loading dock areas.
- Perimeter patrols should inspect all emergency exits to ensure that they remain closed and secure.

II. SPECIAL PARKING AREAS/VALET

- Signs should be posted indicating that the inside of vehicles, trunks, and cargo areas are subject to inspection prior to vehicles being permitted to use special parking areas or valet.
- Hospitality security should patrol and post personnel in key areas such as designated vehicle drop off areas and valet to conduct inspections of vehicles dropping people off or vehicles that are parked in these areas.
- Any person arriving who does not grant permission to have his or her vehicle inspected will be advised to park off site.

Valet/Special Parking Sign Example:

> For your safety and security, all vehicles are subject to a visual security inspection that includes, but is not limited to, the following areas:

Emergency Procedures & Response Plans: 000	**Effective Date:**
HEIGHTENED PROPERTY SECURITY ALERT PROCEDURES	**Revision Date:**
Approval:	**Page 2 of 2**

- Interior
- Exterior
- Trunk
- Cargo areas

For those who do not wish to participate in this inspection, the vehicle may not park on site, and off-site parking should be utilized.

III. INTERIOR PERIMETER OF THE PROPERTY

- Hospitality security should patrol the interior perimeter establishing a back-of-house perimeter patrol to detect persons who are unauthorized to be in this area.
- Anyone who is not displaying the proper credentials should be identified and his or her employment/access status confirmed.

IV. DELIVERY AREAS/LOADING DOCKS

Hospitality security should patrol these areas, being extra vigilant when these areas are closed in order to detect and prevent unauthorized access.

V. ENTRANCES

Hospitality security patrols should be implemented at the entrances to regulate large items entering through this area and to be observant for suspicious or unusual activity.

VI. ACCESS ROADS

Hospitality security patrols should be conducted on access roadways leading into the property. Visual inspections should be conducted, and any suspicious or unusual activity should be immediately reported to a member of the hospitality security leadership team.

The following is an example of the implementation of these procedures and processes. These are general guidelines and, if necessary, should be modified to meet the specific needs of your property.

- **Implement Sections I, II, and III.**—When intelligence information is received from law enforcement that warns of a credible threat.
- **Implement Sections I, II, III, IV, V, and VI.**—When intelligence information is received from law enforcement that indicates that there is a credible, specific, and impending threat.

Emergency Procedures & Response Plans: 000	**Effective Date:**
EVACUATIONS	**Revision Date:**
Approval:	**Page 1 of 5**

Evacuations are a critical area as it pertains to the safety and security of guests, patrons, and employees. Any time an announcement is made to evacuate, there is always a chance that someone may become hurt or injured during the evacuation process. People may become frightened or scared and do whatever they feel is necessary to exit. This may result in other guests being knocked down or even trampled. Especially susceptible are the elderly or those who are unable to ambulate freely without the assistance of others or devices. For this reason, caution should be taken prior to instituting the announcement of an evacuation. Maximum safety of guests, patrons, and team members should be paramount when contemplating an evacuation. On the other hand, every second matters in the event that there is an actual emergency that requires an evacuation. The reasons that a property should be evacuated include general fire alarms that will cause a property to evacuate automatically and other events and situations that may arise that require removal of the occupants for life and safety reasons.

Evacuations should be made based on reliable information received pertaining to the protection of life, the safety of occupants, and the confirmation of the received information. In certain situations, it may be prudent to conduct an investigation regarding the information received prior to the commencement of an evacuation. In the event of a false report, an evacuation could create a danger and risk that could result in serious injuries to the evacuees. When possible, confirmation of the information received should be completed in a thorough, efficient, and expedited manner. Methods that can be used to confirm the information received include the following:

- Activation of initiating devices
- Confirmation from credible sources via phone, radio, etc.
- Confirmation from CCTV cameras

Once confirmed, an evacuation announcement should be made using the public-address system (PAS). Announcements should be brief, clear, and concise. Some events may activate an automated announcement, others may require manual operation of the PAS. The announcement should state which location(s) are being evacuated and where and how to exit the property. Words or phrases that could induce panic and fear are to be avoided. For example, words like "bomb," "fire," etc., should not be used. Also, consideration of the popular languages spoken in the property should be taken into consideration. The announcement should be in English and, if possible, in another language that is known to be dominant at the property. This will expedite the evacuation process and help to reduce confusion.

The evacuation announcement should be reviewed and approved prior to any evacuation and announced over the public address system. The announcement should be communicated in a

Emergency Procedures & Response Plans: 000 **Effective Date:**

EVACUATIONS **Revision Date:**

Approval: **Page 2 of 5**

calm and clear voice. When the order to evacuate is announced, it is to begin immediately in a calm and professional manner. The evacuation announcement should be brief, clear, and concise. The following is an example of an evacuation announcement:

> "May I have your attention please. May I have your attention please. There has been an emergency reported in the property. Please proceed calmly to the nearest emergency exit. Thank you."

Repeat the emergency evacuation message as needed. All employees should direct guests to exit the property—providing it is safe to do so. Once guests have exited the property, nonessential team members should exit and meet at the pre-established team member meeting place. All guests and nonessential employees should exit the property and be directed a safe distance away from all exits for their own safety and to allow for the entry and exit of emergency responders.

If warranted, a Command Center should be established in a safe location. The Command Center may be established inside the property or at an off-site location. The Command Center should be equipped with a telephone, television, security radio, table, chairs, access to CCTV, etc. Transmissions and communications should be regulated, received, and transmitted through the Command Center.

Hospitality security evacuation procedures include being responsible for overseeing and coordinating the evacuation of the property. The responsibilities of the hospitality security team include the following:

- Top priority is the protection and safety of guests and team members.
- The protection and safeguarding of assets is second priority.
- The leader of the hospitality security team, or designee, is the person-in-charge during an evacuation, emergency, or any crisis.

When an evacuation is imminent, members of the hospitality security leadership team should prepare for the evacuation of the property. Preparation should include the following:

- A member of the hospitality security team should be assigned to handle all telephone traffic and make any telephone notifications. This includes:
    - Contacting the fire department, law enforcement, etc.
    - Notifying the leader of each department. The department leader is responsible for notifying appropriate personnel within his or her department.
    - Contacting additional security team members—if needed.

Emergency Procedures & Response Plans: 000	**Effective Date:**
EVACUATIONS	**Revision Date:**
Approval:	**Page 3 of 5**

  - Members of the hospitality security team should be assigned to ensure that the fire lanes, fire hydrants, and helicopter landing sites are clear of vehicles and people.
  - Notifications to fire department, law enforcement, etc.
- Conduct surveillance of the property with CCTV, patrols, etc., to ensure that all occupants have left the premises.
- Post hospitality security personnel at strategic locations to ensure safe evacuation and to prevent vandalism, theft, looting, etc. A member of the hospitality security team should be assigned to keep a log of anyone removed from the property for medical treatment.
- All keys that are needed to ensure the safe evacuation and access to all pertinent areas should be issued to those hospitality security team members responsible for these areas.
- Members of the hospitality security team should be assigned to immediately investigate any reported claims or injuries.
- All available hospitality security team members should assist and direct patrons out the nearest exit, providing it is safe to do so.
- Hospitality security team members should be assigned to the property exits and entrances to assist guests, prevent people from gathering at these areas, and allow entry only to authorized personnel.
- Should it become necessary to vacate any of the vital areas like the Hospitality Security Operations Center, etc., essential records, keys, and other critical items will be removed and immediately delivered to the Command Center.
- When the evacuation is completed, exits and entrance should be secured, and a perimeter patrol should be established and remain in effect until the property is reopened.

When the evacuation order is considered, the decision to evacuate should be made by the general manager, or his or her designee. When the evacuation order is given, the departmental responsibilities should include the following:

The Facilities Department leader's responsibilities should include the following:

- Notifications are to be made to all facility team members advising that an evacuation is in effect.
- Patrons should be directed to exit the property out of the nearest exit, providing it is safe to do so.
- Provide assistance to emergency responders such as the fire and police departments by activating fire pumps, deactivating electrical systems, etc.
- Ensure that support is provided to the Hospitality Security Department.
- Be accountable for verifying that all contractors have completed the sign-in sheet and a physical count is conducted.
- Ensure that all electric and gas in the kitchen and processing areas are turned off.

Emergency Procedures & Response Plans: 000	**Effective Date:**
EVACUATIONS	**Revision Date:**
Approval:	**Page 4 of 5**

The Food and Beverage Department leader's responsibilities should include the following:

- Notifications are to be made to all Food and Beverage Department team members advising that an evacuation is in effect.
- Patrons should be directed to exit the property via the nearest exit, providing it is safe to do so.
- Patrons should be advised that all food and beverage areas are closed.
- Ensure that all Points of Sale are closed, currency is left in the register drawer, and the registers are locked. If possible, disconnect the power cord to the register.
- All keys should be turned over to a member of the hospitality security leadership team and secured.
- Ensure that all electric and gas in the kitchen and processing areas are turned off.

Department leaders of all other areas responsibilities should include the following:

- Notifications are to be made to all members of the department advising that an evacuation is in effect.
- Ensure that all pertinent records are collected and secured.
- Ensure that all electric and power in the area is turned off.
- Patrons should be directed to exit the property via the nearest exit, providing it is safe to do so.
- Ensure that all personnel evacuate the property.

The following are some basic guidelines that should be adhered to regarding an evacuation:

- If necessary, guests with special needs should be escorted.
- Guest should be spoken to in a firm, fair, and polite manner.
- A sense of urgency should be conveyed in a calm and professional manner to ensure complete compliance to the directives given.
- Re-entry into the property is not permitted until an all-clear announcement is given over the public address system.
- In preparation for an evacuation, team members should be familiar with all exits, including emergency exits.
- Predetermined meeting locations should be part of the orientation process for all team members.

In the event of an emergency, all team members should meet at the predetermined location outside of the property where a head count and roll call should occur. Hospitality security should be notified immediately of all persons who are accounted for.

Emergency Procedures & Response Plans: 000	**Effective Date:**
EVACUATIONS	**Revision Date:**
Approval:	**Page 5 of 5**

No one should be permitted to gather near the exit doors or the perimeter of the building. This could jeopardize the lives and safety of those attempting to exit and to emergency personnel responding to the crisis.

Emergency Procedures & Response Plans: 000	**Effective Date:**
FIRE	**Revision Date:**
Approval:	**Page 1 of 4**

This plan should be employed in the event of a fire so that maximum safety may be afforded to patrons, guests, and employees. Employees should be aware of their duties and responsibilities during a fire emergency. If any employee should discover a fire, smoke, or unusual heat, he or she will proceed to the nearest house phone, dial for the operator, or contact the hospitality security emergency extension. The information that should be provided includes the following:

1. Name
2. Exact location of the fire
3. Present fire conditions
4. Is area occupied or vacant? If occupied, approximate number of people.

When fire conditions are discovered by a member of the hospitality security team, the conditions should be reported immediately to the Hospitality Security Operations Center via the portable radio using the appropriate code. Radio contact and condition updates will be reported as long as it is safe to do so. At no time, will the word "fire" be transmitted over the radio.

The following are the steps that should be taken when fire conditions are observed:

- The nearest pull box should be activated.
- If safe to do so, attempt to contain or extinguish the fire with a portable fire extinguisher.
- When exiting the area, use the fire stairs and exits. The elevator should not be used. Elevator shafts and chimneys are similar in that during a fire, smoke and toxic gases can enter the elevator shaft, which may result in the asphyxiation of its occupants.
- Guests and employees should use the emergency exits and fire stairwells.
- Prior to opening a door, it should be determined if the door is warm or hot. If these conditions exist, the door should not be opened.

When security personnel receive a fire alarm, the leadership team members of the Facilities and Security Departments should be contacted immediately. The following should be included in their response:

- A member of the hospitality security leadership team should report to the Fire Command Center and assist with the overall coordination of duties, assignments, responses, and notifications.
- The assignment of appropriate personnel should be detailed to the alarm location to determine the cause.
- Upon arrival to the alarm location, conditions of the alarm area should be reported immediately.
- A representative of the hospitality security team should meet and greet the fire department and provide an escort to the event area, providing it is safe to do so.

Emergency Procedures & Response Plans: 000	**Effective Date:**
FIRE	**Revision Date:**
Approval:	**Page 2 of 4**

To expedite the efficient response to reports of fire conditions, the training received by the hospitality security team should include the following:

- The proper use of the fire protection and detection equipment.
- The locations of fire extinguishers, fire stairs, and fire exits.
- Priority consideration should be provided to persons with special needs during a fire emergency.

Fire Evacuations:

- The leader of the hospitality security team should be responsible for all fire-related operations.
- For fire-related evacuations, the decision to evacuate should be determined by:
    1. The fire official with the highest rank in the fire department
    2. General manager or designee
    3. Leader of hospitality security team
- When notice to evacuate is given, the evacuation plan as outlined in the evacuation procedures should be followed.
- When the fire department arrives on scene, it takes complete command and control of all fire operations and its directives should be followed.
- If an evacuation is announced, it should be completed until all guests and nonessential employees are safely evacuated.
- Remember, the fire department may order, alter, or halt any evacuation once it takes control of the facility.

Telephone Operations:

When an operator receives a call reporting fire conditions, the response should include the following:

- Immediately transfer the call to security via the Hospitality Security Operations Center.
- Advise a member of the telephone leadership team.
- Priority should be given to all calls to the hospitality security team at the Hospitality Security Operations Center.
- Telephone operators should remain at their position during a fire emergency, providing it is safe to do so.

Emergency Procedures & Response Plans: 000	**Effective Date:**
FIRE	**Revision Date:**
Approval:	**Page 3 of 4**

Facilities Operations:

The Facility Department's responsibilities during a fire event should include the following:

- A member of the facilities leadership team should update members of the hospitality security leadership team with all pertinent information regarding the building's various systems.
- Ensure that the monitoring and control of fans, air ducts, air handling units, and dampers occur so that smoke and toxic gases are removed from the property and prevented from recirculating into the property environment.
- Power sources, such as electricity and gas, are shut down in the impacted areas.
- When the order is given to restore normal operations, all fire protection and fire equipment should be refilled, recharged, or replaced.

Most properties are equipped with the following automatic fire detection and fire protection devices:

- Manual fire alarm pull boxes
- Automatic heat detectors
- Smoke detectors throughout the property and in the air handling units
- Public address system for all public and back-of-house areas.

Activation of a manual fire pull box, heat detector, or air handling smoke detector will:

- Automatically sound an audible alarm in the area that the alarm was activated.
- The alarm will appear on the fire panel located in the Hospitality Security Operations Center/ Fire Command Center.
- Security and facilities personnel should be notified and dispatched to the alarm location to investigate for signs of smoke, heat, or fire, providing it is safe to do so.

Fire prevention plays a key role in reducing fire losses, injury, and death. Awareness and correction of fire hazards is a great aid in keeping guests, employees, and the property safe. The causes of most fires include the following:

- Unsafe behavior
- Carelessness
- Improper disposal of smoking materials/matches.
- Improper storage of flammable liquids
- Defective electrical appliances
- Overloading of electrical outlets

Emergency Procedures & Response Plans: 000	**Effective Date:**
FIRE	**Revision Date:**
Approval:	**Page 4 of 4**

It is very important that members of the hospitality security team conduct frequent inspections throughout the building. These inspections should include:

- Inspection of fire exit doors to ensure that they are free of obstructions, debris, and tripping hazards.
- Inspection of evacuation routes to ensure that areas are free of obstructions, debris, and tripping hazards.
- Inspection of exit signs to ensure that they are in place and operational.
- Inspection to ensure that solid combustible and flammable liquids are stored properly.

Emergency Procedures & Response Plans: 000	**Effective Date:**
BOMB THREAT	**Revision Date:**
Approval:	**Page 1 of 5**

In this day and age, it is likely that a property will receive a bomb threat. This can occur at any time of the day or night and is something that is out of the control of security, that is, until the threat is received. This is why it is very important that all personnel on all shifts be well versed with the protocol, responses, and procedures pertaining to this type of event. The initial interaction with the caller is very important in terms of gathering information that can aid in the investigation of this threat, determining where resources will be initially deployed, and attempting to identify the source of the call. Remember, the safety and protection of all guests, vendors, and employees is paramount.

The following are procedures and response plans that should be included in the deployment of the actions taken when a property receives a bomb threat or a device is discovered.

When a bomb threat is received or a suspicious device is discovered, the Hospitality Security Operations Center should be contacted immediately from the nearest house phone. Remember, the device should not be touched, and radios should not be used. When receiving a bomb threat, the information provided should include the following:

- When a bomb threat is received, the person receiving the call should note the phone number displayed on the caller ID screen and complete a bomb threat checklist form while the caller is on the line.
- The person receiving the call—or anyone who is aware that a bomb threat is received, should immediately notify the Hospitality Security Operations Center of the bomb threat via the nearest house phone. Radios should not be used.

One way to visually alert others that a bomb threat has been received is to have the bomb threat checklist form printed on bright paper, for example, neon yellow, and maintained at all areas that receive incoming calls.

- When anyone is observed completing this form, the Hospitality Security Operations Center should be contacted, and the bomb threat response plan should be activated.
- When receiving a bomb threat, the caller should be kept on the line as long as possible. The caller should be encouraged to talk so as much information as possible can be obtained. This includes the phone number displayed, background noises, accent, etc. Encourage the caller to talk, extracting as much information as possible.
- While completing the bomb threat checklist form while the caller is on the phone, attempt to ascertain location, description, and detonation time of the device.

Emergency Procedures & Response Plans: 000	**Effective Date:**
BOMB THREAT	**Revision Date:**
Approval:	**Page 2 of 5**

- A representative from the hospitality security leadership team should immediately go to the location where the bomb threat call was received, speak with the recipient when the call is completed, retrieve the bomb threat checklist form, make notifications, and take appropriate action.

When a bomb threat is received and the pertinent information has been quickly and accurately gathered, the immediate response should include the following:

- Notifications should be made to include the following:
  - Member of the facilities leadership team
  - General manager
  - Member of operations leadership team
  - Law enforcement—bomb squad
  - Leaders of other departments
- Remember, it is always a good practice to direct all inquiries from the media to a specific spokesperson.
- A member of the hospitality security leadership team will determine if the caller identified a location, description of device, or detonation time. This is one of the most critical factors in determining what actions should be instituted. For example, if the caller states, "There is a bomb in your property," and hangs up, a search will be conducted, and if no suspicious devices are located, a decision will be made in regard to the next step. On the other hand, if the caller states, "There is a brown brief case that contains a bomb in the men's restroom at the main entrance in the third stall on the left, and it is set to go off in thirty minutes," and hangs up, and a search of this location reveals a brown brief case or a suspicious device, evacuation procedures should begin. Remember, the safety of the occupants of the property is paramount.
- Search teams and specific areas to be searched are to be assigned by a member of the hospitality security leadership team. It is critical that directions given by the member of the hospitality security leadership team are followed, and a search of each area is completed prior to relocating search personnel to other search areas. Remember, it is always a good practice to assign personnel to areas that they are familiar with because they are more likely to determine if an object or item looks out of place.

Emergency Procedures & Response Plans: 000	**Effective Date:**
BOMB THREAT	**Revision Date:**
Approval:	**Page 3 of 5**

The Security Operations Center, with the use of the CCTV system, should include the following when assisting the hospitality security team in the search for a suspicious object or device:

- Monitor activities and be on the lookout for any suspicious activities, individuals, or groups. These activities are to be reported immediately to a member of the hospitality security leadership team and recorded for review.
- Providing an evacuation order is not in effect, searches should be discreet and conducted in a calm and thorough manner.
- If a suspicious object or device is located, the Hospitality Security Operations Center and the person coordinating the search should be contacted immediately and provided with a description and location of the suspicious object or device. Remember, the suspicious object or device should not be moved, tampered with, or have anything placed over it. This should only be done by law enforcement professionals who are trained in a variety of techniques regarding the disposal of suspicious objects and devices.

When a suspicious object or device has been located, law enforcement should be immediately notified, and the response should include the following:

- The danger area should be identified, and a minimum 300-foot clear zone should be established, including the areas above and below the suspicious object or device.
- Notifications should be made to include the following:
    - Law enforcement—bomb squad
    - Fire department
    - Emergency services
    - Member of the facilities leadership team
    - General manager
    - Member of the operations leadership team
    - Leaders of other departments
- A member of the hospitality security team should be assigned to await the arrival of law enforcement—bomb squad, fire department, emergency services. Upon arrival, escorts should be provided to the responders to the appropriate areas.
- If elevators are involved, a member of the hospitality security team should be stationed at the elevator lobby on the entry level and coordinate the use of the elevator.
- If possible, all doors and windows should be opened to minimize primary damage from an explosion and limit secondary damage from fragmentation.

Emergency Procedures & Response Plans: 000	**Effective Date:**
BOMB THREAT	**Revision Date:**
Approval:	**Page 4 of 5**

- Entry into the area is not permitted until the suspicious object or device has been removed, the device has been disarmed, the property has been declared safe for reentry, and the ALL CLEAR has been announced.

The Hospitality Security Operations Center should document and record all pertinent activity including the following:

- Time bomb threat was received
- Time, name, and title of person who received bomb threat call
- Time law enforcement/bomb squad was notified
- Time fire department was notified
- Time bomb squad arrived
- Time law enforcement arrived
- Time fire department arrived
- Personnel assigned to areas, areas to be searched, status of searched areas
- Time of evacuation
- Areas evacuated
- Time suspicious object or explosive device was detected
- Location where suspicious object or explosive device was detected
- Time bomb squad departed
- Time fire department departed
- Time law enforcement departed
- Time ALL CLEAR given

In the event of a noncontrolled explosion of a suspicious object or explosive device, the response of the hospitality security team should include the following:

- Security personnel should be assigned to respond to the scene to render assistance to those injured and to protect the crime scene for investigation by law enforcement.
- Render first aid and report conditions.
- Ascertain the following of any victims—if possible:
    - Name
    - Time
    - Location
    - Victim—Remember to list all witnesses to the statement

Emergency Procedures & Response Plans: 000	**Effective Date:**
BOMB THREAT	**Revision Date:**
Approval:	**Page 5 of 5**

- All persons found at the crime scene are to await the arrival of law enforcement
- Separate witnesses and suspects
- Prevent conversation between witnesses and suspects
- Be vigilant for any spontaneous admissions or accusations
- Relocate everyone to a safe area to prevent any injury from a secondary device explosion

Emergency Procedures & Response Plans: 000	**Effective Date:**
ROBBERY/ATTEMPTED ROBBERY	**Revision Date:**
Approval:	**Page 1 of 2**

In the event of a robbery, or attempted robbery, the safety of all employees and guests is of paramount importance. Those who commit these acts are usually apprehended in a relatively short period of time due to CCTV, witness statements, and good police work. For these reasons, it is best for those on the receiving end of a robbery to comply with requests for money, etc. Those in areas that have duress alarms should be trained not to activate the alarm until after the perpetrator(s) walk away. There is nothing more important than the safety of all patrons, guests, and employees. Material things like money, etc., can always be replaced whereas the health and well-being of patrons, guests, and employees cannot. The response of hospitality security personnel to this type of event should include the following:

- Upon the receipt of information about a robbery, or robbery attempt, CCTV coverage of the area should commence immediately at the location of the robbery and the surrounding areas.
- Law enforcement should be contacted immediately.
- If CCTV coverage is available, the involvement of weapons and if the perpetrator(s) are at the location or in the area should be determined.
- At any time, if it is determined that anyone is in possession of a weapon, the subject(s) should not be approached. Surveillance of the subject(s) should commence and be maintained (as long as it is safe to do so) until the arrival of law enforcement.
- If the perpetrator(s) are on the property, all patrons, guests, and employees should be routed away from the area. Providing safety and protection to all patrons, guests, and employees is of utmost importance.
- In the event that the perpetrator(s) were not initially identified and subject(s) are later observed, immediately notify the Hospitality Security Operations Center of the location and description.
- Identify, locate, and apprehend the perpetrator(s), if possible and safe to do so without endangering guests, employees, or self.
- If it is not safe to approach the subject(s), keep your distance and maintain observation of the subject(s), as long as it is safe to do so, and await the arrival of law enforcement.
- The area of the robbery, or robbery attempt, should be secured, and the crime scene should be turned over to law enforcement. Implement the hospitality security crime scene procedure.
- Those members of the hospitality security team not directly involved with the investigation or response to this type of event should remain at their post assignments, directing guests away from the incident location while being alert for subsequent incidents.

Emergency Procedures & Response Plans: 000	**Effective Date:**
ROBBERY/ATTEMPTED ROBBERY	**Revision Date:**
Approval:	**Page 2 of 2**

If the perpetrator(s) have fled the area, hospitality security personnel should obtain information from the witnesses, including the following:

- If weapons involved, if so what was used
- Number of suspect(s) involved
- Race, sex, and age of the suspect(s)
- Body type, approximate height and weight of the suspect(s)
- Facial features, facial hair, scars, eyeglasses, etc.
- Hair color, style, and length
- Clothing style, color, etc.
- Direction of travel
- What, if anything, did suspect(s) say?
- If a note was passed, take possession of note and turn it over to law enforcement.

Upon notification of a robbery, or robbery attempt, in addition to law enforcement being contacted immediately, the following should be notified:

- General manager
- Leader of Hospitality Security Department
- Member of operations leadership team
- Leaders of other departments

Emergency Procedures & Response Plans: 000	**Effective Date:**
ACTIVE SHOOTER	**Revision Date:**
Approval:	**Page 1 of 4**

On August 22, 1989, as a New Jersey State Trooper, I was personally involved in a shooting on the New Jersey Turnpike during which I was shot six times. Approximately six months after this incident on Friday, March 9, 1990, Governor Jim Florio made the following remarks pertaining to **assault** weapons ban legislation in Trenton, New Jersey.

> "It's ironic that as the arms race is slowing down in the world between the United States and the Soviet Union, we have another arms race that is literally almost out of control in this country and here in New Jersey. I'm talking about the arms race in assault weapons. The one that's going on in neighborhoods here in New Jersey and across the nation. Drug dealers are turning our streets into battle zones. They're using sophisticated weapons like Mac-10 pistols and some of the other weapons that you see here. Interestingly enough, the colonel and I went to dinner about a week ago when the State Police welcomed back into their ranks for active duty a trooper, Anthony DiSalvatore, whom some of you may remember was almost killed last August when he stopped a car and was shot.
>
> "One of the weapons in the car that was ultimately captured was a Mac-10. So this is not an academic occurrence. We're talking about real live problems that are out on the roads and the highways now that jeopardize the lives of not only the police but jeopardize the lives of all of our citizens. Because drug dealers, particularly, are literally in a position to outgun our police and mow down innocent people. That's unacceptable and it has to end not sometime in the future, not next year, but now. And that's what we're committing ourselves to do. Our families have a right to be safe because without that right, no other right is meaningful ...
>
> "... The legislation being put forward clearly lists what we mean by 'assault weapons.' And the attorney general will have the authority to periodically review and update that list, so we can keep up with the technological innovations that the underworld is capable of putting into the stream of commerce. Common sense is going to start dictating policy. Hunters don't need Uzis to go into the woods. Law-abiding citizens don't need 'street sweepers.' Criminals do ..."

It is difficult to predict what type of weapon will be used in an active shooter event. Intentions and actions of the person committing the act play a significant role in the possible causalities sustained rather than solely the weapon used. Legislative measures, as previously described, are a positive step in deterring this type of behavior. Unfortunately, however, many times, criminals and those who are driven to commit these types of cowardly and horrific acts like those in the active shooter realm, do not usually abide by the laws and norms of society when obtaining their weapons and instruments of death.

Emergency Procedures & Response Plans: 000	**Effective Date:**
ACTIVE SHOOTER	**Revision Date:**
Approval:	**Page 2 of 4**

I have passed on my personal experience about being involved in a shooting incident to various law enforcement agencies and have presented on the topic to a variety of audiences across the country. My hope is that the information presented in these settings helps save the lives of, or prevents serious injury to, those who gave me the honor and privilege to present. In light of recent events, random shootings at businesses of all kinds and the increase of terrorist activity throughout the world and on our homeland, I feel obligated to provide a procedure to you in the event that a situation of this magnitude should arise.

I highly recommend that meetings and **tabletop exercises** be conducted with law enforcement and other agencies that would respond to such an event at your property. The purpose of this active shooter procedure is to identify the role of the Hospitality Security Department if such an event should occur. The following is a brief guideline and does not cover every possible situation but, rather, should serve as an awareness tool with the goal to help reduce the number of injuries or deaths if this type of situation should develop. Active shooter events cannot be predicted to follow any pattern and, therefore, the following protocol should act as a possible sequencing guideline for this type of incident:

When the Hospitality Security Department receives information that shots have been fired—911 should be contacted immediately. Be prepared for the emergency phone system to be overwhelmed when this type of event occurs. Hospitality security personnel should remain calm and speak in a clear manner.

When a call is received and/or information of the call is communicated to the Hospitality Security Department, the CCTV system should be reviewed, and the location of the event should immediately be brought up on the CCTV system. All areas should be scanned in an effort to answer who, what, when, where, why, and how. Some of the information that should be gathered includes the following:

- What is happening
- Where is the caller located—on the property, parking garage, etc.
- Description of perpetrator(s), how many, etc.
- Description and number of people at the caller's specific location
- Types of weapons being used or observed
- How many people are injured and types of injuries
- Callers name and call-back phone number
- Appropriate and immediate external and internal notifications should include the following:
    - Law enforcement
    - Emergency responders
    - General manager

Emergency Procedures & Response Plans: 000	**Effective Date:**
ACTIVE SHOOTER	**Revision Date:**
Approval:	**Page 3 of 4**

- Department leaders
- Affected areas

Hospitality security personnel should continue to perform their duties during this type of event as long as it is safe to do so. The Hospitality Security Department is a key component in providing critical information to responding law enforcement and emergency response agencies.

Only if it is safe to do so, appropriate hospitality security personnel will be dispatched to evacuate guests and employees to a safe area and await the arrival of law enforcement.

For those in areas that are unsafe to evacuate, steps should be taken for proactive cover indoors. This includes the following:

- Turn off the ringer on the cell phone.
- If in a room with a lockable door, lock the door.
- If possible, place a desk, cabinet, etc., in front of the locked door.
- If possible, hide.

Develop a plan of last resort. For example, what actions will be taken by yourself and the group if an active shooter enters the room.

- After the threat is neutralized, law enforcement will make a systematic search of all areas. When approached, display your empty hands in a manner so that both are visible.
- If law enforcement is actively engaging or searching for the shooter(s), do not approach or run towards them. This action puts everyone at risk and could result in injury or death.

Communication between the Hospitality Security Department, law enforcement, and emergency response agencies are critical during and after this type of event. Up-to-date information regarding the event is important to those responding and must be communicated accurately. This information should include the following:

- Description of shooter(s)
- Location of shooter(s)
- Actions of shooter(s)
- Types of weapons used and in possession of shooter(s)
- Identification of shooter(s)

Emergency Procedures & Response Plans: 000	**Effective Date:**
ACTIVE SHOOTER	**Revision Date:**
Approval:	**Page 4 of 4**

Remember, active shooter situations demand an immediate response to the situation by law enforcement and responding agencies to stop the shooting and prevent further harm. The goal is for the Hospitality Security Department to assist law enforcement in any way possible as long as it is safe to do so.

Remember, in active shooter situations, law enforcement is trained to neutralize anyone who has a weapon. Years ago, a leader in the law enforcement community where I was in charge of a security department in a metropolitan area advised that law enforcement, generally, will not risk life and injury to themselves or others in determining if a nonlaw-enforcement person at the scene of an active shooter event carrying a weapon is the active shooter, an accomplice, or someone trying to assist the police. For this reason, it is best for everyone to use extreme caution during active shooter situations.

Emergency responders will provide treatment to the injured. Hospitality security personnel will assist in these processes and roll out the appropriate portable triage stations as needed. For situations such as these, and other types of emergency situations, it is a good idea for all employees to program the Hospitality Security Operations Center emergency phone number into their cell phones.

Emergency Procedures & Response Plans: 000	**Effective Date:**
POWER OUTAGE	**Revision Date:**
Approval:	**Page 1 of 3**

Over the decades, I have been involved in numerous power outages. The one big takeaway from these experiences is that employees in all departments should instill a sense of confidence and assurance to the occupants of the property. The safety of guests, employees, and assets are paramount. When a power outage occurs the uninterruptible power supply **(UPS)** and backup generators should power the lights, life-safety systems, CCTV surveillance system, etc. Emergency generators supply power to the UPS system. If the power outage will be for an extended period of time, ensure that periodic fuel deliveries are scheduled to the fuel tanks that supply power to the UPS system.

In preparation for power outages, the following list of items that should be included in the emergency event portable container:

- Flashlights
- Batteries
- Glow sticks
- Glow in the dark tape
- Floor plan marked with shutoffs for electricity, gas, water, etc.
- Hand crank/solar/battery/adapter powered multifunction radio. It should include features to charge cell phones, receive AM/FM/LW/SW/NOAA channels, and provide NOAA emergency/weather alerts.
- First aid kits
- Trauma kits
- CPR kits
- First aid gloves
- Instant ice packs
- Chargers for cell phones, etc.
- Megaphone
- Dust masks
- Pry bars
- Duct tape
- Emergency whistles
- Heavy duty work gloves
- Caution tape
- Survival blankets

Emergency Procedures & Response Plans: 000	**Effective Date:**
POWER OUTAGE	**Revision Date:**
Approval:	**Page 2 of 3**

- Highly visible safety vests
- Hard hats
- Goggles

A list of items should be maintained and displayed on the emergency event portable container indicating the dates of expiration or the shelf life of products. As these dates approach, the items should be replaced, and the list should be updated. Remember, it is a best practice to store the emergency event portable container under the view of the CCTV system. If the emergency event portable container is utilized, it should be replenished as soon as possible.

Power failures may occur for numerous reasons. A power failure can be caused internally, externally, or a by a combination of both. Regardless of the reasons, the end result is that hospitality security personnel are on the front lines when it comes to addressing this type of issue, and the response should include the following:

- Hospitality security personnel should have specific job duties and responsibilities. Duties should include the reporting of any unusual activity, suspicious persons, and the physical inspection of badges, identifications, and access levels of those in back-of-house areas.
- Members of the hospitality security leadership team should be assigned to specific areas of the property.
- A member of the hospitality security leadership team should make an assessment of the available lighting and the occupancy of the property. If the UPS does not respond to the power outage, resulting in inadequate lighting, hospitality security personnel should distribute flashlights and glow sticks accordingly. The use of candles can cause fires and are prohibited.
- A member of the hospitality security leadership team should contact a leader of the Facilities Department and work together in implementing and coordinating the response plan.
- Hospitality security and facilities personnel should inspect all **emergency lighting** and power systems to assure that all equipment is functioning properly.
- Facilities personnel should maintain a watch of the emergency generators and electrical systems until normal power and operations are **restored**.

Emergency Procedures & Response Plans: 000	**Effective Date:**
POWER OUTAGE	**Revision Date:**
Approval:	**Page 3 of 3**

- Hospitality security personnel should inspect all elevators to ensure that no one is entrapped. If anyone is discovered entrapped, the elevator entrapment procedure should be implemented.
- A member of the hospitality security team should continuously monitor the news and weather on the radio and television for any updates concerning the power outage that could impact the property.
- A member of the hospitality leadership team should be notified immediately upon receipt of any new developments including restoration of power, rioting, looting, etc.
- In the event that violence or criminal activity has been reported in the surrounding areas of the property, increased security patrols may be needed at the perimeter of the property, entrances and exits, and other areas deemed necessary by members of the hospitality security leadership team.

Emergency Procedures & Response Plans: 000	**Effective Date:**
DEATHS	**Revision Date:**
Approval:	**Page 1 of 3**

In my career, I have discovered unattended deaths and suicides and have witnessed unfortunates who lost their lives before my eyes. For example, I received a phone call late one night at approximately 4:40 a.m. advising that a person was on the ledge of a property on the 14th floor. I rushed from home to the scene where a police officer was speaking with the subject on the ledge. I stood by the police officer while he was pleading with the subject to come towards him and off the ledge. The subject shook his head yes and said, "Okay." The subject began inching along the ledge with his back against the wall while moving ever so slowly towards us. The subject was a few feet away as the police officer was reaching his arm out when the wind began to pick up. The subject stopped and attempted to crouch down to maintain balance when a strong gust of wind swept the subject off the ledge to the ground fourteen stories below, landing between two security officers.

Many times, when someone in the Hospitality Security Department becomes involved in the discovery of or witnesses to a death, it is often the first time that he or she has observed this type of event firsthand. This is why it is important to implement postcrisis programs, which are usually driven by the human resources team, for those involved in this type of incident to ensure that they receive a proper and professional debriefing. It is not enough, as I have experienced in the past, for a property to merely advise in general terms, "If anyone needs help, call the employee assistance hotline." My recommendation is that a professional crisis counselor should be on-site as soon as possible after such an event and all of those who were involved have appointments immediately scheduled that they must attend. This is paramount in enabling those who have witnessed horrific events to come to terms with what happened and to learn techniques and resources that can help them address any emotional or personal issues that they may develop as a result.

Another important aspect that is important to remember is to treat the deceased with dignity and respect. The removal of the body should be through the back-of-house and service areas so that the family of the deceased does not feel additional anguish, pain, or humiliation. By treating the deceased with care and taking into consideration the possible consequences of not using the back-of-house and nonpublic areas, the transition of a horrific event back to the normal operations of a property can be a smooth one.

For example, at a property in which I had overseen security for several years and then moved on, my successor did not follow the previously mentioned guidelines. A short time after the transition, a celebrity's death occurred, and the decision was made to ignore protocol and do things a different way by removing the deceased celebrity out of the main entrance doors. As you can imagine, this created quite a commotion with guests' videotaping and photographing the removal of the body. Images of the deceased being removed from the main entrance were shown by the media, and I can only imagine the pain it caused to family and friends.

Emergency Procedures & Response Plans: 000	**Effective Date:**
DEATHS	**Revision Date:**
Approval:	**Page 2 of 3**

In another case that occurred early in my career when I was a security supervisor, I arrived to work in the morning and received the following information regarding an incident that occurred on a prior shift. Security personnel responded to a guest room where a guest had expired. To make a long story short, the person was not clothed and was on the floor. The responding security personnel moved the body and placed a blanket over the deceased. Then, to make matters worse, the room phone was used to contact the Hospitality Security Command Center. The potential crime scene had been contaminated, and, as far as I know, law enforcement has never been able to determine who may have been involved with this crime. Needless to say, extensive crime scene protection training was provided to the security team after this unfortunate incident.

When property personnel discover a death, the response should include the following:

1. The Hospitality Security Operations Center should be contacted immediately. The phones in the immediate area where the deceased is discovered should not be used. For example, if the deceased is discovered in a room, use a telephone that is located outside of the room.
2. The person discovering the deceased should remain at the scene until a member of the hospitality security leadership team arrives and clears the person to leave.
3. Nothing should be touched, removed, or altered at the potential crime scene.
4. Information and details should only be discussed with the appropriate hospitality security personnel or law enforcement authorities investigating the incident.
5. Remember, the information that you have is very important to the investigation of the incident.

When the Hospitality Security Operations Center is notified of a death, the response should include the following:

- Contact a member of the hospitality security leadership team.
- Contact law enforcement.
- Record the date and time of notifications to law enforcement, emergency responders, and all agencies involved.
- Record the date and time of arrival of law enforcement, emergency responders, and all agencies involved.
- Record the date and time of departure of law enforcement, emergency responders, and all agencies involved.

Emergency Procedures & Response Plans: 000	**Effective Date:**
DEATHS	**Revision Date:**
Approval:	**Page 3 of 3**

The responsibilities of members of the hospitality security leadership team should include the following:

- Notifications should be made to include the following:
  - Emergency responders
  - General manager
  - Law enforcement
- A member of the hospitality security leadership team should make internal notifications to the appropriate property leaders.
- The area should be secured using the crime scene procedures.
- A Command Center should be established in close proximity to the scene.
- Written statements should be obtained from all employees identified at the scene.
- A review of the CCTV should be conducted to determine the most recent actions and activity of the deceased and the identification of any employees that may have accompanied the deceased.
- Ensure that all witnesses are separated and pertinent information from each is gathered.
- Ensure that the area is secured and turned over to law enforcement upon its arrival.
- The area should be secured until the investigation by law enforcement is completed.
- Law enforcement is in charge of the investigation. Members of the hospitality security leadership team should, when possible, assist and comply with law enforcement's requests for information and assistance until the determination of the cause of death is established.
- The medical examiner, ambulance personnel, etc., should be escorted through the back-of-house and service areas whenever possible.
- The removal of the body should be through the back-of-house and service areas whenever possible.
- Immediate arrangements should be made with the human resources team to coordinate and facilitate the arrival of a professional crisis counselor.
- Information of those involved should be gathered, and mandatory appointments to visit the on-site professional crisis counselor should be made for those that were involved in responding to the incident and for others who may have been impacted.

Emergency Procedures & Response Plans: 000	**Effective Date:**
CRIME SCENE PROTECTION	**Revision Date:**
Approval:	**Page 1 of 2**

The protection of a crime scene is critical for the proper investigation and subsequent prosecution of those who violate the law at a property. At times, it may not be immediately understood by hospitality security personnel that a crime has been committed, and potential evidence and witness statements may not be properly gathered. To be proactive in this approach to incidents and crime scene protection, it is recommended that all responses by the hospitality security team should be treated as if a crime has been committed in terms of protecting the scene until proven otherwise. A crime scene, or scenes, can be explained as the immediate or extended area in which a crime may have occurred and could contain physical evidence pertaining to the identity of a suspect.

Signs or indicators that can help to determine if an incident is a possible crime scene include the following:

- Broken glass
- Blood
- Cutting instruments, knives, razors, box cutters, etc.
- Unattended weapons
- Damage to property
- Discarded clothing
- Threatening demeanor or attempts to intimidate
- Statements or actions of nearby guests to incident—advising or pointing in the direction of a person who fled area or was involved in an incident

The member of the hospitality security team initially responding to an incident may be advised by the Hospitality Security Operations Center that a possible crime has taken place. Other times, the initial responding hospitality security personnel may need to be responsible for evaluating the incident scene and observing the surroundings and actions of those at the location to determine if the elements of a possible crime exist. It is not an easy task, and the observations and appropriate response should occur quickly and accurately regarding the determination of a potential crime scene and the immediate preservation of the evidence. Persons within the crime scene area should be identified and escorted from the potential crime scene to a safe location. Potential witnesses or suspects could include guests, patrons, vendors, employees, etc. A member of the hospitality security leadership team should ensure that a list of all persons at the potential crime scene is obtained as quickly and efficiently as possible.

Emergency Procedures & Response Plans: 000	**Effective Date:**
CRIME SCENE PROTECTION	**Revision Date:**
Approval:	**Page 2 of 2**

When protecting a possible crime scene, it is important not to contaminate any of the physical evidence. If possible, hospitality security personnel on this type of assignment should stand in one place, in a strategic location where the scene can be protected, and not touch anything. In confined spaces, all entrances and exits to the crime scene should have a member of the hospitality security team protecting the area until the arrival of law enforcement. In situations where a limited area of space is identified as a possible crime scene, that area should be isolated by the use of stanchions with the appropriate number of hospitality security representatives needed to insure the protection of the area. Remember that when a potential crime scene is located outside, efforts should be made to protect possible evidence from the wind, rain, etc.

In any case, a crime scene log should be maintained that documents all persons entering and leaving a potential crime scene, including the name, date, and time that the security representative began the crime scene protection assignment. A member of the hospitality security team should maintain this log and protect the crime scene until relieved by law enforcement. When relieved of the assignment, the security representative should document this relief of responsibility on the crime scene log with the name, date, and time of the law enforcement agent who took over the assignment and the name of the security representative who was relieved.

A member of the hospitality security leadership team should be responsible for the overall security and protection of the crime scene. This should include the following:

- Notifications made to include the following:
  - General manager
  - Law enforcement
  - Leader of Hospitality Security Department
  - Leaders of affected areas
- Security assignments of personnel.
- Establishing a Command Center within close proximity to the crime scene.
- Communicating updates from law enforcement and actions taken by the security team to the appropriate property leaders.

Emergency Procedures & Response Plans: 000	**Effective Date:**
CROWD CONTROL	**Revision Date:**
Approval:	**Page 1 of 2**

During the course of my career, there have been times when the proper implementation of crowd control procedures was paramount to the safety and protection of those caught up in a wave of humanity when people respond in great numbers to an event. If you have never experienced this firsthand, it can be quite an experience. When crowd control procedures and protocol are not in place or acted upon, the results can be catastrophic and can lead to serious injuries. I recall one specific incident on New Year's Eve at a very large property when the whole area was closed by design and only foot traffic was permitted. Being my usual hands-on self, I was at an entrance of the property that was experiencing a great influx of people. Crowd control emergency procedures that I had trained and practiced with the security team were working, but the situation was reaching a critical point.

In an attempt to assist a security team member with the closing of a gate that would prevent people from entering, and to get others to follow my lead, I led the charge and thrust myself into this mass of humanity to reach and close a gate that was a mere ten feet away. I suddenly was shoulder-to-shoulder with guests without having the ability to move about. I felt as if I was in an ocean being carried and bounced about by the current. I was literally being taken by a tide of people away from the gate and entrance to the property. Suddenly, one of the very large members of my security team—who was about seven feet tall—grabbed me by the shoulders, picked me up, and placed me into the safety of the property entrance. I then attempted to navigate my way back through the crowd in an attempt to close the gate again so that we could temporarily prevent guests from entering. At this point, the security officer who had pulled me from the sea of humanity like a little child made his way out to me, put his hand up and said, "I got this," and forged his way through the crowd with me behind him. We secured the gate and reestablished control of the entry, and we both began to laugh, celebrating our success.

The preceding story demonstrates how teamwork, communicating with your team, being aware of your surroundings, and practicing procedures prior to an actual event are important to provide for the security and safety of everyone. When crowd control procedures are implemented to provide patrons safe access and the freedom to enter, exit, and move about, the security team should include the following:

- Prior to the crowd control procedures being activated, notifications should be made to include the following:
    - General manager or designee
    - Member of the hospitality security leadership team
    - Member of the hospitality security operations leadership team
    - Only after those listed above have been consulted and agree, should crowd control procedures should go into effect.

Emergency Procedures & Response Plans: 000	**Effective Date:**
CROWD CONTROL	**Revision Date:**
Approval:	**Page 2 of 2**

- Crowd control procedures should be considered any time the number of people on the property reaches such levels that it begins to restrict free access through the aisles, entrances, and exits of the property.
- When conditions require the temporary closing, or the restriction of entry, to the property, hospitality security personnel should place stanchions in a switch-back fashion outside of the entrances.
- Hospitality security personnel assigned to the entrances of the property should be issued a bullhorn and a handheld clicker used for recording the number of guests who enter.
- Hospitality security personnel assigned to the exits should be issued a handheld clicker used for recording the number of guests who exit and should ensure that no one enters through this area.
- A member of the hospitality security leadership team should gather the number of people who have entered and exited at selected intervals from those possessing the handheld clickers.
- Based on the information gathered at the selected intervals regarding the number of people who have entered and exited, a member of the hospitality security leadership team should advise the hospitality security personnel at the various entrances to permit entry of a specific number of people based upon the number of people who have exited.
- Monitoring of the property should be ongoing. Only after those listed below have been consulted and are in agreement, should crowd control procedures be discontinued:
    - General manager or designee
    - Member of the hospitality security leadership team
    - Leader of the operations leadership team

The previous emergency procedures, response plans, and intertwined stories depict why it is always important to try to consider as many outcomes as possible when making decisions. Whenever I encounter a situation, I always think of the worst-case scenario; that way, I am prepared for anything, up to and including the worst case. This may be one reason why I have been referred to at the many properties I have worked at as the "vice president" or "director of doom and gloom."

I have always taken this as a compliment, as any security professional should, because it illustrates that you are doing your job by providing for the safety and security of all and by having a plan or a course of action for any event or situation. Remember that procedures and response plans are living, breathing documents that are there to help provide direction on the correct choices. My hope is that the procedures and policies contained in this book are helpful in assisting you in making the right choices and doing the right thing when situations arise at your property and throughout your career.

The previous emergency procedures and response plans should serve as guidelines and be modified to meet the specific needs of your property. The emergency procedures and response plans should be crafted in accordance to, and within the boundaries of, the laws and ordinances that are in effect in the jurisdiction that the property is located. Remember that the protection and safety of people should always be of primary importance; objects and things should be secondary. Additional examples of emergency procedures and response plans can be found in the Appendix located at the end of this book.

Discussion Questions

1. When should the postcrisis/emergency meeting be conducted?
2. What is the purposes of the postcrisis/emergency incident meeting, and why should it be timely?
3. Explain why it is important to review the hospitality security emergency procedures with the agencies that will be responding to the property when emergency situations occur.

CHAPTER

5

FIRE COMMAND CENTER

"Success is not the result of spontaneous combustion. You must first set yourself on fire."

—Fred Shero
A Canadian professional hockey player, coach, and general manager

On November 21,1980, the deadliest hotel fire in Nevada history occurred at the MGM Grand Hotel; it caused the deaths of 85 guests and employees, and approximately 600 other people were injured. The Clark County Fire Department reported that the most probable cause of the fire was heat produced by an electrical ground fault within a combustible concealed space in a waitresses' serving station at The Deli. The hotel was partially sprinklered, but major areas, including the main area and The Deli, which was the origin of the fire, were not.

After the fire started in The Deli, a flame front moved through the property. Smoke spread to the high-rise tower through stairways, elevator shafts, and air handling systems. The means of egress from the high-rise tower was impaired due to smoke that spread into stairways, exit passageways, and through corridors. The fire department confined the fire to the area of origin in a little over an hour. It was approximately four hours before all guests were evacuated. Unfortunately, there were 85 fatalities as a result of this fire incident. The major factors that contributed to the loss of life as a result of the fire incident include the following:

- Rapid fire and smoke development on the level of origin due to available fuels, building arrangement, and the lack of adequate fire barriers.
- Lack of fire extinguishment at the incipient stage of the fire.
- Distribution of smoke throughout the heating, ventilating, and air conditioning (HVAC) equipment.
- Smoke spread through the elevator shafts to the high-rise tower.

- Unprotected vertical openings contributed to smoke spread to the high-rise tower.
- Substandard enclosure of interior stairs, smoke-proof towers, and exit passageways contributed to heat and smoke spread and impaired the means of egress from the high-rise tower.

The previous details were a result of an investigation report prepared by Richard Best and David Demers into the MGM Grand Hotel fire and investigated and prepared by the National Fire Protection Association(NFPA) under a contract with the Federal Emergency Management Agency. This horrific incident demonstrates the importance of having life-safety systems in place, life-safety systems in good working order, and a hospitality security team knowledgeable of its duties and responsibilities if such an event should occur.

In another fire-related incident that occurred in Las Vegas 35 years later in July of 2015, a fire erupted and quickly engulfed the high-rise hotel swimming pool area located on at the 14th floor of the Cosmopolitan of Las Vegas Hotel. Approximately 110 firefighters responded to combat the fire and to help evacuate persons safely from the area. As a result of the advancement and implementation of technology, new codes, and a robust county fire inspection program, no serious injuries were reported.

The previous two examples illustrate the evolution of fire protection programs and systems over the past few decades. The proactive measures that were developed, implemented, and reinforced by county inspections played an important role in the positive outcome of the fire that occurred in 2015. It is critical that the Hospitality Security Department develops a rapport with fire departments, emergency responders, and law enforcement agencies. Remember to incorporate them into your training and response programs to ensure that the hospitality security team receives the proper training and is able to demonstrate knowledge of the training received.

This chapter is designated for Hospitality Security Departments that operate the Fire Command Center (FCC) for their property. When the Fire Command Center falls under the realm of the Hospitality Security Department, it increases the ability for quick confirmation and recognition of an alert on the fire panel as being an actual event or an alarm malfunction. In the past, and at properties where the fire alarm panel location is not associated with the Hospitality Security Department, the chances of the response to an activation on the panel being disjointed increases as does the risk to life and property. These are reasons that, if possible, it is best to locate the Fire Command Center in the same area as the Hospitality Security Operations Center.

Importance of an On-Site Fire Command Center

Think about this for a minute. For properties that do not have a Fire Command Center located in the same area as the Hospitality Security Operations Center, which is staffed 24/7, when an alarm sounds, a responder goes to the fire alarm panel and identifies the location of the alarm. The location of the event is communicated via radio or telephone. Those operating the CCTV system should first confirm the location and then attempt to locate the event while other personnel are dispatched to the alarm location. This takes time, and, unfortunately, in a worst-case scenario, a few seconds or even minutes mean the difference between a quick response, identification of the issue, and the dispatch of appropriate emergency personnel or a total catastrophe.

On the other hand, when the Fire Command Center is located within the framework of the Hospitality Security Department, the needed information is gathered instantly as the fire panel alert is transmitted. This saves time, which results in a quick, efficient, and effective response regarding the identification of the alarm. This, in turn, provides safety and protection to guests, employees, and company assets.

The Fire Command Center should be intertwined with the Hospitality Security Operations Center. The hospitality security personnel responsible for this area should be familiar with the basic operations and components of the fire alarm system. The following are the basic operations of a fire alarm system:

- **Automatic fire detection**: Includes smoke and heat detectors; when activated, they trigger audio visual devices.
- **Building controls:** Designed to interface with various systems that control electrical and mechanical systems within a building. These include electrical lights, back-up power, fire pumps, water pumps, air control, vent control, etc.
- **Intelligent or addressable analog fire detectors:** Microprocessors and microcomputer-controlled panel and devices.
- **Manual fire alarm**: Includes pull stations; when the bar is pulled, it activates audiovisual devices. This is a Type 1 alarm—when activated, it automatically activates horns, strobes, speakers, etc. The area of alarm should be physically inspected and cleared prior to the resetting of this alarm type.
- **Sprinklers and fire suppression systems**: Interfaced with the fire alarm system to automatically recall elevators, activate sprinklers, etc.
- **Voice alarm and activation**: A public address system that communicates information by a human voice providing instruction to evacuating a structure or status of an alarm condition.

Basic Components of the Fire Alarm System

The following are the basic components of a fire alarm system that should report to the Fire Command Center located in the Hospitality Security Operations Center.

- **Annunciator status panel:** The annunciator status panel identifies the following:
  - Condition status of an alarm
  - Alarm type
  - Alarm location
  - Location of trouble

  When there is an alarm, an indicator light flashes on the annunciator status panel, identifying the location of the alarm. Depending on the type of alarm and providing it has been verified as being a nonevent, an authorized representative of the Hospitality Security Department can control the alarm system by using a reset switch, silence the alarm, or reset the system.
- **Control panel**: The control panel has many functions; basically, it is the brains of the system. The control panel processes information from field devices, such as pull stations and water flow sensors. When the system recognizes that there is an alarm condition, it

triggers the preset audio-visual devices. The control panel also monitors and supervises the integrity of the power supply and circuitry.

- **Field devices**: Field devices are used in the initiating zone and include the following:
    - Heat detectors
    - Smoke detectors
    - Pull stations
    - Audiovisual devices

  There are two basic types of fire alarm systems used in the Fire Command Center of a Hospitality Security Department; they are single-stage and two-stage systems. The following is an explanation of each:

- **Single-stage system**: A single-stage system means that when a device is activated, it is designed to immediately transmit an alarm signal throughout the entire property to warn occupants that a fire emergency exists. For example, in most jurisdictions, a pull station is categorized as a single-stage device.
- **Two-stage system**: A two-stage system means that the system is designed to transmit a distinct alert signal to the Fire Command Center located in the Security Operations Center. When this type of alarm is received, responders are to be immediately dispatched to the alarm location to investigate and determine the source of the alarm. If fire conditions are present, audible and visual alarms are to be activated and fire procedures implemented. Two-stage alarm systems are used to reduce the possibility of risk and injury when investigating whether a property should be evacuated.

  Evacuating a property due to an alarm malfunction could result in endangering the safety of patrons, guests, and employees of a property due to a nonevent. With this in mind, if the proper personnel do not activate or reset the fire alarm system, a predetermined time to investigate an alarm signal should be established during which the alarm system is automatically activated. It is essential that Hospitality Security Department personnel responsible for the Fire Command Center have a thorough knowledge and are trained in the proper procedures to follow before silencing an alarm. In most jurisdictions, the activation of two or more devices will activate the fire alarm system in the same manner as if it were a single-stage alarm. An example of this would be that when two or more smoke sensors are activated, the audible and visual fire alarm system activates.

- **Standby power supply**: In the event of a power outage, the standby power supply is designed to keep the fire alarm system operational for a predetermined amount of time. The standby power supply can consist of the following:
    - Battery-charged back-up power.
    - Essential equipment and areas are connected to the back-up power supply system (UPS) that supplies power to all emergency systems in the event of a power outage.
    - A back-up power redundancy system; for example, if the UPS system fails, the battery back-up power would supply power to the fire alarm system.

Science of Fire

The following are the four phases of fire:

- **First phase—incipient phase:** There is no noticeable smoke, heat, or flame. During this phase, flammable gases and/or combustion products are emitted.
- **Second phase—smoldering phase:** There is no substantial amount of flame or heat, but smoke is visible.
- **Third phase—flame phase:** Usually involves less smoke, but flames break out and generate substantial heat.
- **Fourth phase—high-heat phase:** Fire spreads rapidly, producing extensive flames and extreme heat.

The three elements needed for fire are oxygen, heat, and fuel, which make up what is known as the fire triangle. If one of these elements is missing in the fire triangle, a fire cannot exist. The removal of one or more sides of the fire triangle can be achieved by using fire extinguishers and fire extinguisher systems. The following are classifications of fire:

- **Class A:** Involves cloth, rubber, wood, paper, or other solids containing carbon. Water is used to the stop the fire and cool the material.
- **Class B:** Fueled by flammable or combustible liquids which include oil, gasoline, or other similar materials. The oxygen supply of the fire triangle can be smothered by the use of dry powder, foam, or carbon dioxide.
- **Class C:** Involves energized electrical equipment. Always deenergize the equipment and use a nonconductive extinguishing agent such as carbon dioxide or dry powder.
- **Class D:** Involves combustible metals such as magnesium and titanium. Dry powder extinguishing agents work by absorbing heat and smothering the fire.
- **Class K:** Involves cooking oils and greases such as vegetable oils and animal fats. Fire extinguishers rated for this type of fire contain a wet chemical agent that turns the cooking oil and fat that is serving as fuel to soap.

Using the proper fire extinguisher on a fire is very important for the safety and protection of guests, patrons, employees, and the property. Failure to do so can have catastrophic results. All employees should be required to know the locations of the nearest exits and emergency exits and the locations of the nearest fire extinguishers in their work areas. All employees should know how to select the proper fire extinguisher in their work area and should know how to operate them in the event of a fire emergency. As I stated in an earlier chapter, the acronym **PASS** can be helpful in remembering the proper steps when using a fire extinguisher. PASS stands for the following:

> **P**—Pull the pin of the fire extinguisher that is located at the top by the handle.
>
> **A**—Aim the fire extinguisher at the base of the fire.

S—Squeeze the handle of the fire extinguisher.

S—Sweep the fire extinguisher from side-to-side at the base of the fire

When writing this chapter about the Fire Command Center component of the Hospitality Security Department, I struggled with the best way to present this material. I wanted this section to be useful, uncomplicated, and easy to understand while not wanting these policies to be simply used verbatim. My reasoning was that the rules, regulations, codes, and laws governing the areas that the Fire Command Center is responsible for while being part of the Hospitality Security Department may be unique and different in every jurisdiction. Either way, I have decided to include the general process and procedures of a Fire Command Center.

Remember that these are designed to cover the basics for a variety of jurisdictions and are to be used as a guide. They are designed to provide a starting point for your own Fire Command Center procedures. It is very important to review and understand the equipment used; how it operates; and the rules, regulations, codes, and laws that govern all areas of the Fire Command Center of your property.

I have always had great success when I have met with and consulted with local jurisdictional representatives of fire departments, law enforcement, and emergency responders. When meeting with the various agencies, I was able to develop a great rapport with those responsible by providing a copy of the properties emergency procedures for their review. Afterwards, I would meet again and review and discuss the emergency procedures, answer any questions, and update the emergency procedures accordingly. This was very helpful for me, and it should work to your advantage to ensure that everyone is on the same page as to what the protocol, policy, and procedures are regarding the specific requirements and responsibilities for your property in the event of a fire emergency.

The goal of standard operational procedures is to be able to establish communications between all the entities involved in addressing fire events and fire evacuations or any other type of emergency resulting in the protection of life and property. Prior to an actual fire, or event, it is critical to establish mutual assistance protocols and maintain communications with the fire department, law enforcement, and emergency response personnel. One way to develop and create a working rapport with them is to invite them to participate in your emergency exercises and training programs. Also, with the approval of the leadership team of your property, invite the fire department, law enforcement, and emergency services to conduct training exercises on your property in which the Hospitality Security Department can participate. This will help to increase the cohesiveness between all involved and develop a sense of team spirit.

By the same token, too, there may be training exercises that are specific only to the fire department, law enforcement, and emergency services, which do not afford the opportunity for others to participate. Welcome this with open arms and embrace it by providing a location on the property where training exercises can be conducted. When it comes to life and safety, there can never be too much communication and interaction between all departments and should be encouraged. Although the response to any emergency event requires responders from various departments and agencies, all have the same objective in mind and that is to protect life and property. As I always like to remind everyone involved in this great endeavor, "one team—one goal."

Case-by-Case Examples

Standard Operational Procedure: 000	**Effective Date:**
FIRE COMMAND	**Revision Date:**
Approval:	**Page 1 of 3**

The Fire Command Center responsibilities, systems, types of alarms, and equipment include the following:

FIRE ALARM PRINTOUT

- Any fire-related alarm received by the Fire Command Center via the fire alarm computer system will be automatically printed out. The information contained in this printout will include the following:
  - Type of alarm
  - Location of alarm
  - Time of alarm
  - Date of alarm
- The various types of alarms received in the Fire Command Center include the following:
  - Priority one (fire)—Activates audible and visual devices, recalls and activates fire suppression systems.
  - Priority two—Supervisory alarms and trouble alarms. Does not automatically activate audible and visual devices, recalls elevators, or activates fire suppression systems.
- Alarm Malfunctions—When an alarm is activated, and there is no sign of smoke, flame, heat, or the indicators of fire, the ALL CLEAR will only be reported to the Fire Command Center when the responders to the alarm location are 100% certain that there is no sign of smoke, flame, heat, or the indicators of fire.
- During the investigation of any emergency, life-safety event, or investigation of alarms only, the radio traffic related to the emergency, life-safety event, or alarm investigation should be communicated. All other radio traffic should cease until the ALL CLEAR has been declared by a member of the hospitality security leadership team.

Priority 1—(pull station, water flow, multiple smoke detectors)

- Alarm received and acknowledged on Fire Command Center panel.
- The Fire Command Center panel is not to be reset until after an alarm investigation has been completed, and it has been 100 % determined that it is not an actual alarm.
- An actual event—the Fire Command Center panel may be reset only with the approval of the fire department.

Standard Operational Procedure: 000 | **Effective Date:**

FIRE COMMAND | **Revision Date:**

Approval: | **Page 2 of 3**

- Notification to fire department.
- Member of hospitality security leadership team to respond to alarm location.
- Member of facilities leadership team to respond to alarm location.
- Those responding to the alarm location will do so, providing that it does not jeopardize their safety.
- Those responding to the alarm location will maintain radio contact with the Fire Command Center and report conditions.
- The Fire Command Center personnel will confirm that a representative of the hospitality security leadership team conducted a meet-and-greet with the fire department and provided an update of the situation to the fire department chief.
- A representative of the hospitality security leadership team will provide an escort to Fire Department personnel to the alarm location or event, providing that it is safe to do so.
- Fire Command Center personnel will record the date, time, and any comments when the ALL CLEAR is given by the fire department in the daily activity log.
- The ALL CLEAR will be announced over the two-way radio system, and normal radio traffic may resume.

Trouble Signals—(ground fault—power failure)

When a trouble signal is received in the Fire Control Center, the response should include the following:

- Notification to a member of the hospitality security leadership team and maintenance leadership team.
- Acknowledgement that the signal was received at the Fire Control Center panel.
- An investigation to determine the cause of the signal and the action taken regarding the signal will occur and be documented in the daily activity log.

Standard Operational Procedure: 000	**Effective Date:**
FIRE COMMAND	**Revision Date:**
Approval:	**Page 3 of 3**

Supervisory Alarms—(tamper switch)

When a supervisor alarm is received in the Fire Control Center, the response should include the following:

- Notification to a member of the hospitality security and maintenance leadership team.
- Acknowledge that the signal was received at the Fire Control Center panel.
- An investigation to determine the cause of the signal, and the action taken regarding the signal will occur and be documented in the daily activity log.

Remember—All alarms received at the Fire Command Center will be recorded on the daily activity log.

Standard Operational Procedure: 000	**Effective Date:**
FIRE WATCH	**Revision Date:**
Approval:	**Page 1 of 3**

Throughout my career, I have had to implement fire watch details at properties that were being built or at properties that were already open and operational. The point is that fire watches may have to be implemented at any time for a variety of reasons. It is always a good idea to have conversations on a periodic basis with the leader of the local fire department responsible for responding to your property regarding this and other fire response-related topics prior to having to implement a fire watch. When a fire watch detail is implemented, the procedures should include the following:

- Fire Command Center notifies the fire department and the alarm monitoring company that a fire watch will be implemented.
- The information regarding date, time, and who was notified is recorded in the daily activity report by a Fire Command Center representative.
- A member of the hospitality security leadership team will receive updates regarding all information pertaining to the fire watch by a Fire Command Center representative.
- A representative of the hospitality security leadership team will establish a fire watch detail which will include the following:
    - One hospitality security representative per three floors.
    - The Fire Command Center will report any gaps in coverage to a representative of the hospitality security leadership team.
    - Hospitality security representatives will have knowledge, location, and use of fire protection equipment such as fire extinguishers.
    - Hospitality security representatives will maintain a fire watch log of activities which, upon request, will be available to the fire department during the fire watch.
    - Hospitality security representatives who are on fire watch cannot have other duties while assigned to fire watch. The only exception is that the fire department may designate other duties to security personnel assigned a fire watch detail. If this occurs, the hospitality security representative must immediately notify the Fire Command Center of the details which, in turn, will inform a member of the hospitality security leadership team and log the information into the daily activity log.
    - Hospitality security representatives assigned to a fire watch will not perform firefighting duties beyond the scope of an ordinary citizen.
    - Hospitality security representatives assigned to a fire watch detail will conduct fire watch patrols every fifteen to thirty minutes and document these patrols on the fire watch log of activities.
    - Hospitality security representatives must maintain radio communications with the Fire Command Center.

Standard Operational Procedure: 000	**Effective Date:**
FIRE WATCH	**Revision Date:**
Approval:	**Page 2 of 3**

- Hospitality security representatives must have specific knowledge of any warning devices that are out of service.
- In the event of an emergency, hospitality security representatives must know the evacuation routes from the area of the fire watch.
- The Fire Command Center will maintain a fire watch log during the fire watch that will be available for the fire department to review at any time during the fire watch.
- In addition to the name and address of the property, the fire watch log will include the following:
    - Name and identification number of the hospitality security representative conducting the fire watch.
    - Time that the hospitality security representative completed each fire watch patrol tour of assigned area.
    - Recording of the date, time, and who was spoken to in regard to communications to the fire department and monitoring company.
    - The recording of any information requested by representatives of the fire department.
    - At the completion of the fire watch, a Fire Command Center representative will notify the fire department and the monitoring company of the cancellation of the fire watch. The date, time, and person notified will be recorded in the daily activity log.

The following is a guideline that should be utilized and distributed to all hospitality security personnel who are participating in a fire watch.

WHAT IS A FIRE WATCH?

- A fire watch is the action of a hospitality security representative whose sole responsibility is to watch for the signs of any of the stages of fire and if any are observed, to report it immediately to the Fire Command Center.

WHAT ARE THE REQUIREMENTS OF A FIRE WATCH?

- When a required fire protection system is out of service for four hours or more in a twenty-four-hour period, the authority having jurisdiction will be notified, and the property will be evacuated, **OR** an approved fire watch will be implemented for all areas left unprotected until the fire protection system has been returned to service.

Standard Operational Procedure: 000	**Effective Date:**
FIRE WATCH	**Revision Date:**
Approval:	**Page 3 of 3**

- A fire watch will involve some special action beyond normal staffing. Additional hospitality security personnel, who are specially trained in fire prevention, will be assigned to conduct documented patrols the areas requiring a fire watch.

WHAT ARE THE DUTIES OF THOSE INVOLVEDIN A FIRE WATCH?

- Periodic documented patrols of the affected areas and property will be conducted by those assigned to a fire watch detail.
- The Fire Command Center will communicate with the fire department.
- Those assigned to a fire watch detail will be able to recognize and identify any life, fire, or property hazards.
- If an emergency is discovered, the Fire Command Center will notify 911 with the exact address and specific type of emergency.
- If the property needs to be evacuated, emergency evacuation procedures will commence.
- Hospitality security personnel assigned to a fire watch detail and the Fire Command Center will maintain a log of fire watch activities available for inspection by the fire department.
- Hospitality security personnel assigned to a fire watch detail and the Fire Command Center will have knowledge of the location and use of fire protection equipment, fire extinguishers, etc.
- Hospitality security personnel assigned to a fire detail cannot be assigned any other duties.
- Hospitality security personnel assigned to a fire watch detail will not perform firefighting duties beyond the scope of an ordinary citizen.

HOW SHOULD THE FIRE WATCH BE DOCUMENTED?

- A fire watch log should be maintained at the Fire Command Center. At all times, the fire watch log must be available to the fire department during the fire watch. The fire watch log should contain the following:
- Name and address of the property, name of hospitality security personnel conducting the fire watch, and the times that each patrol was completed.
- Any communications that are made to the fire department and monitoring company.
- Any other information as directed by the fire department.

HOW TO CANCEL A FIRE WATCH

- When a member of the hospitality security leadership team confirms that the fire protection system has been fully restored, the Fire Command Center will cancel the fire watch by notifying the fire department and monitoring company.

Standard Operational Procedure: 000	**Effective Date:**
FIRE EVACUATIONS	**Revision Date:**
Approval:	**Page 1 of 8**

In the event of a fire alarm or actual fire, it will be the responsibility of the Hospitality Security Operations Center and the Fire Command Center to ensure that the safety of the property—occupants, first, assets, second—are paramount and that the emergency procedures and policies are implemented and followed. Members of the hospitality security leadership team will be the primary source for coordinating the emergency response plan. It will be the responsibility of the hospitality security leadership team to ensure that all hospitality security policies and procedures are adhered to.

It is essential that the Fire Command Center and all hospitality security personnel communicate and assist the fire department, law enforcement, and other emergency responders when requested. Remember that the fire department is the governing authority whenever its services are needed and its instructions are to be followed. In the event of an emergency, a member of the hospitality security leadership team will designate a command post. Command post locations should be predetermined prior to any actual event or emergency. The equipment located at the command post should include the following: telephone, table, chairs, other items as needed, and adequate space to accommodate key representatives of the property, law enforcement, and emergency response agencies.

ALARMS

When an active alarm is received, the response from Fire Command Center personnel will include the following:

- A member of the Fire Command Center will immediately go to the fire alarm panel and determine the location and type of alarm.
- The Fire Command Center will immediately dispatch hospitality security personnel to the alarm location to investigate and determine if it is an actual fire event.
- A member of the hospitality security leadership team will be notified.
- In some jurisdictions, there is an allotment of time given to respond to determine if an alarm is an actual fire event before the fire department is notified. The maximum amount of time given for security representatives to respond and report conditions of the alarm is 180 seconds. The 180-second countdown begins immediately upon receiving the alarm notification. If there is not one hundred percent certainty that the activated alarm is not a fire event, the fire department will immediately be contacted by the Fire Command Center.
- The audio (horn and PA system) and visuals (strobes) of the fire alarm system will be activated with announcements to evacuate the property.

Standard Operational Procedure: 000	**Effective Date:**
FIRE EVACUATIONS	**Revision Date:**
Approval:	**Page 2 of 8**

- A member of the hospitality security leadership team will direct the Fire Command Center to assign security personnel to report to the fire lanes. The fire lanes will be cleared of all bystanders, vehicles, and any other obstructions and await the arrival of the fire department.
- Upon arrival, the fire department will be apprised of the situation and escorted to the alarm location—providing it is safe to do so—by a representative of the Hospitality Security Department

FIRE

When a fire or evidence of a fire is discovered by a member of the Hospitality Security Department, it will immediately be communicated—by code name or signal—over the two-way radio system and/or the Fire Command Center will be contacted over the telephone. Radio transmissions must include the **exact location**, nature, and status of the fire condition. To help prevent panic and chaos, the word "fire" should never be transmitted.

Fire Command Center personnel will include the following in their response to notification of a reported fire event or actual fire:

- The Fire Command Center will immediately notify the fire department, members of the hospitality security leadership team, and dispatch hospitality security personnel to the location of the fire event.
- Providing it is safe to do so, those responding will attempt to extinguish the fire.
- A member of the hospitality security leadership team will direct the Fire Command Center to assign security personnel to report to the fire lanes. The fire lanes will be cleared of all bystanders, vehicles, and any other obstructions and await the arrival of the fire department.
- A member of the hospitality security leadership team will establish a command post and await the arrival of the fire department.
- Upon arrival, the fire department will be apprised of the situation and escorted to the alarm location—providing it is safe to do so—by a representative of the Hospitality Security Department.
- All members of the Hospitality Security Department will be familiar with the overall layout and physical aspects of the property. Knowing the unique, distinctive, and overall layout is important for the expeditious handling of fire and other emergency situations. Remember that panic poses a serious threat to the safety of all involved in a fire event. To help induce a general calming effect on others, it is very important for hospitality security representatives to remain calm, convey an attitude of reassurance, and maintain a professional demeanor when dealing with a fire event or other types of emergency situations.

Standard Operational Procedure: 000	**Effective Date:**
FIRE EVACUATIONS	**Revision Date:**
Approval:	**Page 3 of 8**

EVACUATIONS

During an evacuation, to maximize the protection to the occupants of the property, it is very important that evacuations occur in a safe, efficient, and orderly manner. The goal of the Hospitality Security Department during an evacuation is the protection of patrons, guests, employees, and the company assets. From time to time, on-the-spot decisions may be necessary when unique incidents or events occur, and a decision must be made to provide for the safety of the occupants and the protection of lives. Any time this occurs, the hospitality security procedures and processes should be updated to include the type of event involved with the prescribed response.

When the Fire Command Center receives a General—Priority One Alarm, the fire alarm system's audio and visual devices will activate automatically. The Hospitality Security Department will immediately investigative and confirm the fire event. Once confirmed, the Fire Command Center will make an announcement in a calm, clear manner to evacuate the property.

In the event of a hotel evacuation, the following should be implemented—providing it is safe to do so:

- A member of the hospitality security leadership team should report to the Front Desk and obtain copies of the occupied rooms list—by room number—from a member of the front desk leadership team. The occupied rooms list should include notes pertaining to guests with special needs and pets so that appropriate measures can be taken to ensure the safe evacuation of all.
- Providing it is safe to do so—a systematic approach should be implemented, utilizing a system that indicates that a guest room was checked and cleared by placing an indicator at the center of the door. Some indicators I have utilized in the past were large "X" chalk marks and brightly colored round stickers. This evacuation system will provide the ability to quickly determine which rooms were checked. The items used as indicators should be stored in the fire extinguisher cabinets on each hotel floor hallway. As part of their normal duties, hospitality security personnel should check the fire extinguisher cabinets while conducting documented tours of the hotel floors to ensure that the brightly colored round stickers and chalk have not been removed and will be available when needed.
- Hospitality security personnel should be posted in the stairwells to direct and reiterate the message to evacuate in a clear and calm manner.
- Hospitality security personnel should await the arrival of the fire department and be prepared to issue radios and detailed information.
- Hospitality security personnel should have in their possession emergency keys, including hotel master keys, access to floor plans of the property and provide escorts as needed—as long as it is safe to do so.

Standard Operational Procedure: 000	**Effective Date:**
FIRE EVACUATIONS	**Revision Date:**
Approval:	**Page 4 of 8**

Upon receiving the evacuation order, it will be the responsibility of each department leader to notify the appropriate personnel within his or her department and execute his or her departmental evacuation procedures. Remember that all windows and doors should be checked in each area to ensure that they are closed to prevent ventilation to the fire, providing that it is safe to do so. Doors between stairways and floors will remain closed to prevent drafts. Do not use the elevators. The leader of the Hospitality Security Department, or designee, will immediately notify the general manager—or designee. The following is a list of departments and evacuation roles and responsibilities for each. Remember that these are examples and should be modified to meet the needs of your property.

PBX DEPARTMENT

The PBX Department will be responsible for coordinating all telephone communications during any fire event or emergency and to prioritize incoming calls in the following manner:

- Call all guest rooms—starting with the affected floor. Call all guest rooms on the affected floor(s) twice.
- Systematically call all guest rooms that are located above and below the location of the reported event beginning with the floor above and the floor below the area(s) of the reported event.
- Any guest room in which a guest does not answer the phone will be highlighted on the rooms list and called again after all guest rooms have been called.
- Hospitality Security Department and Fire Command Center extensions.
- Extensions in the fire event or emergency area.
- In-house telephone extensions.
- Outside calls.

FRONT DESK

- Provide copies of the occupied rooms list—by room number—to a member of hospitality security leadership team. (This should include notes pertaining to guests with special needs and pets.)
- Provide copies of the occupied rooms list—by room number—to a member of PBX leadership team. (This should include notes pertaining to guests with special needs and pets.)
- Distribute evacuation maps to guests.
- Secure front desk, keys, and key cabinets.
- Assist with the evacuation as long as it is safe to do so.

Due to the critical nature of the PBX Department, personnel should remain in their work area as long as it is safe to do so. At any time that there is a concern for safety, all personnel will exit in a calm, orderly manner and report to the predetermined staging area.

Standard Operational Procedure: 000	**Effective Date:**
FIRE EVACUATIONS	**Revision Date:**
Approval:	**Page 5 of 8**

BEVERAGE AREAS

The Beverage Department leader's responsibilities should include the following—providing it is safe to do so:

- Notifications are to be made to all beverage department team members advising that an evacuation is in effect.
- Patrons should be directed to exit the property via the nearest exit.
- Ensure that all Points of Sale are closed and locked and that currency is left in the register drawer. If possible, disconnect the power cord to the register.
- All keys should be turned over to a member of the hospitality security leadership team and secured.

Beverage personnel responsibilities will include the following, providing it is safe to do so:

- Secure and lock any cabinets containing bottles of liquor.
- Secure and lock all Points of Sale.
- Give the register keys to member of the beverage leadership team.
- A member of the beverage leadership team should ensure that all registers are locked.

Beverage personnel will immediately leave their work areas without retrieving personal items in a calm and orderly fashion. If safe to do so, beverage personnel will assist guests by providing directions to the nearest exit while departing the property in a calm, orderly manner and report to the predetermined staging area.

FOOD AREAS

The Food Department leader's responsibilities should include the following, providing it is safe to do so:

- Notifications are to be made to all Food and Beverage Department team members advising that an evacuation is in effect.
- Patrons should be directed to exit the property via the nearest exit.
- Ensure that all Points of Sale are closed and locked and that currency is left in the register drawer. If possible, disconnect the power cord to the register.
- All keys should be turned over to a member of the hospitality security leadership team and secured.
- Food personnel will immediately leave their work areas without retrieving personal items in a calm and orderly fashion. If safe to do so, personnel will assist guests by providing directions to the nearest exit while departing the property.

Standard Operational Procedure: 000	**Effective Date:**
FIRE EVACUATIONS	**Revision Date:**
Approval:	**Page 6 of 8**

Operators of equipment will turn off equipment and machinery in their work area and immediately leave their work areas without retrieving personal items in a calm and orderly fashion. If safe to do so, personnel will assist guests by providing directions to the nearest exit while departing the property.

Those operating ranges, grills, and ovens will immediately turn off equipment in their work area and leave their work areas without retrieving personal items in a calm and orderly fashion. If safe to do so, personnel will assist guests by providing directions to the nearest exit while departing the property in a calm, orderly manner and report to the predetermined staging area.

If possible and safe to do so, food personnel who work out of a register will secure and lock their register and give the register keys to member of the food leadership team and immediately leave their work areas without retrieving personal items. While exiting the property in a calm and orderly manner, if safe to do so, personnel will assist guests by providing directions to the nearest exit while departing the property.

Providing it is safe to do so, the leader of the area will conduct a check of equipment to ensure that all equipment and machinery has been turned off, that all Points of Sale are secure, and that all personnel have exited the area.

HOUSEKEEPING

The Housekeeping Department leader's responsibilities should include the following—providing it is safe to do so:

- Notifications are to be made to all Housekeeping Department team members advising that an evacuation is in effect.
- Patrons should be directed to exit the property via the nearest exit.
- All keys should be turned over to a member of the hospitality security leadership team and secured.
- Housekeeping personnel will immediately leave their work areas without retrieving personal items in a calm and orderly fashion. If safe to do so, housekeeping personnel will assist guests by providing directions to the nearest exit while departing the property in a calm, orderly manner and report to the predetermined staging area.

MAINTENANCE

- Assist the Hospitality Security Department and the fire department in evacuation and emergency operations.
- Shut down gas and power as requested by the fire department.
- Will be responsible for ensuring that immediate access is available to any affected area at the request of the Hospitality Security Department.
- Will be on alert and ready to immediately shut down power, gas lines, etc., to any area.
- Members of the maintenance leadership team should report to the command center.

Standard Operational Procedure: 000	**Effective Date:**
FIRE EVACUATIONS	**Revision Date:**
Approval:	**Page 7 of 8**

BELL STAFF

- Providing it is safe to do so, a member of the bell staff should be stationed in the lobby area distributing evacuation maps to guests while assisting and directing guests to the muster area.
- A bell staff team member should assist the Hospitality Security Department by ensuring that the fire lane in front of the property is clear of all vehicles. Any vehicles located in these areas must be immediately removed.

HUMAN RESOURCES

- Retrieve employee-on-property report and visitor log.
- Report to predesignated meeting point.

ACCOUNTING

- Providing it is safe to do so—ensure that the area is secure and gather all pertinent information.
- Report to predesignated meeting point.

OTHER DEPARTMENTS

All department heads should ensure that their employees know:

- Where the emergency exits are in their immediate area and where the fire extinguishers are kept in the event of a fire/emergency.
- The location of the primary and secondary staging areas.
- Any specific duties before they leave their work area.
- Assistance should be provided to elderly, handicapped, or physically disabled persons out of the building.
- Speak politely to guests; insist on complete compliance.
- Convey an attitude of total assurance so that your requests and directives go unquestioned.
- Employee behavior during an emergency evacuation may well be the key to a successful operation.
- Calm and professional expertise in the handling of guests will reduce panic and injuries.
- Anyone who has been evacuated is not to be allowed reentry until the property is deemed safe and the all-clear announcement is given.

Standard Operational Procedure: 000	**Effective Date:**
FIRE EVACUATIONS	**Revision Date:**
Approval:	**Page 8 of 8**

- It is of the utmost importance that when evacuation procedures are in progress, evacuees cannot be permitted to cluster around the immediate exterior of the building.
- Emergency egress areas must be clear of debris and obstacles to allow for a quick and efficient evacuation.
- A head count of all personnel should be conducted at the staging area to ensure that everyone is present and accounted for.

HOSPITALITY SECURITY DEPARTMENT ASSIGNMENTS

In addition to the previously mentioned details pertaining to the hospitality security personnel response to a general alarm, the following should also be included:

- Secure any crime, fire, or other emergency scene—permitting only those with proper authorization access to these areas.
- Direct guests and patrons to the nearest exit.
- Providing it is safe to do so, those assigned to fixed posts will remain on their posts to ensure the orderly evacuation of occupants of the property.
- Back-of-house areas will be patrolled to assist those evacuating and to prevent access back into the employee areas until the fire alarm is cleared.
- Employees will be directed to the predetermined staging area.
- Only after the ALL CLEAR is given by the fire department to members of the hospitality security leadership team will reentry be permitted onto the property.

Emergency responders will provide treatment to the injured. Hospitality security personnel will assist in these processes and roll out the appropriate portable triage stations as needed. For situations such as these, and other types of emergency situations, it is a good idea for all employees to program the Hospitality Security Operations Center emergency phone number into their cell phones.

Standard Operational Procedure: 000	**Effective Date:**
IMPAIRMENT OF LIFE-SAFETY SYSTEMS	**Revision Date:**
Approval:	**Page 1 of 1**

The impairment notification form must be legibly completed when the fire control system is serviced or tested or any part of the system is placed into the bypass mode. An entry must be made into the daily activity report, which will include the following:

- Date
- Time
- Information regarding:
  - Who authorized the work to be completed on the life-safety system?
  - What is being done to the life-safety system?
  - When is the work scheduled to be completed?
  - Where is the work being conducted?
  - Why is the life-safety system being impaired?
  - Any additional pertinent information.

The impairment notification form is kept and maintained by the Hospitality Security Department in the Fire Command Center. Upon completion of service, test, or bypass, the impairment notification form must be immediately updated by the person(s) or company that initially made the impairment notification. An entry must be made into the daily activity report indicating the following:

- Date the work was completed on the life-safety system.
- Time the work was completed on the life-safety system.
- Who completed the work on the life-safety system?
- Is the life-safety system 100% operational or are additional repairs needed?
- Is a fire watch needed?
- Any other pertinent information.

Discussion Questions

1. What is the single-stage system, and what is an example of a single-stage device?
2. What are the three elements needed for fire, and what is this known as?
3. What are the four phases of fire?
4. What are the classifications of fire?
5. Explain the acronym PASS, and when it should be used?
6. List and explain the basic components of a fire alarm system.
7. Define and explain what a fire watch is and the requirements and duties of those involved in a fire watch.

CHAPTER

6

POLICIES, PROCESSES, AND BEST PRACTICES

"If people knew how hard I worked to get my mastery, it wouldn't seem so wonderful at all."

—Michelangelo

An Italian sculptor, painter (Sistine Chapel), architect, and poet during the Renaissance

Over the years, I have been involved in developing policies, processes, and best practices that have increased the effectiveness and efficiencies of security departments. Periodic reviews of these areas should occur at least every 12 months. However, sometimes a situation will occur, something may come to light, or an idea may be so good that it may require the immediate revision or creation of a policy, process, or best practice.

During a normal periodic review, one of the first things that should be done is to observe current practices and conduct one-on-one meetings with members of the hospitality security team. The topics of discussion should include the following:

- What are we doing well?
- What can we improve upon?
- What should we start doing?
- What should we stop doing?

When completed, and the responses to these questions are composed, group meetings with the members of the hospitality security leadership team should be conducted to review and discuss the departments policies, processes, and best practices. After all areas have been vetted, action should be taken to create, modify, start, or discontinue specific policies, processes, or best practices of the Hospitality Security Department. When the policies, processes, and best practices have been updated, Hospitality Security Departmental meetings should be conducted, focusing on a review and discussion of the polices, processes, and best practices that are currently in place. At these meetings, the information should be communicated, reviewed, and acknowledged by the hospitality security team. My teams particularly enjoyed the meetings when I served pizza and soda to those in attendance.

The following are some of policies, processes, and best practices that I have found to be helpful in the hospitality security arena. This chapter will also contain discussions that are relative to areas of hospitality security. It is recommended that these be reviewed to determine if they contain any information that may be useful for the overall operation and performance of your Hospitality Security Department. Remember to confer and confirm with your legal department, general manager, and key members of the executive leadership team to determine if the following abide by the laws, policies, processes, best practices, and guidelines that have been established and have jurisdictional control over your property.

Setting up Your Hospitality Security Department

During the opening phases of the many properties I have worked on across the country, I believe it is eight at last count, one of the first things to determine is staffing needs. Anytime there is a project regarding staffing levels, post locations, etc., I have always found it helpful to obtain a blueprint plan that provides an overview of the entire property or area in which security will be needed. Once this document is obtained, the next step is to determine which hospitality security post assignments require 24/7 coverage. I usually use round ¼″ diameter color coding labels in assorted colors—red, blue, green, yellow—to identify the various hospitality security post assignments. For example, the use of a red round ¼″ diameter label can be used to designate all 24/7 hospitality security posts. Other colors of the round ¼″ diameter labels can be utilized to designate other hospitality security posts that are utilized for other specific hours, etc. A legend should be provided as a reference that indicates what each round ¼″ diameter color label represents. When this project is completed, the final product should provide a visual representation of the hospitality security coverage provided by referring to the color-coded labels and the legend.

Once the hospitality security post assignments and staffing needs have been determined, the next step is to calculate the hours and personnel needed to staff these areas. To determine this, the term "full time equivalents" (FTEs) is utilized. An FTE is the absolute bare minimum that will be needed to cover a post 24/7. Keep in mind that this does not account for vacations, sick leave, etc. To account for instances such as these would usually require a bare minimum of 4.5 FTEs to cover a post on a 24/7 basis. FTEs are determined by performing the following calculation: 24 hours a day multiplied by 7 days a week equals 168 hours; 168 hours is divided by 40 hours which equals 4.2. ($24 \times 7 = 168$, $168/40 = 4.2$).

Once the number of FTEs are calculated, the costs involved of staffing the property at these levels can be determined. Don't forget that an additional calculation will need to be done for the members of the leadership team. These wage expenses should be compared to the designated budgetary funds available to see if there is enough money in the budget. If there is, great, if not, then a meeting should be scheduled with an executive leader at the property who has the authority to modify the budget to meet the needs of the department and the property.

Prior to any meetings regarding the budget of the Hospitality Security Department, double check all of your facts, figures, and post assignments. Be prepared to defend, describe, and explain each and every position/post in the Hospitality Security Department. One tool that I have found useful over the years has been the staffing level form that I created for circumstances like this. Basically, the form lists staffing levels by post assignment, position by shift—day, swing, grave—and by business volume—normal volume (level 1) and high-volume levels (level 2). Remember to staff to volume. For example, in the jurisdictions in which I was the leader of security teams, the high-volume days varied from shift to shift. For example, day shift usually experienced its high-volume days on Saturday and Sunday. Whereas, swing and grave shifts usually experienced their high-volume days on Friday and Saturday.

At the bottom of the page of this form (see Chapter 10: Forms), the total calculations are listed for normal volume and high-volume days for each shift, categorized in the following manner:

- Hours per day
- Hours per week
- FTE total per week
- Total for all shifts—day, swing, and grave

Remember to be on guard anytime the top leader of an organization, like a general manager or president or a corporate representative, invites you to lunch away from the property. On one such occasion, I was invited to such a lunch by two top staffers with the following caveat, "Oh, by the way, be prepared to discuss your staffing levels." So, prior to the lunch, I gathered and made copies of all the previous types of information discussed and answered question after question while trying to eat lunch. An explanation was asked why each post was needed, what the function was, was it really needed, etc.

At one point, near the very end of the lunch, I referred to the staffing level form and stated, "If you want to cut the budget—the staffing levels are in front of you—I explained why each is needed and you see the expenses that will be incurred staffing to these levels." At this point, they both looked at each other, and the Spanish Inquisition, I mean the questions regarding staffing levels, was over. At this point, it was revealed to me that the projected staffing numbers that were put together prior to my arrival were way off and needed to be justified—which they were. Then, they both thanked me and commented that I was the best x's and o's person in the industry. I am sure that you will receive similar accolades if you use the previous methods described in developing your game plan, determining staffing levels, and presenting the information with the staffing level form as a guide in a clear and concise manner.

Hospitality Security Departments are considered proprietary security and are generally considered to be nonrevenue generating departments. One area that I have had success in, in generating revenue for properties involved offering property security services for meeting rooms, conventions, exhibits, etc. This was done in an effort to provide the clients of the property an opportunity to use the in-house proprietary security department personnel to safeguard, protect, or provide other services as needed at a lower rate than an outside security service and a higher rate than the pay rate of the in-house security representative providing the service. Clients generally utilized this in-house service for a variety of reasons, including the familiarization of the area that hospitality security personnel possess, at a cost less than an outside service, and with the professionalism of the Hospitality Security Department. In the event that a client would rather use a property-recommended nonproprietary contract security guard service, a meeting would be held to include the following:

- Review property and emergency procedures
- Review safety protocol, location of fire extinguishers, fire stairs, emergency exits, AED units etc.
- Review the activities and events
- Hospitality Security Department contact phone numbers and radio call signs for the Security Operations Center, leaders of the Hospitality Security Department, etc.

In any event, when providing meeting rooms, conventions, exhibits etc., consideration for handling these areas should include the following:

- Hours that security is needed
- Functions to be performed
- Areas of special interest or concern
- Items of high value
- Escorts of persons or items
- Changing of the core locks of meeting, convention, or exhibit doors
- Issuance of keys to areas as approved by the person-in-charge of the event

At times, I have used nonproprietary security personnel in conjunction with my proprietary security team. Whenever this occurred, a meeting was held with the owner of the nonproprietary security company prior to its staff working on property—which included a review of policy, procedures, expectations, uniforms, appearance, etc. After the owner of the company advised that he could abide by the conditions and trained those who would work on the property, were they permitted to do so. Afterwards, when the nonproprietary security personnel were at their assignments, I would walk with the owner or designee and observe their performance, uniform, and grooming to ensure that they were in compliance with the expectations discussed. In the event that they were not, the person from the nonproprietary security company would be relieved from his or her assignment. This is one of the processes I have implemented in the past which attributed to the success of having proprietary and nonproprietary security personnel working side-by-side without the guests being able to distinguish the difference between the two.

It is a good policy to review and implement security posts that are needed to provide sufficient coverage of your property. These posts should include the following:

- **Security Operations Center—**This is the nerve center of the Hospitality Security Department. This area maintains the shift activity sheet which is utilized to refer break schedules, post assignments, and aids in the assignment of security-related assignments. It monitors the life-safety system, including alarms and fire alarm system and maintains a daily activity log.

- **Employee entrance—**Ensures that employees are in possession of employee badge and issues temporary employee, visitor, and vendor badges to persons with company-related business. It issues keys and ensures that all are signed out and returned with all of the logs completed accurately and legibly. Performs baggage checks and ensures that property passes are used when removing property from the premises.
- **Main entrance—**This area is usually the first and last point of contact a patron has with the Hospitality Security Department and may set the tone for the sense of safety and security the guest may have of the property and of the department. Hospitality security personnel posted at this post greet guests and thank them for coming to the property; they are vigilant about suspicious activity, unusual behavior, fire and safety hazards. Any unusual activity or hazardous conditions are to be immediately reported to the Security Operations Center. Unattended children must be immediately reported to the Security Operations Center and kept under observation until reunited with their parent or guardian.
- **Property rover—**Property rovers are to continuously patrol the property and respond to other duties as assigned. Responsibilities include patrolling food and beverage areas and cash handling areas, handling assignments, etc. Property rovers are vigilant of suspicious activity, unusual behavior, underage consumption of alcohol, fire and safety hazards. Any unusual activity or hazardous conditions must be immediately reported to the Security Operations Center. Unattended children must be immediately reported to the Security Operations Center and kept under observation until reunited with their parent or guardian. Rovers should provide guest service to patrons by providing directions, answering questions, and conducting proactive patrols.
- **Hotel rover—**Hotel rovers are to continuously patrol hotel floors and respond to other duties as assigned. Responsibilities include patrolling and responding to incidents involving guests, guest rooms, guest room floors, fire stairs, etc. Guest room doors should be inspected for pry marks and to ensure that they are closed. Pry marks can be a result of a criminal using a large screw driver to jimmy or attempt to pry open a guest room door. Be alert for frequent activity into guest rooms—this could indicate unacceptable behavior such as prostitution, drugs, etc. Proactive patrols of all areas of the hotel should be documented by recording the date and time each floor was patrolled utilizing an electronic hotel tour documentation system or, if unavailable, a manual hotel tour documentation system.
- **Hotel elevators—**Those posted at the hotel elevators and areas that provide access to the guest floor areas should be vigilant in their duties by requesting guest room cards from those entering the area. Observations of the items being brought into these areas should be scrutinized, and the Security Operations Center should be immediately notified if any unusual, suspicious, or prohibited items are observed. Providing it is safe to do so, the person(s) in possession of these items should be tactfully approached to obtain information that is then provided to the Security Operations Center and to a member of the hospitality security leadership team upon arrival to location.
- **Back-of-house rover—**Back-of-house rovers patrol the rear house areas and address other duties as assigned, while being vigilant for unauthorized persons, ensuring that fire exits are clear of obstructions, identifying safety hazards, etc. All anomalies—including any of the previously listed items—must be immediately reported to the Security Operations Center.

- **Breaker—**Breakers are usually your best all-around hospitality security representatives since they will be providing post relief to various assigned areas. When a breaker relieves someone from a post, he or she assumes all responsibilities of the post being relieved. It is important that the breaker follows the break schedule issued and must advise a member of the hospitality leadership team and the Security Operations Center anytime there is a deviation to the break schedule.

Another area that needs to be constantly on the radar is ensuring that the hospitality security team has the tools and equipment to perform its job in an excellent manner. I have seen, in the past, where a department was being held accountable to perform at a certain level but was not provided with the proper tools and equipment to achieve the expected standard. Some of the reasons that this occurs is that the "bean counters" do not want to release funds to purchase equipment. Sometimes, what is needed is not clearly communicated or the supplies needed were depleted and members of the leadership team of the department did not reorder them.

To prevent the previously mentioned situations from occurring, it is always a good policy to take proactive steps, which should include the following:

- At every roll call and preshift meeting, ask if any tools or equipment are needed. Part two of this inquiry is to ask, "Are there any tools, equipment, etc., needed to perform the job better?"
- When tools or equipment are needed, members of the hospitality security leadership team should ensure that it is clearly communicated to those who control the purse strings and establish a timeline of expected delivery of the items.
- A repair, maintenance, and replacement schedule for items should be established, budgeted, and executed.

This is critical for the morale and synergy of the Hospitality Security Department. Nothing can be more frustrating than having a team that really wants to be the best but is not allocated the proper tools and equipment to perform at its highest level. Sometimes, it involves a piece of equipment needed to conduct thorough checks of state or federal identification presented by guests and patrons. Other times, it can simply be pens or paper that are needed to perform basic tasks. Regardless, it is the responsibility of the leader of the Hospitality Security Department to ensure that all tools, equipment, and any other items that are needed are acquired, maintained, and replenished, as needed, to ensure the top performance of the team.

Types of Communication

Communication is always a critical area in the hospitality security arena. It is vital, especially in security and emergency-related matters, that hospitality security personnel focus on all communication to ensure that what was heard was actually said and what was said was actually heard. If, at any time, there is any uncertainty, the facts should be confirmed before communicating to others. There are many types of communications that occur which involve members of the Hospitality Security Department, including:

- **Conversational communications—**These interactions occur within and between departments, guests, employees, etc.
- **Directional communications—**These generally occur during roll call and preshift meetings. Direction is provided when an assignment is received. This also occurs when an event of an incident occurs—direction is given to guests, employees, etc.
- **Informational communications—**Information is given regarding assignments; be on the lookout (BOLOs); what to do if certain subjects, incidents, or situations are encountered. Information is also gathered and provided to guests, employees, etc., in regard to incidents, directions, processes, etc.
- **Two-way radio communications—**These should be short and to the point, using 10 codes on plain talk. When a crisis or emergency occurs and involves the joint efforts of multiple agencies and departments, plain talk may be the best way for all agencies and departments to communicate with each other to all areas. Oftentimes, the 10 codes used by the various responding agencies and departments may not be the same.

It is a good policy that during an emergency or other significant event, only information related to the emergency or significant event should be communicated. The implementation of restricted two-way radio communication is stated at the start of emergency or significant event and rescinded at the completion of emergency or significant event. When communicating words, names, etc., that sound similar, spelling using the phonetic alphabet helps to prevent miscommunication. The following is an example of a phonetic alphabet:

A—Alpha	N—November
B—Bravo	O—Oscar
C—Charlie	P—Papa
D—Delta	Q—Quebec
E—Echo	R—Romeo
F—Foxtrot	S—Sierra
G—Golf	T—Tango
H—Hotel	U—Uniform
I—India	V—Victor
J—Juliet	W—Whiskey
K—Kilo	X—X-Ray
L—Lima	Y—Yankee
M—Michael	Z—Zulu

- In addition to the hospitality security leadership team primary channel, secondary and emergency channel members should have the capability to change to the two-way radio channels of other departments. All other hospitality security personnel will remain on the primary hospitality security channel and use the secondary channel and the emergency channel as needed.

- During emergency situations, all members of the Hospitality Security Department will monitor all radio transmissions and respond accordingly.
- Hospitality security personnel will only make hospitality security-related radio transmissions. The misuse, mishandling, or damage of two-way radios will subject a hospitality security representative to disciplinary action up to and including termination.
- To provide for a pleasant environment for patrons, and to avoid broadcasting the actions of the Hospitality Security Department, earpieces will be worn by all hospitality security personnel and will be considered a part of the hospitality security uniform.
- One neat option that I request when ordering two-way radios is an emergency activation button. The emergency button is usually orange, or associated with another bright color, and is generally located on the top of a two-way radio. It should be programmed in a manner that when it is activated by depressing the button, it sends an emergency signal to the Security Operation Center. The emergency button should only be used in cases of emergencies when it is not possible to transmit in any other manner.
- **Emergency communications—**These are issued in a variety of ways, including telephone, radio, person-to-person, person-to-group, etc. For example, at the Hospitality Security Operations Center, there should be at least two telephone extensions. General calls to the Hospitality Security Department should be received on a telephone extension that has a normal ring tone. The Hospitality Security Department emergency phone extension should be easy for all team member to remember—for example 555—and have a unique and distinctive ring tone. When a call is received on the Hospitality Security Department emergency phone, it should simply be answered, "What is your emergency?" These numbers should be communicated to all employees of the property and should appear on the phone display screen as Emergency: Ext. ### and Nonemergency: Ext. ###. For phones that do not have a display screen, a label should be placed on the handset, "In case of emergency, call Ext. ###."

At various properties, I have implemented a policy that I have found to be very useful, the designation of a cell phone to a member of the security leadership team—besides the one issued to the leader of the department. This designated cell phone should be passed along shift-to-shift to the highest-ranking member of the security team. This enables the leader of the Hospitality Security Department who is on property to be contacted immediately. In the event of emergency situations, the leader of the Hospitality Security Department has the ability to receive and communicate detailed information without broadcasting it over the two-way radio system. As events unfold, direction and information can be provided—in real time—which will enable the best decisions to be made based on the information received at the time. This also is a great benefit in aiding communications with the Hospitality Security Operations Center, law enforcement, emergency responders, and other agencies.

In the past, I have created security pocket manuals that were designed to be on the person of members of the security team. The pocket manual should post assignments, two-way radio 10 codes, policies, procedures, best practices, property information, important phone numbers, etc. With the current technology available, the pocket security manual should evolve into being placed onto a mobile phone app that can be issued to members of the Hospitality Security Department. If the information is provided in this manner, it can be easily updated, viewed, and utilized.

Guest Room Procedures

Another area of importance is the creation and securing of guest room key cards that are to be used in situations when the property is unable to create new guest room key cards. This can occur when the guest room key card-making machine loses the ability to make key cards. To prepare for such an event, the Hospitality Security Department should implement a program where key cards to enter each individual guest room are created and secured. The creation of these emergency guest room key cards is a proactive precautionary measure that should be implemented in the event that guest room key cards are unable to be produced. These key cards will provide for the seamless operation of the property, enabling guests to receive guest room key cards to enter their guest room.

Three sets of these key cards—each packet should contain two key cards—should be produced, properly labeled, stored, and safeguarded by the leader of the Hospitality Security Department. The hospitality security representative creating these key cards should begin with the lowest guest room number and (2) two key cards should be created for each guest room. Key cards should immediately be placed into the prelabeled, designated binder for each individual guest room. In the past, I have found that placing the key cards into labeled baseball-card binder sleeves maintained in large three-ring plastic binders labeled Binder 1 Sequence A, Binder 2 Sequence B, and Binder 3 Sequence C worked well. Remember, do not place the guest room number on the key card. The guest room number should be placed on the corresponding card binder sleeve containing the respective key card. Once a guest room key binder is completed, it should have a zip tie tightly secured horizontally around the binder and another zip tie tightly secured vertically around the binder. This helps to eliminate the accidental use of the guest room key binders and allows for the quick and easy identification of the guest room key binders that are or have been activated. This also aids the leader of the Hospitality Security Department in conducting frequent inventories of the key cards and binders.

The activation of the guest room key cards contained in the binders should only be used when the inability to make new guest room key cards occurs. After approval has been obtained from the leader of the Hospitality Security Department, a member of the hospitality security leadership team should retrieve Binder 1 Sequence A and conduct an inventory of the contents. If no discrepancies are noted, this key card book will be provided to a member of the front desk leadership team who will utilize these key cards for guest check-in.

Use of any guest room key cards contained in Binder 1 Sequence A, Binder 2 Sequence B, or Binder 3 Sequence C must be approved by the leader of the Hospitality Security Department. After approval has been obtained, a member of the hospitality security leadership team should retrieve Binder 1 Sequence A from the designated area where the key cards are secured. In the event that there are delays in the repair or replacement of the guest room key card equipment, Binder 2 Sequence B and Binder 3 Sequence C may have to be utilized. It is imperative that the sequence listed above be adhered to at all times. Remember that the replacement of any guest room key card binder utilized should be completed as soon as possible.

Throughout my career, I have been responsible for hotels that range from hundreds to thousands of rooms. A critical area of providing a feeling of safety and security should include the visible presence of security personnel in main through fares, corridors, entrances, elevator lobbies, etc. This security presence has a positive impact on several levels, which includes adding another layer of security that persons with bad intent must by pass, acting as a deterrent, identifying unacceptable behavior, and providing guests with a feeling of safety and security.

Hospitality security professionals should be posted at the entrance of the elevator bank or entrance areas to guest floors with signage indicating that a guest room key must be displayed to gain entry. A second layer of protection should involve key card access to activate the elevator bank. This prevents those without active guest room keys from being able to easily access the guest room floors. This should be used in conjunction with CCTV placed in the elevator and monitored by a member of the Security Operations Center. When someone is observed not to have a valid guest room key, requesting others to use their keys, or piggy backing an elevator ride with legitimate guests, security personnel should be immediately dispatched to the last known location of the subject and provided with a detailed description.

When hospitality security personnel come in contact with a person who attempts to enter a guest floor or elevator and does not have a valid room key, the response should include the following:

- A valid room key should be requested from the guest.
- If the guest does not have a valid room key—identification should be requested.
- If a guest indicates that he or she is not a hotel guest, notification should be made that only hotel guests are permitted on guest floors or the elevators.
- If a guest indicates that he or she is a hotel guest—directions should be provided to the Front Desk.

Hospitality security professionals posted at the entrance of the elevator bank or entrance area to guest floors should also be on the lookout for persons attempting to bring large quantities of items, such as alcohol, suspicious items, prohibited items, etc. When any of these items are encountered, the response should include the following:

- A valid room key should be requested from the guest.
- If the guest does not have a valid room key—identification should be requested.
- Contact a member of the hospitality security leadership team.
- Depending on the nature of the items—law enforcement may be contacted.
- Appropriate action should be taken as it relates to state laws, federal laws, and local ordinances.
- The Security Operations Center should be kept abreast of all activity that occurs in these areas.

Lost and Found

The care and custody of items lost and found in a property generally fall under the control of the Hospitality Security Department. The following will review best practices and policies that should be implemented in the lost and found environment. One of the first things that I have done anytime that I was responsible for the lost and found area at a property was to inspect the storage location to ensure that there was adequate space. On occasion, I have had to clearly explain to executive leadership that a larger area was needed. Fortunately, every time a larger area was needed, it was located and provided to meet the needs of lost and found.

The next steps involve the ordering of thirty-one large containers, ordering a safe, installation of shelving to support the containers, installation of CCTV, and securing access to the lost and found area with a proximity card or other design or process to target-harden this sensitive area. The thirty-one containers represent each day of the month. Items received are placed into the bin corresponding with the day the item turned into the Hospitality Security Department. For example, if an item is turned into lost and found on March 19th, it would be placed into bin 19. If, when April 19th rolls around and the item is not claimed, it would be removed and processed; items turned into lost and found on April 19th would be placed in the bin labeled 19. This is a cyclical and continuous process that is very useful for the tracking, retrieving, storing, and disposing of lost and found items. Items of high value—cash, jewelry, etc., should be stored in the safe located in the lost and found area. In order to maintain the integrity of the lost and found area, access should be limited to as few members of the Hospitality Security Department as possible.

Even when all measures are in place, and lost and found is administered by the leaders of the Hospitality Security Department, there are occasions when theft will occur from the lost and found environment by persons in positions of trust. For example, I once had a leader of my hospitality security team steal cash from a safe located in the lost and found storage area. Basically, what had happened was that a guest advised that he or she had lost a specific amount of cash at the property. After confirmation of the facts, the authorized hospitality security leader went into the lost and found safe and completed the proper procedure and process for the retrieval of the guest money—but also took money that was unclaimed. As this person was walking through a mantrap where the leader thought there was not adequate CCTV coverage, the money was placed into his or her inside jacket pocket. This was discovered hours after it occurred because this leader forgot to turn in the lost and found keys at the end of the shift, and there was a discrepancy in the lost and found safe log, which in and of itself is suspicious. I reviewed the CCTV coverage of the lost and found area and discovered that one of my security leaders was a thief.

The following are some of the types of theft scams that can occur in the lost and found environment with tips and best practices for preventing them.

- Checkbook theft scam
  - Checkbook is recovered by employee.
  - Check is removed from the middle or back of the checkbook.
  - Check is written and cashed.
  - Owner of check does not usually discover loss until a withdrawal shows up on his or her statement.

  - Bank may not elect to prosecute due to the expenses incurred and/or bank insurance may cover the loss.
  - If the owner and the checkbook are reunited, advise the owner to inspect his or her bankbook to ensure that all checks are accounted for. It is also a best practice to advise the guest to contact his or her bank.

- Credit card theft scam
  - Credit card information is recorded by an employee prior to being logged into lost and found or afterwards by a rogue employee. Information is passed on to an accomplice who uses the card and splits the proceeds with employee.
  - Credit card gets "lost"—is not properly recorded and documented as being turned over to a hospitality security representative or into the lost and found. When the credit card is discovered, the person responsible usually advises that he or she was told that the guest was going to be stopping by to pick up his or her credit card.
  - To help deter this type of behavior, it is a best practice that any credit card received must be immediately logged into the lost and found log and stored.

- Staging items theft scam
  - When lost and found items are discovered not processed by a member of the hospitality security team, it is an indicator that the system is being tested.
  - When an inquiry is made pertaining to the lost and found item not being logged in, the hospitality security representative will usually claim something like the following:
    - Informed that guest would pick up the item.
    - Keeping the item for safe keeping until the owner arrives.
    - Owner of the item never showed up.
    - Forgot to log the item into the system.
    - Was so busy, forgot the item was here.
  - If the lost and found item goes unnoticed, the rogue hospitality security member may steal the item.
  - To help deter this type of behavior, members of the hospitality security leadership team should implement a best practice of making frequent inspections of the locations that lost and found items are turned into at the property.
- Other theft scams
  - Lost and found item is turned over to security representative at lost and found.
  - Hospitality security representative follows the lost and found procedure and records item into lost and found.
  - Hospitality security representative advises co-conspirator of item information. Co-conspirator contacts lost and found and claims the item.
  - A best practice for this type of scam is to check lost and found logs to determine if a specific person claims an inordinate amount of lost and found property or if there are inquiries regarding lost items that were released.

  - Another type of theft scam involves the disposition of unclaimed lost and found items when they are sold to an outside agency like a pawn shop.
  - The hospitality security representative may:
    - Put high value items aside and steal the items.
    - Not turn in all the items and steal the items.
    - Be paid partially in cash, which the hospitality representative keeps and is issued a receipt for the difference that is returned to the property.
  - Even though hospitality security leaders and administrators are in positions of trust, the following best practices should be observed to prevent the creation of an opportunity for theft in these types of situations:
    - Separation of duties
    - Checks and balances
    - Reconciliation processes
- The following policies should be implemented in lost and found environments to reduce and prevent theft from this area.
  - CCTV in lost and found room—with a specific location for processing all paperwork and activities.
  - Security notified immediately upon the discovery of any lost or found item.
  - Hospitality security representative retrieves lost and found item.
  - When a lost and found item is transported, it should be under constant CCTV coverage until the item is secured.
  - Proper completion and documentation of the life cycle of a lost and found item.
  - Separation of duties.
  - Checks and balances.
  - Reconciliation processes should be reviewed to insure compliance.
  - Integrity inspections.
  - Inspect the trash containers for lost and found paperwork. (I discovered torn up lost and found paperwork in a trash can located in the lost and found area, which led to the admission of theft by a security representative.)
  - When anomalies are uncovered, those who are responsible for the lost and found area should be investigated and interviewed.

It is important that guests and employees perceive the property as a place that ensures a reasonable safeguard for treatment of personal possessions. Found items should be delivered to the lost and found and tagged in a property bag. In situations where it is impractical for an employee to personally deliver an item, the Hospitality Security Department should be contacted to pick up and transport the item to the lost and found. A tracking mechanism should be utilized. One method is to use a three-part receipt that, when completed, is distributed in the following manner: one copy is retained by the Hospitality Security Department, the second copy will stay with the lost and found item, and the third copy should be given to the person turning in the item. Every attempt should be made to find the rightful owner of any items turned into the lost and found.

Flyers, Outside Businesses, and Unwelcome Visitors

On occasion, outside businesses will attempt to deliver flyers under guest room doors advertising their business, menus, special offers, etc. I can remember during the first days of being in charge of a Hospitality Security Department in a large city, the general manager called me into his office and told me that vendors from restaurants were constantly sending people over to slide menus under the guest room doors—and he wanted it stopped immediately. The proactive measures I implemented resulted in stopping this type of behavior in a relatively short period of time. One measure taken was that I would check into a guest room and sit in front of the door. As soon as a menu was placed under a door, I would exit the guest room. Sometimes, the vendors would be working in a group or they would run. When the subject(s) were identified and stopped, they would be questioned, information gathered, and the person(s) would be evicted from the property.

Another measure implemented involved frequent patrols of the hotel floors and fire stairs. Many times, people who were involved in this type of activity would not walk in through the front doors of the property or would attempt to use the fire stairs, as previously mentioned, as a means of escape when they were observed. When information was received that menus were being slid under guest room doors, the subject(s) would be questioned, information gathered, and the person(s) would be evicted from the property.

In an effort to deter this type of behavior and to protect the privacy of guests from unwelcomed visitors, deliveries being made by outside vendors to guest rooms (delivery food items, as an example) should be screened. When a delivery person claims to have a delivery that was ordered by a guest, the destination guest room should be contacted, and the guest should be asked if he or she is expecting a delivery from the company that the delivery person represents. Remember that it is essential that the vendor supply the name and guest room that the order was placed under. The hospitality security representative should not confirm or deny the information that is provided.

If the order is not confirmed by the guest, the delivery person should be asked to identify him- or herself. The location of origin of the delivery should be contacted and the guest room number confirmed to determine if the person had an actual delivery. When the information is not able to be substantiated, it usually is an indication that the delivery person was attempting to execute another type of activity, such as delivering menus to guest rooms, etc. If the delivery does not match a registered guest name or if the guest named by the delivery person indicates that he or she did not place such an order, a member of the hospitality security leadership team should be contacted and the identification of the delivery person should be verified. Afterward, the vendor should be escorted off the property, and the incident should be documented.

If this order is confirmed, the guest should be advised that the delivery person will be escorted to his or her guest room and should be arriving shortly. Hospitality security personnel should accompany the delivery person directly to the room, knock on the door, and identify themselves as hospitality security representatives. After the transaction is completed, the delivery person should be immediately escorted off property. The delivery person should not be allowed to enter any areas of the property outside of the path of travel to and from the destination.

The unauthorized removal of items from a property can result in large losses to a company. A robust program that requires employees to make available for inspection all items, including personal bags, boxes, briefcases, etc., by the Hospitality Security Department can act as a deterrent to this type of behavior. Some techniques used and uncovered in my career by those attempting to steal company property involved minibar liquor items stored in portable beverage containers and expensive food items like steak, lobster, etc., in backpacks. Sometimes those committing these acts attempted to walk past the authorized exits where security personnel are posted; other times subjects attempted to use unauthorized exits like back doors and are detected.

To prevent the unauthorized removal of property assets from the premises, all items removed from the property must have written approval from a member of the department's leadership team in the form of a property clearance form. Remember that if a person did not bring an item into a property, he or she must have a property clearance form to leave the property with it. When an employee has cause to remove property assets from the complex, the employee must receive authorization (in the form of a property clearance form) from a member of the department's leadership team. The property clearance form must be completed by a member of the department's leadership team, indicating the materials/articles to be removed. This form should also contain the date, description of materials/articles, name of person removing items, the signature, and title of the member of the departmental leadership team who authorized the removal of the items.

Upon leaving the property, all employees will make all items—personal bags, boxes, briefcases, etc.—available for inspection by the Hospitality Security Department. When an employee wishes to leave the property with item(s), he or she must first stop at the Hospitality Security Departments area, located at the employee entrance, and present the property clearance form. The hospitality security representative will inspect the property clearance form along with the contents of the package, parcel, or bag. The hospitality security representative will compare the signature of the member of the departmental leadership team authorizing the removal of the items with the property removal signature list to ensure its authenticity. If the items on the property clearance form matches the items being removed from the property, the hospitality security representative will sign the form, retain a copy of the form, and provide a copy of the form to the employee. Copies of the signed property clearance form are to be turned over to a member of the hospitality security leadership team for review and retention.

Upon the employee exiting the building, the property reserves the right to inspect any or all packages, parcels, or bags, including personal items and property of employees. At no time will hospitality security representatives place their hands in other people's belongings. If there's an obstruction, the person will be asked to move the obstruction. Baggage checks should always be in view of the CCTV cameras. The frequency of these checks is at the discretion of a member of the hospitality security leadership team. If an employee or vendor is leaving the complex from an unauthorized exit with items that could possibly conceal company property, he or she should be escorted immediately to an area with CCTV coverage where the items should be inspected. In the event that a person is discovered attempting to exit the premises with company property without a property clearance form, a member of the hospitality security leadership team must be immediately contacted, and all subsequent events pertaining to the incident must be documented.

If employee lockers are used at a property, I have found that the best practices should include:

- Having the Hospitality Security Department issue the combination locks.
- Maintaining accurate records.
- Securing the lock combinations with access limited to the leader of the Hospitality Security Department.
- Ensuring that the locker inspection program is clearly communicated and documented.

The lock issued for use on the property should contain a feature that has a key override for supervisory access. This is useful in the event that there is a bomb threat or other type of circumstance that requires the opening of employee locks without having to cut off the lock or retrieving the lock combination.

The communications of the locker inspection program should include the following:

- The property reserves the right to open and inspect employee lockers, including the contents, effects, or articles that are contained in the lockers.
- Locker inspections can occur at any time, with or without advance notice or consent, and may occur during, before, or after working hours.

Locker inspections must have a minimum of two property representatives in attendance and must include the following;

- A member of the hospitality security leadership team must be present.
- A witness from the Hospitality Security Department can be present, or
- A witness from the Human Resources Department can be present.

All locker inspections must be properly documented and must include the name of the member of the hospitality security leadership team who was present, witness(es) present, and the name of the owner of the locker. In the event that an illegal item is discovered, law enforcement must be immediately notified. If any items are discovered that violate property policy, the item may be confiscated and appropriate action is to be taken. Any time that an illegal item or an item in violation of property policy is discovered in a locker, all events and details pertaining to the incident must be properly documented.

It is important that hospitality security representatives are trained and acknowledge that their authority is the same as an ordinary person. Sometimes, when people new to the security world are informed of this for the first time, they are a little surprised to hear that they do not have any special powers. Hospitality security representatives have a perceived authority by patrons and guests and have a responsibility to provide a safe and secure environment for guests, patrons, employees, and company assets.

With this in mind, the Hospitality Security Department should be vigilant while conducting proactive patrols and immediately report any life-safety issues, suspicious activity, criminal behavior, etc. The reasonable anticipation is that the hospitality security representative will take appropriate measures so that some harm or injury will not result due to action taken or a failure to act in a given situation. This is an important concept because it ties into possible liability issues as they relate to Hospitality Security Departments. The following are some of the key terms as they relate to the proper care provided to guests and patrons.

Negligence is a failure to exercise care, or not exercise care, toward others that a reasonable or prudent person would. Basically, a Hospitality Security Department never wants to be deemed by the courts that there was a failure to act or an inadequacy in any area including training, staffing, scheduling, policy, procedure, supervision, etc. If this should happen, the result usually involved something occurring to a guest or patron that was not good. Negativity towards the Hospitality Security Department and possible criminal, civil, or financial penalties could result.

Generally speaking, a tort can be defined as an act, or failure to act, that wrongly causes harm to someone. Torts can be negligent or intentional in nature. Negligent torts include instances when there is inadequate or negligent hospitality security, supervision, training, etc. Intentional torts can occur when action is taken that violates the rights of a person, which include wrongful arrest, wrongful imprisonment, assault, etc. If this should happen, the result usually involved something occurring to a guest or patron that was not good. Negativity towards the Hospitality Security Department and possible criminal, civil, or financial penalties could result.

Report Writing

To safeguard against your Hospitality Security Department being impacted by the previous situations, a proactive approach should include the following:

- Provide adequate training
- Ensure there is proper supervision
- Maintain proper staffing levels
- Know and follow policies and procedures
- Write proper, complete, and fact-driven reports

Report writing is essential to the proper documentation of incidents and events that occur at the property. Remember that reports are important because they may be relied upon for legal matters and may be utilized by attorneys, police, etc. I have found that a process should be developed in writing the narrative of a report which should include the following:

- Origin and detail:
  - The first sentence of report should start with "On (date) at approximately (time) (job title, first and last name and identification number of hospitality security representative responding to scene)."
  - Identify the person(s) involved in the incident by name.
- Investigation revealed:
  - Who, what, when, where, why, and how should be addressed and answered.
- Review of CCTV revealed:
  - Should provide a timeline listing and describing the sequence of events with a brief description of exactly what occurred according to the review of the CCTV. For example:
    - 1740 hours—Male subject LUCKY and Male subject UNLUCKY observed having a verbal altercation
    - 1741 hours—UNLUCKY pushed LUCKY
    - 1742 hours—LUCKY struck UNLUCKY in the face with his right fist.
    - Note the Security Operations Center representative who provided the CCTV footage.

- Interviews and statements:
  - Note if there were any witnesses.
  - Obtain written statements.
- Attachments:
  - Photos of subject(s), area, items, etc.
  - CCTV coverage of incident
  - Forms
  - Logs

Underage Drinking

The prevention and detection of those who are under the legal age to consume alcoholic beverages is an area of great concern in the security industry. Failure to keep underage persons from consuming alcohol may result in harm to the underage person consuming the alcoholic beverage. All states prohibit underage drinking and a property may incur serious fines. For example, in an article that appeared in the Associated Press on June 24, 2014, titled, "Harrah's Atlantic City fined for underage drinking and gambling," provides instances where underage drinking occurred. In one incident, a nineteen-year-old was permitted to drink for nine hours, consuming eight alcoholic drinks. In another incident, an eighteen-year-old was given eight bottles of beer and was later found unconscious at the property. Paramedics were called, and the eighteen-year-old was taken to a nearby hospital.

To illustrate this point, an article appeared in the *Las Vegas Review–Journal* written by Howard Stutz, "Caesars to pay $100,000 fine to settle underage gambling, alcohol charges."

The article describes incidents where a seventeen-year-old and twenty-year-old consumed alcohol without employees requesting to see identification. The twenty-year-old was at a property bar for two-and-a-half hours and consumed alcohol. The incident involving the seventeen-year-old involved the consumption of six alcoholic beverages over five-and-a-half hours. He came into contact with approximately twenty employees during the time and none asked to see identification. As these examples illustrate, it is very important that properties enliven the enforcement of their policies regarding the prevention of underage consumption of alcohol in all areas. Policies regarding this area should include the following:

Anyone who appears under the age of 30 must present valid identification indicating that he or she is of the legal age to consume alcoholic beverages. The following are examples of acceptable nonexpired photo identifications:

- State-issued driver's license
- Passport
- United States military identification card
- State-issued identification
- United States Office of Immigration naturalization card
- Federal identification

The following are examples of unacceptable identification:

- Student identification card
- Social security card
- Birth certificate
- Counterfeit identification
- Student identification card
- Altered identification card
- Expired identification
- Copies of identification

Indicators of altered or fraudulent identification include the following:

- Suspicious changes in date of birth.
- Distorted appearance of state seals.
- Font and type are not consistent throughout the identification. Variations could indicate that the identification was altered.
- The word "duplicate" on the front of the identification could indicate that someone else may have the original.
- Bumpy surface by the photo or birth date could indicate tampering of identification.

Always ask the guest to remove the identification from any container, case, etc. This will allow closer inspection of the identification. The following are areas that should be included when attempting to detect a fraudulent identification:

- Match the photo, height, and weight on the identification with the person. Many times, the identification will be valid—but it belongs to someone other than the person who has it in his or her possession.
- Verify the birthdate to ensure that the person is of legal age to consume alcoholic beverages.
- Check the expiration date—an expired identification is not valid.
- Remember to check both sides of the identification. Many times, a fraudulent identification will have an excellent front but may lack detail on the back.
- Ask for a second form of identification; those presenting fraudulent identifications rarely carry a second form of identification.
- Ask person to sign his or her name; compare to the signature on the identification.
- Ascertain from the person presenting the identification about basic information such as:
    - Date of birth
    - Age
    - Middle name

- Address
- Zip code
- Zodiac sign

A member of the hospitality security leadership team must be contacted if there are any questions pertaining to the authenticity of an identification or if any time a patron is unable to provide proper identification. If it is determined that an identification is fraudulent, a member of the hospitality security leadership team will notify the Security Operations Center and the appropriate law enforcement entity and evict the subject from the property.

If a minor is discovered consuming alcohol, the proper authorities must be notified, a member of the hospitality security leadership team will be contacted, and an incident report will be completed. The prevention of allowing underage persons to consume alcohol is the responsibility of all employees. To aid in the recognition of those who are underage, the current legal date of birth should be posted in strategic areas such as where alcoholic beverages are served.

It is a delicate balance that hospitality security representatives must try to keep when addressing young-looking guests who are of the legal drinking age. On one hand, they need to provide exceptional guest service, and, on the other hand, they need to enforce the policies, rules, regulations, and the law. To prevent a young-looking person from having a bad experience at the property by constantly being asked to show his or her identification, I have implemented the use of hand stamps or wrist bands being offered to maintain the balance between enforcement and guest service after the identification of an individual has been confirmed that indicates that he or she is not underage. The guest can be offered to receive a hand stamp or a wrist band. It is not mandatory or required that the guest accept a hand stamp or wristband, it is merely an option and offered as a convenience to the guest.

This process requires a different hand stamp and wristband that is changed every 24 hours. When I have instituted this program in the past, a minimum of seven types of hand stamps and wristbands of each were selected and were unique in nature. The color or stamp of the day should be communicated at all preshift roll calls and through the internal communication network of the property. The random selection of the hand stamps and wristbands being used on any given day and the uniqueness of the stamps and bands help to prevent the counterfeiting of these items. In the event that an underage person is observed wearing a wristband or displaying a hand stamp, a member of the hospitality security leadership team must be contacted immediately. Identification will be requested from the person. Information regarding who issued the wristband or hand stamp and where it was issued from will be determined, policies will be adhered to, and an incident report will be completed.

Unattended children are different than those minors previously described who are brought to the property by adults. It is very important that when unattended children are reported or discovered, a hospitality security representative stays with them until they are reunited with their parents or guardians. When addressing situations of this nature, the policy should include the following:

- Upon discovery of an unsupervised child, a member of the hospitality security leadership team will be contacted and attempts will be made to identify his or her parent or guardian.
- The Security Operations Center will be notified, and CCTV will be reviewed in an attempt to ascertain who was with the child and the location of the parent or guardian.

- If a parent or guardian is located and provides proper identification, the unattended minor policy will be explained—which states that children must be accompanied by an adult at all times, and the child will be returned to the parent or guardian.
- If a parent or guardian cannot be located, hospitality security personnel will attempt to locate the parent or guardian, and a member of the hospitality security team will remain with the child.
- If a parent or guardian cannot be located within a reasonable amount of time, the proper authorities will be contacted, and the child will be turned over to their care and custody.
- An incident report will be completed.

Security processes as they relate to minors is an area of paramount importance for the Hospitality Security Department. First and foremost is the protection and safety of the minor. It is prudent to keep abreast of the laws, ordinances, and industry standards involving this area and that your legal rights and obligations are vetted through the legal team, executive team, and general manager of the property. The following are some guidelines that should be taken into consideration when developing procedures, processes, and protocols as they relate to the protection and impact of minors on the property.

- Enforce the property rules and regulations in a strict, uniform, and nondiscriminatory manner.
- Require all minors staying in a guest room to register as guests.
- Impose and enforce a maximum number of guests per room.
- Require all minor guests to present valid identification at check-in. Confirm name and address.
- Require all minor guests to provide the name, address, and telephone number of their parents or legal guardians.
- For proms and other school-related activities, all minor guests should be required to provide the name and telephone number of a school administrator.
- Require a refundable security deposit. If a credit card is presented, confirm minor is the card holder. If a parent is the card holder, require parent to sign the credit card authorization.
- Provide minor guests a copy of the property rules and regulations and have them sign same indicating they have read, understand, and agree to comply.
- Property should not issue honor bar keys to underage guests. If honor keys are not key controlled, remove all alcohol from the honor bar.
- Room service should not deliver alcohol to guest rooms used exclusively by minor guests.
- Require all minor guests to obtain a signed authorization form from their parent or guardian accepting liability for room charges and any room damage.
- Anticipate proms, graduations, formal dances, sorority and fraternity parties, and other special events; contact local schools and colleges; and prepare a calendar.
- Communicate to all property personnel on how incidents involving minors will be addressed.
- Distribute a list of rules and regulations to all guests during prom season and other special events.

- Create a room block where minors will be located so that the hospitality security team can easily monitor and provide for a safe and secure environment.
- If a minor guest is removed from the property, exercise reasonable care. Parents, guardians, school administrators, and/or police may be contacted for the protection of the minor guest and the property.

Many times, in my career as the leader of a security department, I have been responsible for the formation and designated as the champion of safety committees. You may already be responsible for a safety committee; if not, you may be in the future. The reason I say this is that properties everywhere are trying to do more with less for economic reasons and profit margins. With this said, ensure that an enlivened safety committee is in place at your property, conducts monthly meetings, and has representation from all departments. An area that should be reviewed and discussed is the identification of Occupational Safety and Health Administration (OSHA) regulations and the steps taken to ensure that the property is in compliance. Some of the key areas that the Hospitality Security Department should receive training in to be in compliance with OSHA regulations involve the following:

- Blood-borne pathogens
- Lockout/tagout
- Fire extinguishers
- Hazardous material

These are critical areas that all members of the Hospitality Security Department and team members of the property should be trained in because it directly impacts the safety of all occupants of the property. The testing of the training received in these areas should include a pretest that should be administered prior to any training. When the training is completed, a post-test should be administered to determine what was learned as a result of the training.

Safety Committees and Security

Effective safety committees are important because they prevent accidents; increase compliance; and improve teamwork, productivity, communications, and morale. Polices addressing this area provide a return on investment that results from an effective safety committee program that outweighs initial costs and operating expenses. Greater productivity and fewer lost workdays contribute measurably to the bottom line and usually result in savings that can be realized by reductions in insurance premiums and injury rates.

An area where safety is of paramount importance is swimming pools. Pools are usually one of the biggest attractions to guests. Unfortunately, this area can pose dangers, including the following:

- Drowning
- Electrocution
- Slip and falls

- Injuries from diving, jumping, or pool drains
- Reactions to chemicals

One way to prevent accidents from occurring in the pool and the pool area includes the following:

- Signage should be posted in the pool area and should include the following:
  - Children should not be left unattended in the pool area. Signage should be posted stating, "Children should not use pool without adult supervision."
  - Diving is not permitted into the pool. Signage should be posted stating, "No diving" with the international warning symbol for no diving.
  - If no lifeguard service is required, signage should be posted stating, "Warning—no lifeguard on duty."
  - Location of safety equipment.
  - The depth of the pool.
  - An emergency phone should be within 200 feet of the pool. Signage should be posted stating, "In case of emergency, call 911." If the phone is not easily visible from the pool, the signage should include a clear description of where the phone is located.
  - Running is not permitted in the pool area.
  - Glass is not permitted in the pool area.
    - In the event that broken glass is discovered in the pool, the pool must be evacuated immediately and drained, cleaned, and vacuumed. Only when all glass has been removed should the pool be placed back into use.

Other proactive measures that can be taken to increase the safety of the pool and the pool area include the following:

- Use of nonslip materials on the pool deck.
- Use of nonslip materials on diving boards.
- Use of nonslip materials on the egress areas of the pool.
- A Red Cross-approved first aid kit in the pool area.
- Flotation device that can be easily placed into the pool.
- A fiberglass safety hook that can be easily used to pull someone out of the pool. A fiberglass safety hook is preferred because it prevents electrical current from passing between the rescuer and the person in need of assistance.
- Keep areas free of electrical appliances.
- Do not use extension cords.
- Proper chemical levels of the pool water should be maintained.
- Pool and pool area should be placed on a preventive maintenance schedule.
- Train staff on pool safety, circuit breaker locations for pool equipment, lights, etc.
- Remove or replace items that can conduct electricity from in and around the pool. For example, replace metal ladders and railings with sturdy plastic ones.

Some key points to remember regarding accidents include the following:

- An incident can develop into an accident. If someone has a relatively minor cut and does not need medical attention or lose work time, it is an incident. If, for example, the minor cut becomes infected and medical attention is needed or work time is lost, it changes status from an incident and becomes an accident. This is one reason why it is important to follow up with employees when they have an incident to ensure they are okay and that their incidents do not develop into an accident. It demonstrates that you and the property really care about everyone's well-being.
- Unsafe acts and unsafe conditions are contributors to accidents. Many accidents are a result of unsafe acts; if you are able to reduce unsafe acts, you will reduce your accident rate. Unsafe acts usually occur as a result of knowingly or unknowingly violating accepted safe practices. Some of the reasons why unsafe acts occur are due to lack of knowledge about the proper operation of equipment, not wearing safety equipment, and bad habits and behavior that were permitted in the past and were not addressed.

When an incident or accident occurs, it should be investigated to determine why it occurred and, if necessary, proactive measures should be taken to prevent it from happening again. Accident investigations determine how and why they occur. The information gained helps prevent a similar or, perhaps, more serious accident from occurring in the future. A good investigation exposes processes that may have contributed to the accident and provides information for correction of unsafe acts or unsafe conditions

There are two types of accidents—those that involve guests or nonemployees and those that involve employees. The Hospitality Security Department personnel should provide the contact information for the property's Risk Management Department to the person involved in any accident. Many times, I have provided a business card with the contact information of the Risk Management Department to the person involved in an accident. The information contained on the risk management business card included the following:

- "RISK MANAGEMENT" at top of business card in large font and bold lettering.
- Message beneath Risk Management Department advising, "Please contact the Risk Management Department for follow-up information regarding your report."
- Phone number to be contacted.
- Days of week and hours to contact the Risk Management Department. For example, "Monday–Friday, 9:00 a.m.–5:00 p.m."
- Email address of the Risk Management Department.
- Name and address of the property.

All accidents should be immediately reported to the Hospitality Security Department. A hospitality security representative should evaluate the severity of the injury with the injured party and decide upon the level of medical attention that will be required. If, at any time, there is a complaint of chest pain, numbness in the arm, shortness of breath, dizziness, or any other indicators of a possible heart attack, stroke, or other serious condition, 911 will be contacted immediately, and an automated external defibrillator (AED) unit will be brought to the location and readied for use.

In the event that an ambulance is requested or needed, the following should be included in the policy regarding this event:

- Hospitality security personnel will be dispatched to the closest access entrance to stand by for the ambulance or medical unit.
- A hospitality security representative will keep the area free of traffic and attempt to ascertain the nature of the injury, illness, and general information—name, age, medications, medical history, etc., to be relayed to the responding emergency medical technicians (EMTs)
- A member of the Hospitality Security Department will meet and greet the responding EMTs and provide an escort to the ill or injured person.
- The Security Operations Center will be kept updated with the patron's condition, arrival, and departure of ambulance and patron.
- Hospitality security personnel should avoid comments that could be misconstrued or misinterpreted indicating an admission of culpability or the acceptance of liability for any injury or accident.
- Incident will be documented, and an incident investigation and report will be completed, which should include CCTV coverage, witness statements, etc.

Another area that applies to creating a safe and secure property environment is the training and certification of all members of the hospitality security team in the use of an (AED), cardiopulmonary resuscitation (CPR), and basic first aid. This policy is very important since the lives of others may depend on the quick response and actions taken by members of the hospitality security team until the arrival of the emergency medical technicians. AED units should be strategically located throughout the property, including the Security Operations Center, which ensures a relatively quick response from any area of the property.

This policy played out in real life in the quick response and use of an AED on one of the leaders of my security team. The story goes like this, while having a conversation with one of my security leaders, the leader stiffened up and fell out of a chair and onto the floor. I immediately had 911 called and had an AED unit brought to the location. The heart of the security leader stopped and was restarted five times by those in the room with the aid of the AED unit. An emergency medical technician arrived and transported the security leader to the hospital. The emergency medical technician advised that if it were not for the quick response and actions taken by those in the room, the security leader would not have survived. The story has a happy ending in that the security leader returned to work and continued to have a productive career after his heart attack.

Hospitality security professionals must provide safety and protection in environments where people come to visit to have fun. Sometimes, people have so much fun that their behavior borders on the dangerous or becomes undesirable and disruptive to other guests. When people are involved in these types of incidents, the hospitality security representative should addresses the situation in a professional, polite, and courteous manner. These guests may not be aware that they are being disruptive or creating a problem. The hospitality security representative should tell them that this behavior will not be tolerated and attempt to correct the behavior with verbal requests, assisting them, and listening to them. Hopefully, these people will settle down, realize and discontinue their problematic behavior, and have a good time within the boundaries of acceptable behavior.

However, if unacceptable behavior persists, the hospitality security representative will have to take steps to address this situation, which could lead to an eviction from the property. For example, when responding to an incident where a guest is uncooperative or escalating a situation to the point where the subject may be trespassed, I have found it best to include the following when addressing this type of incident:

- Ensure that the Security Operations Center has been advised of the situation and is observing and documenting the incident on CCTV.
- Advise the guest that if his or her behavior continues to exceed the bounds of accepted behavior, that he or she will be trespassed from the property for a year, and if he or she returns, that person will be subject to arrest for trespassing.
- When this is communicated to the guest, the hospitality security representative should raise a hand up in the air and point the index finger upwards. This indicates to those witnessing the event, the Security Operations Center, and to those in a court room if the CCTV coverage is subpoenaed, that the subject was given a first warning regarding being trespassed for his or her behavior.
- If the subject does not comply with the first request and continues to exhibit behavior that exceeds the bounds of acceptable behavior, repeat the message, and the hospitality security representative should raise his or her hand up in the air again and point two fingers upwards. At this point, the subject may ask why the hospitality security representative is pointing his or her fingers in the air. The subject should be advised that this indicates to those witnessing the event that the eyes in the sky, and the Security Operations Center, are watching the subject, and if the situation is not resolved and the unacceptable behavior continues, once three fingers are placed in the air, the trespass will go into effect and law enforcement may be contacted to respond to their location. This also provides an alert to the hospitality security team that a situation may escalate where law enforcement may be needed.

Any time money is handled by members of a security department, care and caution must always be exercised. One of the many areas in the security environment that requires the strictest adherence and execution of policy and procedures is the transfer of monies and assets. This process is a joint effort executed by the Hospitality Security Department in conjunction with an armored car company. Both are responsible for the safeguarding of company assets. Generally, the Hospitality Security Department is responsible for the monies and assets while they are being escorted to the armored car location or to armored car personnel until they are turned over to the armored car company's representatives. Sometimes, during this process, things can go horribly wrong when a person has bad intent and a firearm.

For example, a couple of decades ago, a security representative was escorting money, and while the money was being transported to it destination, a subject attempted to grab a bag of cash from the cart that the security representative was using to transport the money. While the perpetrator was grabbing the bag of money, the security representative instinctively also grabbed the bag of money. This resulted in the perpetrator drawing a gun and shooting the security representative in the face. The security representative fell to the ground, and the perpetrator fled the premises. While exiting the property, the perpetrator discarded his jacket into a trash can, which was retrieved. A search of the jacket revealed the driver's license of the perpetrator in the jacket pocket. A short time later, the subject was apprehended by law enforcement at his residence and was convicted of the crime based upon the evidence and CCTV coverage of the incident.

After being hospitalized, the security representative who was shot during this incident eventually returned to work as a security representative. Afterwards, procedures were implemented to ensure that any carts used to transport money and assets were locked and secured with the keys to unlock the transportation cart being located only at the destination of the pick-up and drop-off points. At no time, should anyone involved in transporting the money have the key that unlocks the cart containing the money. The key to unlock the cart should be in a secure area and should only be used to unlock the cart containing money when both are in a predesignated secured area. If the handling and transporting of money at your property does not exercise these best practices, they should be implemented immediately for the protection and safety of all.

Discussion Questions

1. What is considered to be the nerve center of the Hospitality Security Department?
2. Explain the steps that should be implemented to ensure that the hospitality security team has the tools and equipment needed to do its job and why it is important.
3. List some of the circumstances and steps that should be included when conducting a review of policies, procedures, and best practices.

CHAPTER

7

INVESTIGATIONS

"An excuse is worse and more terrible than a lie, for an excuse is a lie guarded."

—Pope John Paul II

Pope of the Catholic Church from 1978–2005 who promoted greater understanding between nations and religions

This chapter will review some of the various types of investigations that may be encountered in the realm of the hospitality security world. Incident types and descriptions of the investigative steps that should be taken are discussed. There are many different types of investigations that the Hospitality Security Department may need to conduct or be involved in, ranging from the relatively mundane like maintaining the chain of custody of evidence up to protecting a crime scene of deaths that could possibly be linked to murder.

There are many types of investigations that may fall under the umbrella of the Hospitality Security Department, including those that involve employees, guests, and vendors. Investigations may involve the perpetrator acting alone or with others. An example of multiple persons committing a theft can occur when perpetrators conspire and execute scams that involve the misappropriation or theft of funds between an employee, guest, or vendor. Other types of investigations involve guest and employee accidents. Generally, the Hospitality Security Department will conduct initial investigations involving employees. Once all of the facts are established or if it is uncovered that there is guest involvement in committing a crime, law enforcement should be notified.

Other times, when crimes of a more serious nature are uncovered, such as armed robbery or when a deceased person is discovered, law enforcement should be immediately notified. The responsibilities of the Hospitality Security Department should include the protection of the crime scene, gathering information, separating witnesses, etc. Regardless of the type of investigation, CCTV coverage should be reviewed, and any pertinent coverage should be saved immediately. This is very important because after a certain amount of time, usually a couple of weeks, the CCTV coverage may not be available due to storage limitations. Failure to secure

CCTV coverage of an incident or event could prove detrimental to the investigation, identification of those involved, the sequence of events, or the prosecution of a case.

Remember to confer and confirm with your Legal Department, general manager, and key members of the executive leadership team to determine if the following abide by the laws, best practices, policies, and guidelines that have been established and have jurisdictional control over your property. Below are some of the types of investigations that may occur. It is imperative that members of the hospitality security leadership team are notified when these incidents happen.

Guest and Employee Accident Investigations

An accident can be defined as an unplanned or uncontrolled event in which the action or reaction of a substance, object, energy, or person results in injury. It is important that a report be completed by a representative of the Hospitality Security Department on all reported incidents involving guests and employees. Accident investigations determine how and why failures occur. The information gained from these investigations helps prevent a similar or, perhaps, a more serious accident from occurring. A good investigation should expose errors in processes that may have contributed to an accident, provide a basis for elimination of identified hazards, decreases accident rates, lower workers' compensation costs, and provide information for correction of unsafe acts or unsafe conditions.

Some components of accident classification include the following—a loss of work time or an injury requiring medical attention. Remember that an incident can categorically develop into an accident if the person involved needs to seek medical attention from a doctor or hospital at a later date due to infection, etc. Accidents can occur for many reasons, including unsafe acts and unsafe conditions. The following are some of the reasons why people may commit unsafe acts which could result in a person sustaining an injury:

- Lack of knowledge of proper use of equipment, products, etc.
- Incentive to perform duties within a certain timeframe.
- Physical or mental impairment
- Behavior permitted in the past that was not addressed

Sometimes, incidents initially identified as accidents are associated with some type of criminal activity. For this reason, during the investigation, the protection of the scene is important because it will assist investigative personnel in the reconstruction of the event in an attempt to identify times, suspects, victims, causes, contributing factors, and criminal liability. The following are some measures that should be taken when investigating an incident that may involve some type of criminal activity.

During an incident, people may attempt to gain access to the area of the possible crime scene. Those who should have access include first responders—medical personnel, essential hospitality security personnel, law enforcement. Those who should not be permitted access include news media, nonessential hospitality security personnel, employees, and guests. Remember that the protection of life overrides all considerations of physical evidence. Every attempt should be made to protect the evidence; however, if evidence is disturbed in the care of a victim, the disturbance should be noted in the hospitality security report.

Slips and Falls—Observations are Critical

Guest or employee slip-and-fall accidents that the Hospitality Security Department may encounter include guests or employees slipping or falling indoors or outdoors. Those accidents may include slippery surfaces, ice, foreign objects, debris, sidewalks, escalators, stairs, bathtubs, etc. Report guidelines should include the following:

- Who was involved or contributed to the accident?
- Who witnessed the accident?
- What actions and/or conditions led up to the accident?
- When did the accident happen?
- Where did the accident happen?
- Why did the accident happen?
- How did the accident occur?

Remember to demonstrate empathy and concern towards the guest or employee. Offer immediate medical assistance. Conduct a thorough and immediate investigation and complete the required reports. For employee work-related injuries, contact a member of the Hospitality Security Department's leadership team as soon as possible. Provide the workers compensation contact information to the employee. For guest accidents, provide claim-processing information and the risk management contact number.

For all slips and falls, your observations are critical. Always notice the type of surface involved, the location of the fall, the presence of any foreign objects or substances, and the actions of the guest or employee who may have contributed to the fall. A minimum of three photos should be taken from various vantage points that capture the accident area. Photos should also be taken of the shoes worn, capturing both the shoe and bottom of the shoe tread. The hospitality security report should note the type of shoe worn, size of heel, rubber sole with no heel, safety shoe with no heel, etc., by the person involved in the accident.

The following highlights some of the critical investigative items that should to be preserved in the event of slips and falls indoors, in bathtubs, outdoors, on ice or snow, and in the pool area.

Bathtub

- Take photos of the exact location of fall.
- Obtain a copy of the owner's manual to determine the instructions on cleaning, policy and procedure for cleaning, materials that are recommended to be used in cleaning the bathtub.

- Determine if slip-resistant treatments were used on the bathtub. If slip-resistant treatments were used, obtain the invoices and contracts of those vendors who provided the slip-resistant treatments.
- Determine the height of tub off of the floor.
- Determine who last cleaned the tub.
- Determine if there was any water or any other substances on the floor.
- Was there a mat in the tub?
- Were grab bars present; if so, note their location.
- Was the bathroom a handicapped bathroom?
- Did the fall occur inside or outside of the tub?

Indoor

- Take photos of the exact location of the fall.
- Obtain logs and determine who and when last cleaned, swept, or mopped the area.
- Determine if "wet floor" signs were posted.
- Take photos of the "wet floor signs" and their positions at the time of the accident.
- Determine and document the type of surface involved (carpet, tile, marble, rug).
- Determine the proximity of signage to the location of the fall. Determine if the signs were visible from the site of the fall.
- Determine the type of shoes worn at time of incident.
- Determine if CCTV coverage of the area is available.
- Determine if there were any defects, foreign objects, or substances on the floor.
- If a foreign substance is present, determine what it is and describe it.
- Determine who last cleaned the area and when.

Outdoor and Pool Areas

- Take photos of the exact location of the fall.
- Determine who and when last cleaned, swept, or mopped the area.
- Determine if there was water on the surface where the fall occurred.
- Determine if wet floor signs were posted and their proximity to the fall.
- Determine the proximity of signage to the location of fall. Determine if the signs were visible from the site of the fall.
- Take photos of any "wet floor" signs positioned at the time of the accident.
- If the fall occurred on tiles, obtain the invoices and contracts with the company that installed the tiles.
- Take photos of the "POOL RULES" signs.
- Determine if CCTV coverage of the area is available.

- How close to the edge of the pool was the guest when the accident occurred?
- Are there any contributing factors to the accident, for example, was the guest running?

Ice

- Take photos of the exact location of fall.
- Obtain salt and sand logs and determine when and who performed the salting and sanding.
- Obtain salt and sand logs and purchase invoices
- Obtain contracts and invoices for snow removal to determine when and who removed the snow.

Escalator Malfunction

When an escalator stops with guests or employees on the escalator, the investigation should include the following:

- Why did the escalator stop?
- If the Facilities Department or vendor was contacted, determine date and time notified, date and time responded, and determination of why the escalator malfunctioned.
- Obtain statements from witnesses.
- Obtain statement from facilities representative and responding vendors.

If available, obtain and save CCTV coverage of any incident or accident area for a period of time prior to the incident or accident and a period of time after incident or accident. Usually, a minimum of fifteen minutes on each side is recommended. However, a complete CCTV review of the areas and persons-of-interest will determine if a greater amount of CCTV coverage will be needed. For example, I had one case where an employee advised he or she hurt his or her knee when walking on a brick service area. The employee advised that his or her knee buckled, he or she stumbled, and almost fell. After reviewing the hours that this employee worked, the CCTV revealed the employee walking across the area where the employee stated the event occurred throughout his or her shift. Each and every time, the employee walked normally across the area without exhibiting any sign of stumbling. It is a best practice to confer with your Legal and Risk Management Departments for the specific standard time period required on each side of the incident or accident.

Theft From Guest Rooms

There are various methods that perpetrators use to commit theft from guest rooms. Those who commit these crimes include employees, guests, unauthorized persons, etc. The theft triangle is a model designed to explain why employees might steal from a property and is composed of the following three elements that are perceived from the perpetrator(s) perspective: motive, low risk, and opportunity. To impact the perception of safety and security, a Hospitality Security Department should conduct proactive patrols in all areas, including the guest room floors and fire stairs, to detect suspicious items, persons, and behavior.

One method that is used by those who commit guest room theft is forced entry into the guest room by inserting a large screw driver or other type of instrument between the door and the locking mechanism. Pry marks on the door frame are telltale signs that a tool has been used to gain entry into a guest room.

Another type of theft from a guest room that can occur involves employees. This can occur when an employee gains access to a guest room and removes items, usually, jewelry, cash, credit cards, checks, and other items of high value. For example, one case I investigated involved a guest reporting that a check had been cashed after staying in a guest room at the property. Part of my investigation included a lock interrogation of the room the guest occupied.

A lock interrogation report can be obtained electronically or manually by inserting a device into the guest room door. The information gathered from the lock interrogation includes who entered the guest room by date and time, if and when the dead bolt was activated, and type of key used to enter the guest room. Some of the types of keys include a floor keys section key, floor master key, supervisor key, emergency key, security key, etc. From the lock interrogation report, a determination can be made regarding which key was used to enter the guest room during the window of time that a theft occurred. A review of the housekeeping schedule and those who used keys to enter the room should be examined. A list of all who entered the guest room should be compiled and analyzed.

For the previous investigation, the lock interrogation revealed that a housekeeping employee had entered the guest room and had also entered another guest room where an item was also reported missing. Part of my investigation included reviewing the initial pre-employment application of the person-of-interest in this theft. A handwriting comparison was made of the letters and numbers written on the application and those on the check that was cashed. I noticed that the way the employee wrote the number "8" was very unique, and it appeared on both the employee application and the cashed check. The police were contacted, and I presented the findings of the uniqueness of the number "8." At this point, the police agreed to pursue this matter. During the subsequent interview, the employee revealed that she had removed a check from the checkbook located at the back of the victim's checkbook to avoid easy detection. She also added that she was involved with a group that worked in housekeeping departments throughout the area that has made hundreds of thousands of dollars by committing theft in this manner.

When investigating guest room thefts, I recommend following these procedures:

- Meet with the complainant, obtain all of the details (who, what, when, where, why, and how); when the guest noticed the damage, if any; the last time the guest was in the room; a description of items missing; and when item(s) were discovered missing. Determine the window of opportunity for when this crime was committed.
- Provide all of the pertinent information regarding the incident to the Security Operations Center.

- CCTV coverage should also be examined for any potential witnesses or perpetrators in the area during the timeframe that the incident is reported to have occurred. Remember, witnesses and perpetrators could be other employees, guests, vendors, etc.
- The area should be examined for clues to determine how the guest room was entered. The inspection for signs of forced entry should include the following:
  - Check locks for signs of tampering
  - Pry marks on door
  - Physical evidence—i.e., screwdriver marks, etc.
- If CCTV coverage is available, obtain coverage.
- Take photos of any damage to the guest room.
- A member of the hospitality security leadership team will be updated with details, and law enforcement should be notified.
- The incident report is to be completed and reviewed by a member of the hospitality security leadership team.

Remember, in this type of investigation, the housekeeping staff might have used the door latch to keep the door open while cleaning the guest room. This is never a good practice and could result in others entering the room besides the employee who used his or her key card to open the guest room door. When this occurs, it increases the scope of the investigation as well as the list of potential persons-of-interest. Housekeepers should keep their supply cart in front of the door of the guest room while they are inside cleaning the guest room. This helps to prevent others and unwelcomed visitors from entering the guest room and provides for a safer environment for the person cleaning the guest room.

Theft From Vehicles

From Vehicle Parked by Guest

- Meet with the complainant; obtain all of the details (who, what, when, where, why, and how) as to when the vehicle arrived on property, the last time items were observed in the vehicle, when the vehicle was discovered missing; and obtain identification, i.e., driver's license, vehicle registration, and vehicle insurance card.
- Provide all of the pertinent information regarding the incident to the Security Operations Center.
  - If possible, the time the vehicle arrived on the property and the time the person who is filing the report entered the property should be verified.
  - CCTV coverage should also be examined for any potential witnesses in the area, and the timeframe that the incident is reported to having occurred should be reviewed. Remember, witnesses could be other employees, outside patrols, guests, etc.
- The vehicle should be examined for clues to determine how the vehicle was entered. The inspection for signs of entry should include the following:

    - Check locks for signs of tampering
    - Broken glass
    - Pry marks on doors
    - Physical evidence—i.e., screwdriver, hanger, etc.
    - Prior damage
- If CCTV coverage is available, obtain a photo of the incident—i.e., perpetrator removing items from vehicle. If located, allow person to return property to rightful owner.
- Take photos of any damage to vehicle.
- A member of the hospitality security leadership team will be updated with details, and a determination will be made regarding the involvement of law enforcement and the issuance of an eviction to the perpetrator(s).
- A risk management contact card should be provided to the person reporting the incident.
- The incident report is to be completed and reviewed by a member of the hospitality security leadership team.

From Valet-Parked Vehicle

- Meet with the complainant; obtain all of the details (who, what, when, where, why, and how) as to when the vehicle arrived on property, the last time items were observed in vehicle, when the property was discovered missing; and obtain identification, i.e., driver's license, vehicle registration, vehicle insurance card.
- Provide all of the pertinent information regarding the incident to the Security Operations Center.
    - If possible, the time the vehicle arrived on property and the time the person who is filing the report entered the property should be verified.
    - Contact a member of the valet leadership team; the following should be included regarding the information requested:
        - Names of the Valet Department representatives who parked or retrieved the vehicle.
        - Many times, the Valet Department utilizes a computer-generated vehicle tracking system that takes photos of the valet-parked vehicle as it enters and departs the valet parking area. These systems usually record any prior damage to the vehicle, who had care and custody of the vehicle, time the vehicle was parked, who parked the vehicle, what time the vehicle was retrieved, and who retrieved the vehicle. If such a system exists, retrieve all pertinent information from this valet vehicle tracking system. In lieu of obtaining the needed information in this manner, obtain the information from a leader of the Valet Department.
    - CCTV coverage should also be examined for any potential witnesses in the area during the timeframe that the incident is reported to have occurred. Remember, witnesses could be other employees, outside patrols, etc.

- The vehicle should be examined for clues to determine how access was gained to the vehicle. The inspection for signs of entry should include the following:
    - Check locks for signs of tampering
    - Broken glass
    - Pry marks on doors
    - Physical evidence—i.e., screwdriver, hanger, etc.
    - Prior damage

- If CCTV coverage is available, obtain a photo of the incident showing a perpetrator removing items from vehicle. If located, allow person to return property to rightful owner.
- Take photos of any damage to vehicle.
- Speak with the representatives of the Valet Department who had contact with the vehicle.
- A member of the hospitality security leadership team will be updated with details, and a determination will be made regarding the involvement of law enforcement and the issuance of an eviction to the perpetrator(s).
- A risk management contact card should be provided to the person reporting the incident.
- An incident report is to be completed and reviewed by a member of the hospitality security leadership team.

Missing or Stolen Purse or Wallet

- Meet with the complainant and obtain all of the details (who, what, when, where, why, and how) as to a description of the item, a description of its contents, when the item was discovered missing, the location last seen, etc.
- Notify the Security Operations Center, and provide all of the pertinent information regarding the incident.
- Go to the last location where the item was seen.
- Check trash cans and restrooms for a wallet or purse.
- If CCTV coverage is available, obtain a photo of the incident—perpetrator(s) removing the purse or wallet from location. If located, allow person to return property to rightful owner.
- A member of the hospitality security leadership team will be updated with details, and a determination will be made regarding the involvement of law enforcement and the issuance of an eviction to the perpetrator(s).
- If CCTV review is inconclusive or unable to locate wallet/purse, offer to assist guest in making phone calls to cancel credit cards.
- The incident report is to be completed and reviewed by a member of the hospitality security leadership team.

Counterfeit Currency

- Go to the location and meet with the complainant and inspect the suspicious bill. The inspection of the suspicious bill should include the following:
    - Make sure the denomination of the bill matches the portrait on the bill. Many times, lower denomination bills are bleached, then, a high-quality laser printer is used to print a higher denomination bill over the bleached bill. A good way to check for this is to compare the portrait on the front of the bill with the watermark. For example, a bleached $1 bill that was counterfeited into a $100 bill will display George Washington as a watermark instead of Benjamin Franklin. The following are the portraits and watermarks for US currency:
        - $1—George Washington
        - $5—Abraham Lincoln
        - $10—Alexander Hamilton
        - $20—Andrew Jackson
        - $50—Ulysses Grant
        - $100—Benjamin Franklin
    - Examine the watermark on the bill
    - Examine for obvious discrepancies and flaws
    - Examine for red and blue fibers embedded in the bill
    - Security thread
    - Color-shifting ink
    - Microprinting
    - Texture of the bill
    - Color of the bill.
- Obtain all of the details (who, what, when, where, why, and how), manner in which bill was obtained, description of person passing bill, date, time location, etc.
- Notify the Security Operations Center and provide all of the pertinent information regarding the incident.
- If CCTV coverage is available, obtain a photo of the incident—perpetrator(s) passing the counterfeit bill—and determine if others are involved. If counterfeit passing is part of an organized ring, there is usually one person, known as the bagman in the group, who handles the money. The bagman distributes the counterfeits to the others involved. Purchases made with the counterfeit money are usually for low-priced items paid with a large bill denomination for maximized investment. For example, a sign, or "tell," of someone who may be involved in the passing of counterfeit bills would involve the report or observation of someone purchasing a soft drink with a large bill, taking a sip, and throwing it away. Once the purchase is completed with the counterfeit bill, the "clean" money is returned to the bagman and additional counterfeits are distributed. This allows the operation to be mobile, and if a person is caught passing a counterfeit bill, he or she can deny knowledge of the counterfeit bill since he or she only has the one in his or her possession. As soon as there is any sign of trouble, the bagman usually leaves the

area as quickly as possible. Therefore, it is important to identify those involved with the ultimate goal of identifying the bagman.

- In situations where a guest surrenders a counterfeit bill, obtain as much information as possible and request identification.
- Determine if the subject has been involved in previous incidents or evictions.
- The incident report and United States Secret Service counterfeit note report is to be completed and reviewed by a member of the hospitality security leadership team.
- Send the counterfeit bill to the United States Secret Service.

Theft of Service

Some of the areas that theft of service occurs is at retail outlets, food outlets, and other locations that involve cash transactions. Most commonly known is the dine-and-dash in which a person or group of people have a meal in a food outlet and leave without paying their bill. When theft of service situations occur, the response by the Hospitality Security Department should include the following:

- Meet with the complainant, obtain all of the details (who, what, when, where, why, and how), get a description of those involved, determine the amount of money involved.
- Notify the Security Operations Center, and provide all of the pertinent information regarding the incident. If CCTV coverage is available, obtain a photo of the incident—such as the perpetrator walking out of the outlet without paying.
- Communicate a description of the perpetrator(s) to security personnel as a person-of-interest.
- If perpetrator(s) are located, request identification. Determine if the subject(s) have been involved in previous incidents or ejections.
- Offer subject(s) the opportunity to pay what is owed.
- A member of the hospitality security leadership team will be updated with details, and a determination will be made regarding the involvement of law enforcement and the issuance of an eviction to the perpetrator(s).
- An incident report is to be completed and reviewed by a member of the hospitality security leadership team.

Verbal and Physical Altercations

Verbal Altercations

Verbal altercations can occur for a variety of reasons. It is important to de-escalate these situations before they attract a crowd. When a crowd becomes involved, it could morph from a verbal altercation between two people into the worst-case scenario—mob violence. When responding to a situation when people are arguing in an aggressive manner that, if left unattended, might result in a physical altercation, the hospitality security representative should include the following:

- Hospitality security representatives should keep the parties involved separated and ensure that the verbal altercation is discontinued.
- Hospitality security representatives should speak to those involved without taking sides. If possible, this should occur out of the public view. Hospitality security representatives should attempt to resolve the situation.
- Obtain the information of those involved.
- A member of the hospitality security leadership team will be updated with details, and a determination will be made regarding the involvement of law enforcement and the issuance of an eviction to the perpetrator(s).
- If unable to resolve the situation, take actions that will prevent those having the verbal altercation from seeing each other on the property again.
- An incident report is to be completed and reviewed by a member of the hospitality security leadership team.

Physical Altercations

Sometimes a verbal altercation leads into a physical altercation. This is one reason why it is important to nip verbal altercations in the bud as quickly as possible. Physical altercations can stem from incidents that occur on property, although, at times, the dispute between the parties involved may have been ongoing outside of the of the property environment and happened to reach its flash point at the property. For our purposes, a physical altercation is when a patron makes physical contact with another patron in a way that one of the patrons involved feels physically violated. I have seen physical altercations occur that involved two people and others that have involved dozens of people. Thankfully, the security teams involved were well trained and the situations were diffused.

On other occasions, there have been physical altercations during which a person strikes another prior to the arrival of a security representative, and the aggressor departs and leaves the unfortunate victim in an unconscious state at the scene. From an investigative stance, CCTV should be immediately reviewed and notification to law enforcement and the identification and interviewing of witnesses should commence. The mechanics of an assault on a hard surface where one person is struck in the face with a fist and falls to the ground can be life threatening.

As I have seen in the past, when the skull of a person impacts a hard surface like granite, concrete, etc., the force can be greater than being struck in the face by a fist. On occasion, this can result in trauma being sustained to the brain where it can swell, and relief can only be provided at the hospital where holes are drilled into the skull to relieve the pressure. Keep this in mind when providing notifications to others because, initially, the incident may appear to be a physical assault, case closed. However, sometimes the swelling of the brain may not be immediate and may occur when the victim is away from the property at the hospital.

The hospitality security representative should include the following when responding to physical altercations.

- Hospitality security representatives should keep the parties involved separated, and they should not be within speaking distance of each other, providing it is safe to do so, and it does not place the responding security representatives in danger.
- Notify the Security Operations Center, and provide all of the pertinent information regarding the incident.
- Notify law enforcement.
- Obtain medical treatment for those who are injured.
- Secure objects or weapons that may have been used.
- Obtain information of those involved.
- Obtain statements from witnesses.
- A member of the hospitality security leadership team will be updated with details, and a determination will be made regarding the issuance of an eviction to the perpetrator(s).
- An incident report is to be completed and reviewed by a member of the hospitality security leadership team.

The following should be included in the steps that are taken as directed by members of the hospitality security leadership team when crimes of a very serious magnitude such as deaths, sexual assault, domestic violence, etc., occur at the property:

- Members of the hospitality security leadership team should respond, direct security personnel, and treat the incident as a crime scene.
- Protect the crime scene, and secure the area.
- Hospitality security representatives should keep the parties involved separated, and they should not be within speaking distance of each other, providing it is safe to do so, and it does not place the responding security representatives in danger.
- Notify the Security Operations Center, and provide all of the pertinent information regarding the incident.
- Notify law enforcement.
- Obtain medical treatment for those in need of treatment.
- Secure objects or weapons that may have been used.
- Obtain information of those involved.
- Obtain statements from witnesses.
- Maintain a chronological log of arrivals and departures of person(s) and/or agency representatives.
- If deemed necessary, acquire an area or room nearby to establish as a Command Center.
- Suspects should be monitored at all times.
- If possible, it is suggested that the use of the restroom or facilities be delayed until the arrival of law enforcement. Depending on the type of crime, this could help preserve physical evidence.
- Assist law enforcement as needed.
- Obtain written statements of all security personnel involved in the incident.

- Hospitality security personnel will be relieved by law enforcement responding to the scene.
- An incident report is to be completed and reviewed by a member of the hospitality security leadership team.

When a crime is committed at a property, an important aspect is the protection of the crime scene and physical evidence. The difference between evidence and physical evidence is that evidence is anything that can be used to determine whether a crime has been committed, whereas, physical evidence is basically any objects that can used to establish that a crime has been committed or can provide a link between a crime, victim(s), and perpetrator(s). It is important to law enforcement and investigators to analyze and interpret physical evidence clues left behind at the crime scene. These clues could lead to the perpetrator(s) who committed the act, determine the sequence of events, or lead to the identification of those involved.

However, for this to occur, it is critical that hospitality security personnel recognize potential physical evidence, protect it, collect it, or preserve it for those conducting the investigation. If possible, it is best to leave the physical evidence in place until the arrival of law enforcement. There may be times when physical evidence must be gathered by a member of the hospitality security team. For example, if a crime scene is located outside, and it is raining, physical evidence may need to be secured by a member of the hospitality security team to prevent the contamination of the physical evidence.

Another key element regarding physical evidence is the ability to recognize, collect, or preserve it in a timely manner. As in the previous example, failure to recognize or protect the physical evidence could result in the physical evidence being compromised or destroyed which could seriously hamper or compromise an investigation. Remember that every crime scene has a victim, and the proper identification, preservation, and collection of evidence increases the chances of identifying the perpetrator(s) of the crime. If there is ever a doubt as to whether an item or object is physical evidence, treat it as if it is, protect it, and notify law enforcement.

Some types of physical evidence that may be available for recovery at a hospitality crime scene include the following:

- Biological evidence—blood, saliva, hair, semen, etc.
- Tools
- Pry marks
- Firearms and ammunition evidence—weapon, shell casings, etc.
- Weapons—knife, blunt object, etc.
- Fingerprints—located on weapons, paper, etc.
- Toxicology evidence—drugs, poisons, etc.
- Documentation evidence—written notes, paper, ink, etc.
- Explosives
- Drug evidence—left at scene, on person, etc.

The proper identification, collection, and establishment of a chain of custody regarding physical evidence is very important. If any one of these areas is not performed properly, it could result in the physical evidence being contaminated or inadmissible in a court. The basic role of a hospitality security representative is to identify, protect, and, if necessary, collect the evidence. The hospitality security representative who identifies or locates specific evidence should be listed in any reports or in any documentation regarding the incident and the evidence. The information that should be listed includes the following:

- Date physical evidence was located
- Time physical evidence was located
- Exactly where the physical evidence was discovered
- If physical evidence was handled—list by who, date, and time
- To establish chain of custody of physical evidence—list date, time, and the person physical evidence was turned over to. The following should be included regarding the person the physical evidence was turned over to:
  - Name
  - Rank
  - Identification number
  - Name of department

The advantages of following the proper protocol for the handling of physical evidence that is to be utilized in an investigation and eventual prosecution of a case includes the following:

- Physical evidence cannot be distorted.
- Physical evidence is tangible—it can be seen and, possibly, touched by a jury.
- Physical evidence can usually be effective in rebutting statements made by a defendant.
- Many times, physical evidence can help to solve a case.
- Physical evidence can usually confirm the facts of a case and prove that a defendant's statements are false.
- It is advantageous to have physical evidence over the testimony of a witness. Over time, witness testimony is subject to memory loss whereas physical evidence is not.
- A person accused of a crime based upon physical evidence can have the physical evidence tested by an independent expert. This adds to the credibility of the investigation process, the physical evidence, and the judicial system.

Protecting the Crime Scene

Protection of an area varies, depending on the crime, location, and its conditions. The following are the elements regarding the protection of a crime scene:

- Do not touch anything at the crime scene.
- If crime occurred in a room, do not use the telephone in the room.

- Create a log of all persons arriving and entering the crime scene until law enforcement arrives and takes control of the crime scene.
- Protect evidence from physical elements, i.e., rain, wind, traffic, etc.

As you can see, there is more involved than initially meets the eye when it involves the Hospitality Security Department's response to incidents and crime scene protection. The following is an excerpt from a discussion between Monsignor, Theologian, and Author of Detective Stories Ronald Knox (1888–1957) and Scientist John Scott Haldane (1860–1936):

> "In a universe containing millions of planets," reasoned Haldane, "is it not inevitable that life should appear on at least one of them?"
>
> "Sir" replied Knox, "If Scotland Yard found a body in your cabin trunk, would you tell them: There are millions of trunks in the world; surely one of them must contain a body? I think they would still want to know who put it there."

As you should, too, when investigating any incident, always get the facts and don't accept the easy answer or the easy way out. Develop a reputation for the hospitality security team as one that leaves no stone unturned and that always get the person who commits a crime. This will assist in creating a positive reputation for the Hospitality Security Department and have a deterrent effect on those who may have criminal intent or may wish to exceed the boundaries of acceptable behavior. The likelihood is that these types of individuals will be displaced from your property and commit these acts elsewhere at a property that does not have the reputation of being a top-notch Hospitality Security Department such as yours.

Discussion Questions

1. Why is it important to de-escalate verbal altercations?
2. Why is it important to properly identify, collect, and establish a chain of custody regarding physical evidence?
3. What are the elements of protecting a crime scene?
4. What are some of the types of physical evidence that may be available for recovery at a crime scene?
5. List some of the responsibilities of the Hospitality Security Department when responding to an incident.
6. Explain the importance of CCTV coverage of an incident or event and why it should be secured.
7. Explain the elements of properly identifying, collecting, and establishing a chain of custody regarding physical evidence, and what are the advantages of physical evidence?

CHAPTER

8

ETHICS, PROFESSIONALISM, AND LEGAL PERSPECTIVES

"Have the courage to say no. Have the courage to face the truth. Do the right thing because it is right. These are the magic keys to living your life with integrity."

—W. Clement Stone

An American businessman, philanthropist, and self-help author

I have decided to place ethics, professionalism, and legal perspectives together since these topics tend to go hand in hand. If poor ethical decisions and a lack of professionalism are displayed by representatives of the Hospitality Security Department, there is a strong likelihood that they will eventually lead into the legal arena. At a minimum, there will be complaints regarding the performance and behavior of those on the security team who do not always embrace making ethical decisions and perform their duties in a professional manner. Remember, the bar is raised for the Hospitality Security Department. All eyes are on security representatives to determine if they are "walking the walk and talking the talk" and abiding by all of the policies, rules, and regulations. Performing at a minimum level is unacceptable, as is barely doing enough to get by—only the best efforts and performing well above the minimum standard are and should be the norm. This chapter will examine what impact professionalism alongside legal and ethical perspectives have and the important role each plays in the operation and perception of the Hospitality Security Department.

The following is an incident that I was involved in while patrolling the New Jersey Turnpike as a New Jersey State Trooper. On August 22, 1989, while performing my duties during a motor vehicle stop, I was shot six times. God was on my side that day and, after much rehabilitation, I was able to return to society and lead an active and productive life. When I was on the mend, my fellow troopers held a surprise dinner for me and over 200 troopers, dignitaries, the Governor of New Jersey, and past and current colonels of the New Jersey State Police attended. To say the least, it was an honor and privilege to be recognized by my fellow comrades. Among the items presented to me was a framed quote based upon the address delivered at the Sorbonne in Paris on April 23, 1910, by Theodore Roosevelt titled "Dare To Do." It was handwritten in calligraphy and read aloud by the presenter. During the reading, I noticed that a former lieutenant of mine, whom I respected very much, knew the words by heart and was reading along. I have always treasured the memory of the support and kindness demonstrated to me on that day by so many.

Ever since that day, I have placed this gift on the wall of every place I have ever worked. It serves as a reminder of that evening and, in my opinion, pretty much summarizes how I and others, who continuously strive to make the world a better place, feel by never giving up and by not just trying but doing. I also use this as a springboard by reviewing the address with others, by bringing up the topic of ethics, and by discussing the meaning of its words. I enjoy hearing what they mean to the person who reads them for the first time as I describe what it means to me. I have handed out copies and reviewed the following with members of all levels of the teams I have had the pleasure to be part of as their leader.

Dare to Do

It is not the critic who counts, not the man who points out how the strong man stumbled, or where the doer of a deeds could have done them better. The credit belongs to the man who is actually in the arena; whose face is marred by dust and sweat and blood; who strives valiantly, who errs and comes short again and again, because there is no effort without error and shortcoming; who does actually strive to do the deeds, who knows the great enthusiasms, the great devotions, spends himself in a worthy cause; who at the best knows in the end the triumph of achievement, and who at the worst, if he fails, at least fails while daring greatly, so that his place shall never be with those cold and timid souls who know neither victory nor defeat.

—Theodore Roosevelt

An American statesman, politician, conservationist, naturalist, and writer who served as the 26th president of the United States from 1901 to 1909.

Theodore Roosevelt, "The Man in the Arena," 1910.

Ethics, Morals and Values—What are They?

Some say that ethics is what somebody does when no one is watching. Theodore Roosevelt said that "to educate a man in mind, but not in morals is to create a menace to society." These are some of the reasons that the understanding of ethics and ethical behavior is such a vital component to anyone who views him- or herself as a professional. Not only must hospitality security personnel do technical things correctly, but they must also perform their duties in an ethical manner.

Throughout life, on a professional and personal level, everyone encounters moral and ethical dilemmas. To make a solid, reasonable, moral, and ethical decision, it is important to have the understanding, knowledge, and ability to demonstrate that when decisions are made, they are done in a moral and ethical manner. By the end of this chapter, the hope is that when a member of the Hospitality Security Department makes a decision, it is the right one—ethically, morally, and professionally speaking and, if not, understands why.

This is important for many reasons. First and foremost, not performing and executing duties in this manner could impact the safety and security of the guests, occupants, and employees of the property and their perception of the Hospitality Security Department. Other negative consequences include possible civil, criminal, or legal action resulting from a Hospitality Security Department performing its duties in an unprofessional, unethical, and immoral manner. The following is a brief synopsis of ethics, morals, values, and professionalism to aid in the understanding of and shed some more light on the importance of these areas.

Ethics is moral standards and how they affect conduct. The Greek root for ethics is *ethos*, which stresses the perfection of the individual and the community to which he or she belongs. There are many aspects of ethics, including the following:

- Ethics is about what is right and what is wrong.
- Ethics is about vice and virtue.
- Ethics is about benefit and harm.
- Ethics describes what should be.
- Ethics is the way morality is practiced.

In the past, during a discussion pertaining to ethics, one of my great leaders once told me, "Ethics is what a person does when no one is watching." Think about this for a minute—it makes perfect sense.

Morality originates from the Latin word *moralis* which means "traditional customs or proper behavior." Basically, morals refer to a set of rules defining what is considered to be right or wrong and accepted by everyone in a group or society. If someone breaks a rule, he or she is typically considered to be immoral. There are many aspects of morals:

- Morals are values that an individual attributes to a system of beliefs.
- Morals assist an individual in defining right from wrong or good from bad.

For example, Charles Colson, special counsel to President Nixon and founder of Prison Fellowship International, makes a clear and concise synopsis of the difference between morals and ethics. He stated, "Morality describes what is. Ethics describes what ought to be."

Values can be described as beliefs or ideas shared by members of a culture, which include the following:

- Values provide direction in determining right from wrong or good from bad.
- Values are what a person believes to be valuable, have worth, or are important.
- Values influence a person's behavior.

It appears that ethics, morals, and values are interconnected with each other in one way or another. When in a position where action or a decision needs to be made, each of the previously mentioned areas have some weight in the path taken by the person responsible for the outcome. Many times, the areas overlap to varying degrees and frequently impact the final decision. The following will examine and explore in detail these areas and the role professionalism plays.

Ethics in Practice

Merely only knowing the definitions of ethics, morals, and values is not enough to ensure that someone has the abilities to make good decisions. Critical thinking must be applied and demonstrated by consciously using reason to make the best decisions. Making decisions in a repetitive, routine manner or on impulse should be avoided, especially when addressing situations pertaining to areas of ethical concern or the well-being of others.

Where does ethics begin?

- Ethics begins with every person.
- A company or department cannot have ethics; it is the people employed by a company who have ethics.
- It is the leadership team that makes ethical decisions.

I believe, for the most part, most people in businesses and in life desire to be ethical, most companies desire to act ethically, and everyone desires to be treated ethically. However, the larger the group or company, the more challenging it becomes to effectively communicate and calibrate the thinking of everyone in regard to shared values and his or her decision-making processes. Ethically speaking, the following are some of the components that help make people morally better:

- Respecting the rights of others
- Fulfilling obligations
- Being honest
- Treating others fairly

Critical thinking and communication are essential skills that are needed for a successful ethical decision-making program. For any program to work, it must have the buy-in and support of the leaders of the organization and those participating in the program. Knowledge of the following is helpful in the development of a program:

- Personal morality—is an individual's concept of right and wrong. This is developed based upon a person's upbringing and environment. The work environment should be one that is conducive to ethical decision-making.
- Professional ethics—is the organizational and personal standards of behavior that a professional is expected to display and possess.
  - Organizational ethics—are the principals and standards that businesses demonstrate in their operation. These include integrity, responsibility, fairness, and compassion.

Professionalism and Security Certifications

Merriam-Webster defines the root word of professionalism in the following manner:

> A profession is a "calling requiring specialized knowledge and often long academic preparation."
>
> A professional is one that is "participating for gain in an activity often engaged in by amateurs" or one that "engages in an activity professionally."
>
> Professionalism is exhibited by "the conduct, aims, or qualities that mark a profession or a professional person."

Certifications are an important way to establish professionalism. In the past, people have asked me, "Why do you have so many letters after your name?" which would lead to an explanation of each certification. This usually leads to the question again of, "Why?" To this point, I explain that when a person is certified by a recognized organization and the certification is known in the industry, people generally believe that the certification indicates that the person is a professional, is knowledgeable, and is a leader in their field.

There are various types of certifications available to demonstrate that one is a professional in the security field and believes in continuous education and self-improvement. The following are some of the certifications that are recognizable and accepted in the security field.

The following information pertaining to the CLSD certification was ascertained from the American Hotel & Lodging Educational Institute website.

Certified Lodging Security Director—(CLSD)

Overview

> The Certified Lodging Security Director (CLSD®) is the most prestigious certification available to a security executive. It identifies the recipient as being part of an elite group of hospitality professionals who, by combining
>
> education and experience with dedication to the industry, have achieved a high level of expertise.

Globally recognized, the CLSD® is a highly respected professional credential that validates your advanced knowledge in the hospitality industry. It is an honor awarded to security professionals whose leadership and managerial abilities are exemplary.

Achieving the CLSD® certification announces that you have a place among the best in your profession, are abreast of current trends and latest hospitality protocols, and serves as leverage in current and future career opportunities.

Fee includes: CLSD® Exam Preparation Booklet, Resource Materials CD, and Exam, as well as Certificate and Lapel Pin upon successful completion of the Exam.

The CLSD® designation may be used on letterhead, business cards, and other writings.

Recertification

Once certified, designees are automatically enrolled in the CLSD® Recertification Program, which recognizes and rewards continuing efforts toward hospitality career growth. A portfolio to help track professional development activities is provided. Every five years, the certification commission will recertify those who qualify based on their accomplishments. A new jeweled lapel pin (reflecting the number of years certified) and certificate are awarded at the time of each recertification.

Prerequisites

Because individual backgrounds vary widely in the hospitality industry, applicants may pursue the CLSD® designation if currently employed in these qualifying position(s):

Security director at property level or as a corporate executive employed by a firm responsible for the operation of three or more properties, who serves as a regional or corporate director of security, or has ultimate corporate responsibility for security and/or risk management issues.

Candidate Time in Position: 1 year, OR

One current AHLEI *management*, *department head*, or *executive* certification takes 6 months off time requirement (limit 1)

Degree from an accredited academic institution will take 6 months off time requirement (limit 1)

The following pertaining to the ASIS certifications were ascertained from the ASIS website.

Certification Protection Professional—(CPP)

This ASIS credential provides demonstrable proof of knowledge and management skills in seven key domains of security. Those who earn the CPP are ASIS board-certified in security management.

Eligibility requirements—Nine years of security work experience, with at least three of those years in responsible charge of a security function, or a bachelor's degree or higher and seven years of security work experience, with at least three of those years in responsible charge of a security function

Recertification requires earning 60 Continuing Professional Education (CPE) credits every three years. Keep in mind that recertification terms always expire at the end of the year.

Physical Security Professional—(PSP)

This ASIS credential provides demonstrable knowledge and experience in threat assessment and risk analysis; integrated physical security systems; and the appropriate identification, implementation, and ongoing evaluation of security measures. Those who earn the PSP are ASIS board-certified in physical security.

Eligibility requirements—High school diploma, GED equivalent, or associate degree and six years of progressive physical security experience—or—bachelor's degree or higher and four years of progressive physical security experience.

Recertification requires earning 60 Continuing Professional Education (CPE) credits every three years. Keep in mind that recertification terms always expire at the end of the year.

Professional Certified Investigator—(PCI)

This ASIS credential provides demonstrable proof of an individual's knowledge and experience in case management, evidence collection, and preparation of reports and testimony to substantiate findings. Those who earn the PCI are ASIS board-certified in investigations.

Eligibility requirements—High school diploma or GED equivalent and five years of investigations experience with at least two years in case management.

> Recertification requires earning 60 Continuing Professional Education (CPE) credits every three years.

The following pertaining to the CFE certification was ascertained from the Association of Certified Fraud Examiners—ACFE—website.

Certified Fraud Investigator—(CFE)

> The Certified Fraud Examiner (CFE) credential denotes proven expertise in fraud prevention, detection, and deterrence. CFEs are trained to identify the warning signs and red flags that indicate evidence of fraud and fraud risk. CFEs around the world help protect the global economy by uncovering fraud and implementing processes to prevent fraud from occurring in the first place. CFEs have a unique set of skills that are not found in any other career field or discipline; they combine knowledge of complex financial transactions with an understanding of methods, law, and how to resolve allegations of fraud.
>
> Eligibility Requirements—Generally, applicants for CFE certification have a minimum of a bachelor's degree (or equivalent) from an institution of higher learning. No specific field of study is required. Those without a bachelor's degree may substitute two years of fraud-related professional experience for each year of academic study. For example, if college was attended full-time for only two years, an additional four years of professional experience would be needed to meet the education requirements.
>
> Professional Requirements—At the time of certification, applicants must have at least two years of professional experience in a field either directly or indirectly related to the detection or deterrence of fraud.
>
> To maintain the CFE Credential requires the earning of at least 20 hours of Continuing Professional Education (CPE) every 12-month period. At least 10 of these hours must relate directly to the detection and deterrence of fraud, and 2 hours must relate directly to ethics.

In addition to certifications, having membership and being involved in professional organizations like the ASIS Gaming and Wagering Protection Council is paramount in developing a communication and information network. This is useful in keeping abreast of the latest techniques, information, and best practices that are occurring in the gaming sector. This also is another building block in developing, ascertaining, and maintaining a degree of professionalism.

Key Elements of Professionalism

There are many meanings of professionalism; it varies depending on the environment or situation that it is used. There are also many determining factors that influence others when they develop an opinion on whether a person, department, or organization is professional. These factors include the following:

- Appearance
- Performance
- Reaction to pressure
- Communication skills—both verbal and nonverbal
- Confidence
- Focused
- Accountable
- Competent
- Goal oriented
- Respectful
- Sense of urgency

The following are some of the key elements of professionalism:

- Ethics
- Philosophy
- Knowledge
- Guidelines
- Standardization of job performance

When addressing serious or stressful situations, hospitality security professionals should not react emotionally. Rather, these situations should be handled in a serious, effective, and efficient manner. Remember that there is a time and a place for humor. When it is used properly, it has a relieving effect. However, when used improperly, it can have a negative impact on others and the situation that is being addressed. As a hospitality security professional gains more experience, a sixth sense is usually developed that helps to determine when it is appropriate to use humor to alleviate a situation—and when it is not. The best thing to do if unsure whether to use humor is not to use it at all.

There have been times in my career when I have reported to leaders who chose to operate in the marginal areas when it came to conducting business or behaving in an ethical manner. If ever placed into this uncomfortable circumstance, it is best to address the situation. Being the eternal optimist, I always hope that the individual and organization will change their behavior and be thankful that this was brought to their attention.

Unfortunately, however, sometimes leadership may not want to know that there is a thousand-pound elephant in the room and may choose to ignore the questionable ethical behavior by members of its key leadership. If this should ever happen, as I have found myself in the past, the best advice that I can give is to pack your bags and work someplace else. The most important tools that a hospitality security professional have are morals, ethics, and character. These are the key components that separate the wheat from the chaff, the professional from the nonprofessional.

Ethics and professionalism usually go hand in hand. One of the key components of professionalism is a code of ethics. A code of ethics is instrumental in developing synergy and integrating the other skills and components that help establish professionalism. The implementation of a code of ethics is a key component to achieving a higher level of professionalism and credibility in a Hospitality Security Department. A Hospitality Security Department code of ethics should include the following:

- Treating others in a respectful, honest, and professional manner.
- Exhibiting integrity.
- Continuously learning and educating others.
- Being compassionate and empathetic.
- Providing a safe environment.
- Providing for the protection of guests, employees, and company assets.
- Cooperating with local, state, and federal law enforcement agencies.
- Never soliciting any form of compensation or gratuity.
- Presenting all facts of any situation, event, incident, or investigation in a straightforward manner. Failing to disclose all information—or omitting information—could result in a distortion of the facts.

It is important that hospitality security representatives are trained, but they must acknowledge that their authority is, at most times, the same as any private citizen unless authority is obtained through commissioning by a public law enforcement agency. Sometimes, when people are new to the security world and are informed of this for the first time, they are a little surprised to hear that they do not have any special powers. With this said, hospitality security professionals have a perceived authority by the public and have a responsibility to provide a safe and secure environment to guests, patrons, employees, and company assets.

With this in mind, the Hospitality Security Department should be vigilant while conducting proactive patrols and immediately report any life-safety issues, suspicious activity, criminal behavior, etc. The reasonable expectation by the public is that hospitality security representatives will take appropriate measures to ensure that no harm or injury will result due to action taken or a failure to act in a given situation. This is an important concept because it ties into possible liability issues as they relate to Hospitality Security Departments. The following are some of key concepts and terms as they pertain to the proper care that should be provided by hospitality security professionals to guests and patrons.

Know the Bill of Rights

One of the most important concepts for the Hospitality Security Department to understand and apply is the Bill of Rights. The Bill of Rights are the first ten amendments of the US Constitution. The following is a brief synopsis of each:

- **The First Amendment**: Provides for the freedom of speech, religion, the press, the right of the people peaceably to assemble and to petition the government for a redress of grievances.

- **The Second Amendment:** Prohibits the government from interfering with the right of the people to keep and bear arms.
- **The Third Amendment:** No Soldier shall, in time of peace be quartered in any house, without the consent of the Owner, nor in time of war, but in a manner to be prescribed by law.
- **The Fourth Amendment:** Prohibits unreasonable search and seizure.
- **The Fifth Amendment:** Protects citizens against being compelled to testify against themselves, double jeopardy, being deprived of life, liberty or property without due process and being held for a serious crime without presentation to a grand jury for indictment.
- **The Sixth Amendment:** Provides for a speedy trial by an impartial jury, your right to be informed of charges against you, your right to present a defense, and your right to confront witnesses against you.
- **The Seventh Amendment**: Provides for a trial by jury.
- **The Eighth Amendment:** Prohibits excessive bail, excessive fines, and cruel and unusual punishment.
- **The Ninth Amendment**: The enumeration in the Constitution, of certain rights, shall not be construed to deny or disparage others retained by the people.
- **The Tenth Amendment:** The powers not delegated to the United States by the Constitution, nor prohibited by it to the States, are reserved to the States respectively, or to the people.

It should be noted that the Constitution provides little information pertaining to the rights of private citizens in their relationships with other citizens. Most constitutional rights pertain to the citizen's rights in relation to the government. However, constitutional limitations do apply when members of the hospitality security personnel act either in concert with or as agents of governmental law enforcement agencies.

Negligence is a failure to exercise care, or not exercise care, towards others that a reasonable or prudent person would. Basically, a Hospitality Security Department never wants to be in a position where the courts determine that there was a failure to act or inadequacies exist in any area, including training, staffing, scheduling, policy, procedure, supervision, etc. If this does occur, it is usually a result of a hospitality security professional being involved in something occurring to a guest or patron that was not good. Negativity towards the Hospitality Security Department and possible criminal, civil, or financial penalties could result when these types of incidents occur.

Members of the Hospitality Security Department who commit a wrongful act or tort against another person are subject to both criminal and civil penalties. Generally speaking, a tort can be defined as an act, or failure to act, that wrongly causes harm to someone. Torts can be negligent or intentional in nature. Negligent torts include instances when there is inadequate or negligent hospitality security, supervision, training, etc. Intentional torts can occur when action is taken that violates the rights of a person, which include wrongful arrest, wrongful imprisonment, assault, etc. If these types of incidents occur, it is usually a result of a hospitality security professional being involved in something occurring to a guest or patron that was not good. Negativity towards the Hospitality Security Department and possible criminal, civil, or financial penalties could result when these types of incidents occur. The concept of tort liability operates to compensate a victim of his or her loss, acts as a deterrent for future conduct of the same kind, and serves as evidence of society's disapproval of the wrong.

To safeguard against your hospitality security professionals being impacted by the previous situations, a proactive approach should be taken by the Hospitality Security Department which should include the following:

- Ensure that adequate training is provided
- Ensure that there is proper supervision
- Ensure that proper staffing levels are maintained
- Ensure that policies and procedures are known and followed
- Ensure that reports are written in a proper, complete and fact driven manner

Another concept that hospitality security professionals should be familiar with pertains to vicarious liability and the Doctrine of *Respondeat Superior. Respondeat superior* is Latin for "let the master respond." This doctrine indicates that the master is responsible for the actions of a servant while the servant acts on the master's behalf. An employer will be liable for an employee's negligent actions or omissions that occur during the course and scope of the employee's employment. This means that the employee must be performing duties for the employer at the time of the negligence for the employer to be held liable under *respondeat superior.* Hospitality security personnel should understand this concept and the difference between in-house, proprietary, and contract security companies which are considered nonproprietary.

Generally, in-house security personnel and the Hospitality Security Department are servants of the property, whereas, contract security personnel are employees of the supplying company and, therefore, may not be considered servants of the hiring company. Rather, they may be considered clients of the security agency. In certain situations, one person or entity could be liable for the acts or omissions of another person or entity. Vicarious liability is a form of secondary or indirect liability that is imposed when parties have a particular relationship, usually an agency relationship. When this is applicable to a particular situation, a principal is usually required to answer for the negligent or otherwise wrongful actions of a security representative.

The key to liability under *respondeat superior* is whether the security representative was acting within the scope of his or her employment and commits a wrongful act. Some of the factors that determine if a security representative was acting within the scope of employment include the following:

- Did the act occur substantially within the authorized time and space limits of employment?
- Was the person who committed the act motivated, in part, by a desire to serve the master?
- Was the person who committed the act hired to perform the act?

Why Crimes are Committed, and How to Prevent Them

While attaining my master's degree in criminal justice at Rutgers University—School of Criminal Justice in Newark, New Jersey, Ronald V. Clarke was the dean. He developed the crime displacement theory, arguing that crimes are displaced by removing opportunity for crime or by changing the situation of the crime. When this occurs, it does not actually prevent crime but merely moves or shifts the crime to another location. Putting these types of measures in place creates an awareness to those who may wish to cause harm to others that the property implementing these measures has become a hardened target with capable guardians. This should have an impact on those who have intentions of doing bad things at a property by displacing criminal activity from the property to other properties that do not have these proactive preventive measures in place. When this occurs, it does not mean that similar types of crime stop happening everywhere, it merely means that the crimes may continue to occur but not at the property that instituted measures designed to make it difficult to commit a crime without being detected. This is known as the displacement theory and is a valuable tool for Hospitality Security Departments who wish to proactively deter criminal behavior at their property.

Another theory of interest that pertains to this area is the routine activity theory by Marcus Felson and Lawrence E. Cohen. This theory focuses on situations of crimes and is likely to occur when three essential elements of crime converge in space and time:

- Motivated offenders—individuals who are capable and willing to commit crime.
- Suitable target—person or object seen by offenders as vulnerable or attractive.
- Absence of capable guardianship—a person who could intervene, and who, by his or her mere presence, could deter potential offenders from perpetrating a crime.

People commit crimes for many reasons. One theory, as discussed, that attempts to explain why crimes occur is the routine activity theory. Basically, this theory states that a crime occurs when the following elements are present: an accessible target, the absence of a capable guardian, and a motivated offender. The routine activity theory looks at crime from the perspective of the offender's view. The motivated offender assesses a situation to determine if a crime will take place based upon the presence of a suitable target and the absence of a capable guardian. If these are present, there is a strong likelihood that the offender will determine to commit the crime.

The presence of hospitality security personnel is an example of a capable guardian. This is one reason why it is very important that hospitality security personnel be very visible and conduct patrols of all areas. For example, the following should be included in any proactive approach to deterring crime:

- Posts should be established at the entrances of the property.
- Roving patrols should be assigned specific zones.
- Uniforms of the hospitality security team should be visible and distinctive.

When these types of measures are taken, it creates an awareness to those who may have bad intent that the property has become a hardened target with capable guardians. This tends to displace crime from the hardened target area, the property, to other areas that are not located near the property. When this occurs, it does not mean that similar types of crime stop happening everywhere, it merely means that the crimes may continue to occur but not at the property that instituted measures designed to make it difficult to commit a crime without being detected.

This is known as the displacement theory and is a valuable tool for anyone who wishes to proactively deter criminal behavior.

Members of the Hospitality Security Department should be familiar with and understand the differences between the foreseeability approach and the totality of circumstances approach in regard to the role each plays in court decisions. The foreseeability approach is the belief that some harm or injury is likely to result from an act or a failure to act. For example, when an event occurs, a person of average intelligence should have foreseen that his or her negligent act would put him- or herself or others in danger.

Tools that can help with establishing foreseeability are incident report programs used by the Hospitality Security Department. These programs can help provide knowledge regarding who, what, when, where, why, and how crimes have been committed at the property. Other tools that can be helpful in establishing foreseeability information are police statistics. These, too, can provide knowledge of crimes that have occurred in the vicinity of the property and provide knowledge of who, what, when, where, why, and how these crimes have been committed.

Basically, these sources should help to determine location, frequency, and types of incidents that are occurring. With the information gathered from these and other sources, proactive crime prevention and guest safety patrols and posts can be developed Once these facts are gathered, a prevention plan can be developed and implemented. For example, if it is determined that a certain type of unwanted activity is occurring between certain times, days of the week, and locations, resources can be deployed to these areas to address the issue.

Another interesting area to explore is the totality of circumstances approach. In this approach, the courts consider all criminal incidents that occur on a landowner's property and adjacent properties. Also taken into consideration are other types of evidence which include nature of crime, location, condition of property, and the architectural design of the property. This approach places the burden of increasing security measures on the property owners. It is crucial that the leader of the Hospitality Security Department implements security and safety measures that clearly demonstrate that the company is supportive in proactively reviewing and, if necessary, revising procedures, processes, and best practices to demonstrate a commitment to safety and security.

The following are some current trends and practices pertaining to hospitality security that may be of legal concern to properties that have Hospitality Security Departments. The first area that will be addressed is guest property and the responsibilities of both the property and the guest in regard to safeguarding the items that belong to a guest. Under common law, a hotelier was liable for loss or damage to guest property for the full value, unless the loss was caused by the fault of the guest or an act of nature. Today, this general rule still exists; however, with modifications that limit the liability to the property, provided the property complies with legal requirements. Properties generally post conspicuous notices indicating that valuables worth more than a certain amount must be deposited in the property-controlled safe in order to be covered for any loss. Guest room safes are generally recommended only if they contain digital keypads. It is the responsibility of the guest to assume all responsibility for getting into the safe and keeping the combination confidential.

Remember that liability is limited by statute and applies only if the property has followed the requirements, including conspicuously posting notice of the availability of safes. When these requirements are not followed, the property could be responsible for the full value of the stolen or damaged property. It is important that properties and Hospitality Security Departments review the current laws in their jurisdiction with their legal department and are familiar with the laws pertaining to this area.

Hospitality Security Departments must exhibit reasonable care and be vigilant in protecting guests from foreseeable risks. Reasonable care is the degree of caution and concern an ordinarily prudent and rational person would use regarding similar circumstances or events. It is a standard used to determine a legal duty and whether such duty was fulfilled. The responsibilities of a Hospitality Security Department exhibiting reasonable care include protecting guests from other guests and negligent acts committed by the employees of the property. One method of accomplishing this is proactive patrols of the property by the Hospitality Security Department. These patrols should be documented, and any hazardous conditions or safety hazards should be immediately reported and corrected. Areas that hospitality security personnel should address immediately include noncompliance with fire regulations, keeping hallways, passageways, stairways, entrances and exits clear of obstructions and hazards. Other areas include proper lighting levels and the repair, maintenance, and inspection of elevators.

The Fourth Amendment and Guest Room Entry

Over the decades, I have had been part of discussions pertaining to the entering of guest rooms and the protections afforded by the Fourth Amendment of the US Constitution: "The right of the people to be secure in their persons, houses, papers, and effects, against unreasonable searches and seizures, shall not be violated, and no Warrants shall issue, but upon probable cause, supported by Oath or affirmation, and particularly describing the place to be searched, and the persons or things to be seized." It is a delicate balance when it comes to maintaining guest privacy, offering a positive guest experience, and providing for a safe and secure environment for guests, employees, and patrons.

Properties cannot obstruct justice and must comply with police investigations. However, keep in mind that properties that comply with an unreasonable search or seizure that results in harm to the guest could be exposed to civil liability. Guests can bar governmental agents from entering, as in their own home, but these restrictions do not extend to property personnel. Courts have recognized that the Fourth Amendment protection from unreasonable searches and seizures applies to hotel and motel rooms. Consent exceptions allow for warrantless searches and seizures. Basically, the consent exception means that a party's agreement, actual or implied, to a search and/or seizure renders a warrant unnecessary. The courts have upheld that properties do have a right to get into the guest rooms on a regular basis. The expectation and right to privacy in a guest room is less than it is in a person's home, private residence, or even a car.

In general, part of every contract to rent a room has a waiver that is signed, allowing property staff and employees to enter a room for a variety of reasons. These waivers or contracts usually communicate that the property reserves the right to conduct a visual inspection of all guest rooms every twenty-four hours to ensure the well-being of the guest and the condition of the room. If service is refused during this time period, a member of the property leadership team will check the guest room.

Generally, a Do Not Disturb (DND) door hanger does not have any value between the guest and the property unless the signed contract states so. Guests may be able to negotiate alternative arrangements. Many properties that have used DND signs in the past are using signs that indicate that the room is occupied with language that indicates the property reserves the right to enter guest rooms, even when this sign is displayed, for maintenance, safety of guests, security, sanitation, and any other purposes.

Other reasons properties may consider the use of room-occupied signs and when to enter guest rooms may be due to concerns pertaining to drugs, prostitution, human trafficking, meth labs, etc., Properties may also consider the use of room-occupied signs in light of the horrific event that occurred in Las Vegas, Nevada, on October 1, 2017, during which fifty-eight people died and over 500 people were injured. It has been reported that the shooter, Stephen Paddock, smuggled an arsenal of semiautomatic rifles into his 32nd-floor guest room suite at a hotel from which he shot at a crowd from his guest room window while a "Do Not Disturb" sign hung on his guest room door.

This event likely expedited some properties and their Hospitality Security Departments to take proactive measures to add additional layers of protection to provide for the safety of guests staying at their property. There also has been a trend for guest rooms to be inspected on a daily basis by representatives of the property to check on the well-being of the guests and to determine if there are any items that could be involved in the planning of causing harm to others. These items include firearms, explosive devices, detailed maps of the property, etc. The guest room inspection program may have a deterrent effect on those who wish to cause harm or injury to others. Unfortunately, the behavior may still occur, but the chance of it occurring at a property that implements a well designed guest room inspection program in conjunction with a well trained Hospitality Security Department increases the possibility of detecting unwanted behavior by those with bad intentions.

The implementation of a guest room inspection program should include the following:

- Informing guests of the guest room inspection program prior to confirmation of a reservation.
- Acknowledgement of the guest room inspection program by guests prior to the confirmation of reservation.
- Upon arrival to the property, guests should be informed of the guest room inspection program.
- Guest acknowledgement of the guest room inspection program should occur during the check-in process.
- Verbiage should be posted in the guest room regarding the guest room inspection program.
- Verbiage should be posted at property regarding the guest room inspection program.
- The normal protocol should be followed—property personnel should knock on the guest room door and announce their presence prior to entering any guest room.
- Staff should be trained accordingly in regard to the guest room inspection program, which should include the implementation of "See something/Say something."
- Upon observing weapons, unusual items, drugs, suspicious behavior, etc., the Security Operations Center should be immediately notified.
- Upon receipt of any reports of weapons, unusual items, drugs, suspicious behavior, etc., the Security Operations Center should immediately contact a member of the hospitality security leadership team.

Under normal circumstances, the Hospitality Security Department should not allow law enforcement to enter a guest's room without a warrant. However, if a guest's tenancy expires, for example, when the check-out time has passed, or the guest has been evicted, Fourth Amendment protections do not apply, and consent may be given for a search by law enforcement. When this occurs, those with proper authorization, generally members of the hospitality security leadership team, may aid the police and consent to a search of the room. Properties must clearly and consistently communicate the check-out times to guests. In the event that check-out times are extended beyond the posted check-out time, it should provide a process to record these extensions so that team members know if a guest is protected by the Fourth Amendment. The following should be included regarding some of the ways to protect the property and ensure that violations of the Fourth Amendment do not occur:

- Have a clear check-out policy.
- Notify guests at check-in of the check-out time.
- Post the check-out time in the guest room.
- Ensure procedures are consistent.
- Be consistent in communicating the check-out policy.
- Be consistent in enforcing the check-out policy.
- Document extensions provided to guests regarding the check-out policy.
- Communicate extensions to the appropriate team members.

Remember, that if a guest is given permission for a later check-out time or a property practices allowing guests to stay past the posted check-out time, the Fourth Amendment protections will last until the later check-out time.

The following is geared towards addressing hotel guest issues as opposed to tenant situations—which usually involve obtaining court approval for an eviction. At times, a property may be placed in a position by a guest exhibiting unacceptable behavior where an eviction from the property has to be issued. The first threshold that must be cleared is that the property is legally able to evict a person. Generally, the grounds which permit an eviction of a guest include the following:

- Illegal activity
- Disturbing other guests
- Refusal or inability to pay bill
- Refusal to depart guest room

When a guest checks into a property, it is important that the key elements of the law are adhered to, and policies and procedures are instituted and complied with at all times. The property should confirm the agreed upon check-out date and check-out time with the guest. The property must give the guest written notice that the guest room must be vacated in order to accommodate arriving guests who have a contractual right to occupy that room. In the event that the guest fails to completely vacate and leave the room by the agreed upon date and time, the guest room may be entered, the property will take possession of the guest's property, rekey the door, and give the room to the arriving guest who has a reservation. The property must be sure that the guest signs the written notice which should be written in a clear and easily understood manner to thwart claims that the guest was not fully informed at the time of check-in of what would happen if the guest room was not vacated at the agreed upon date and time.

In the event that a guest room must be entered to take possession of the guest's property, the following should be implemented to reduce the risk of a claim that property was stolen or damaged. More than one representative of the Hospitality Security Department should enter the guest room and collect the property belonging to the guest. Remember that the belongings must be safeguarded and returned immediately to the guest upon request.

When a guest refuses to pay for a guest room or services rendered, all attempts should be made to resolve any nonpayment situation. In the event that after all attempts have been unsuccessful, the guest becomes a trespasser and is subject to being evicted from the property. When possible, the removal of the guest should involve law enforcement arresting the trespasser because it minimizes the risk to the property for false imprisonment and any possible injuries resulting from the arrest. When a hospitality security representative demands payment, and a guest refuses either to pay or to leave the property in the presence of law enforcement who witness this crime being committed, law enforcement should make the arrest since the crime was committed in its presence.

The following are some circumstances that indicate when a person can be evicted from a property when refusing to leave a property after being advised to leave the property:

- Upon being requested to leave by a person representing the landlord, usually a member of the Hospitality Security Department, the subject refuses or does not leave a property that is not open to the general public. Most full-service properties and hotels are, typically, not open to the general public.
- The subject is involved in illegal, unlawful, or criminal activity.
- The protection of the safety of other is at risk.
- The subject exhibits disruptive or annoying behavior.
    - Remember, when these types of circumstances occur, the right to evict arises out of the duty of the property to provide for the safety and comfort of the other guests.
- The subject exhibits objectionable or improper behavior.
    - Exactly when objectionable or improper behavior occurs is not always easy to determine; thus, the facts of each situation should be reviewed, and decisions should be made on a case-by-case basis in a consistent manner.
- Remember that the eviction from the property should not place the person in a position of harm.

Hospitality security representatives should use extreme caution when a situation requires the use of reasonable force to evict a person. The use force should only be used as a last resort. If deemed necessary to effectuate an eviction, the use of force should only be used when:

- An immediate eviction is necessary for the safety of others.
- All other methods of accomplishing the eviction have been exhausted.
- The use of force is the only way to accomplish the eviction.

- Only the minimum amount of force that is needed to effectuate an eviction should be applied and should only be used as a last resort.

To limit the liability to the property, the Hospitality Security Department should ensure that improper conduct is not exhibited by members of the hospitality security team when a person is subject to an eviction. Types of improper conduct include the following:

- Humiliation of the subject
- Insulting language
- Intimidating conduct
- Offensive acts
- Excessive force

In my career, I have been invited to be the leader of security teams based on a variety of factors—including the ones previously discussed. Some of the most important included being considered a professional, which encompasses educational background, certifications, reputation, experience, credibility, and confidence that you can get the job done. When a person possesses these traits and talents, he or she adds instant credibility to any Hospitality Security Department. Many times, the selection of this vital position, leader of a Hospitality Security Department, may have ripple effects that carry over into the stockholders, investors, and patrons and creates public confidence of the property being responsible, provides a safe, secure environment, abides by the rules and regulations, and develops a partnership with the local, state, and federal law enforcement community, which, at the end of the day, could have an impact on a property's success, reputation, and bottom line.

Discussion Questions

1. What is ethics? List three aspects of ethics.
2. What do morals refer to?
3. What are values? List three values or beliefs pertaining to values.
4. What is professionalism? List three components of professionalism.
5. What is the crime displacement theory?
6. Explain why a Hospitality Security Department should perform its duties in a professional, ethical, and moral manner.
7. Explain reasonable care and how the Hospitality Security Department should exhibit due diligence in this area.

CHAPTER

9

SELECTION AND TRAINING

"We are what we repeatedly do. Excellence then, is not an act, but a habit."

—Aristotle

An Ancient Greek philosopher, who, with Plato, is considered the "Father of Western Philosophy"

The heart of any Hospitality Security Department is the selection and training of personnel. I have been involved in the openings of many properties from the ground up. The key element to the opening success of each was bringing talented people aboard who, among other things, had the aptitude, ability, and desire to learn and help others. It is of paramount importance that the leader of the hospitality security team be very involved and takes a hands-on approach in the selection process and in the final selection of candidates. This is one of the key reasons why I believe that the properties I opened have been successful. No matter how busy things were, time was always carved out of my hectic preopening schedule to be part of the initial selection of the key and instrumental members of the hospitality security team.

When building the security teams, I always searched for those whom I viewed as being very talented, that I could mentor, and would someday take my place. Some may find the mind-set of succession planning difficult, usually because they are not confident in their abilities or feel threatened in some manner. I have always found succession planning very easy since I always put the best team possible in place and focus energy on the success of the team and property as a whole rather than the success of individuals who put themselves first and others second.

The Hiring Process

This can present an interesting dilemma if you ever find yourself in a position where a key leader of your organization has a self-centered mind-set and believes in rewarding friendships rather than a job well done. Remember, people don't leave companies, they leave bad leaders. So much hard work goes into selecting qualified candidates that it is important to take the following steps to reduce attrition by recognizing a job well done and treating others fairly, with dignity and respect.

Through the years. I have learned to implement the following approach when hiring all members of the hospitality security team. After the Department of Human Resource completes screening of the security candidates, the next phase is a group interview, which consists of the following: Candidates are brought into a classroom setting and asked to stand behind a chair at a desk. All are advised that they will be standing during the entire selection process to simulate being on their feet while on duty. It is made crystal clear to all candidates that being part of the Hospitality Security Department requires being at a standing post and/or walking for an entire shift. All are asked if they can meet this requirement; those who acknowledge that they can, continue in the process. Note that if someone states that he or she cannot perform this duty, I reroute the applicant back to human resources so that another position can be found for the candidate.

The next step in this phase of the process includes "what-if" scenarios. Various scenarios are read aloud regarding situations that occur in the property environment and answers are solicited verbally and in writing. During this interaction between candidates and members of the hospitality security team, many observations are made and noted regarding the candidates, including the following:

- How does the candidate interact with others?
- What is the body language of candidate?
- Does the candidate make eye contact?
- Does the candidate respond appropriately regarding scenarios?
- Does the candidate display dignity and respect towards others?

When creating the questions to ask candidates, make them relevant to the day-to-day operation of the property. For example, ask the question, "Where is the nearest restroom?" The candidate should be advised that this question will probably be asked many, many times a day, and each time it is asked, it should be responded to in a manner as if it were the first time it has ever been heard. I always like to stress that what will take the Hospitality Security Department to the next level is performing the ordinary in an extraordinary manner. This includes interactions and inquiries from guests and patrons that are positive, upbeat, and concluded with words to the effect, "Is there anything else I can help you with today?"

The following are some examples of the questions that require the candidate to take written notes. Prior to starting this section, the candidates should be advised that they are gathering information for a hospitality security report and what actions they think they should take. The questions who, what, when, where, why, and how should be answered in their notes. Advise the candidates that the scenario will be read twice and that questions may be asked. Once a question is answered for a scenario, it will not be repeated again in another scenario. Some things to look for during this exercise are applicants who ask questions that are relevant to obtaining more information and to answer the questions of who, what, where, when, why, and how. Here are some possible questions:

- On March 19th, you are detailed to go to the employee dining area. Upon arrival, you see a female and a male arguing in an aggressive manner. The male is an employee. The female is not an employee. The male tells you that he has a restraining order against the female.
  - Lester Webster, Date of Birth 5-16-1994, 200 pounds, 5'10", black hair
  - Alice Jones, Date of Birth 6-14-1994, 140 pounds, 5'4", blue eyes
    - Anticipate follow up questions on hair color since it is not listed.
    - Anticipate questions on time of incident, how is it determined if a restraining order is in effect, should police be contacted, etc.
- On July 13th, you are detailed to the bar for a report of a person who suffered an injury to her left foot. The guest's name is Sarah Smith and is with her husband, Eugene Smith. Bar supervisor Jones and cocktail server Linda Brown both witnessed the incident and stated that the female appeared to be intoxicated, and Smith mentioned to the server that she had taken pills.
  - Sarah Smith, Date of Birth 2-22-1958, 125 pounds, 5'1", hazel eyes, blonde hair
    - Notice that this answers a lot of the required information.
    - Written statements should be obtained from witnesses.
    - Anticipate follow-up questions on what type of pill was taken, time of incident, etc.
- On November 15th at approximately 1:00 p.m., a patron hands you a gold money clip with the initials "RVD" on it. He stated that he was walking past a restroom and saw the money clip on the floor.
  - Anticipate questions regarding description and information of finder of money clip.
  - How much money, if any, is in money clip, etc.?
- On December 31st at approximately 5:00 p.m., you receive information that a package is at the entrance of a restroom. What would you do?
  - Anticipate numerous questions regarding description of package, etc.
- On November 3rd at approximately 9:00 a.m., you receive a call regarding a female patron who refuses to leave a gaming table. The patron has not placed a bet in over a half hour and is harassing other patrons and the dealer. What would you do?
  - Ask questions regarding information of subject.
  - Anticipate possible eviction of subject, etc.

After reviewing the previously listed questions, it should give you a good idea on how to craft questions of your own that are unique and specific to your property. Remember to keep the questions relevant and to respond to any questions asked by candidates in accordance with the policy and procedures of the property. Be consistent. Do not give answers that are not 100% accurate because if a candidate is selected, chances are that he or she will implement what was learned in this exercise. Remember—first learned, always remembered.

Before any training program can begin, the focus of selecting people to be part of the hospitality security team must occur. The selection of candidates and the training of hospitality security personnel are among the most important aspects of setting the foundation of the department. A mind-set should be created that being a member of the Hospitality Security Department is a coveted position where one does not simply apply for a job but, rather, is invited to have the opportunity to be part of a team. It is important to invest the time, money, and resources into the training of members of the hospitality security team. These reasons include the safety of patrons, guests, visitors, and employees and the protection of company assets.

Candidates who wish to become part of the hospitality security team should have the ability to interact, communicate well with others, and have the aptitude to develop the skills needed for the position. In today's hospitality security world, it is important to select candidates who have the innate ability to interact and communicate with others in a genuine manner while providing guest service to both the external and internal customer. Of equal importance is the ability of a hospitality security candidate to possess the aptitude and the desire to learn the skills needed to perform the essential duties required of his or her position. If there is ever a question regarding the hiring of a candidate, remember the words of Jim Collins, the author of *Good to Great* and my guru of business management , who said, "When in doubt—don't hire—keep looking."

This concept is reinforced in his book by supporting the notion that hiring the right talent has more to do with innate character traits and innate capabilities than with specific knowledge, background, or skills. The following are some other key concepts pertaining to the hiring process presented by Collins.

> "Get the right people on the bus ... and then figure out where to drive it."
>
> "The purpose of compensation is not to 'motivate' the right behaviors from the wrong people, but to keep the right people in the first place."
>
> "The old adage, 'People are your most important asset' is wrong. People are not your most important asset. The right people are."

Once the right people are "on the bus," it is important for the leaders of the hospitality security team to communicate and practice the following:

- An open-door policy
- The inverted pyramid philosophy
- Frederick Herzberg's hygiene theory
- Douglas McGregor's theory X and theory Y

An open-door policy and the inverted pyramid philosophy go hand in hand with developing a sense of esprit de corps in which enthusiasm, devotion, and a strong regard for the performance of the hospitality security team is established. I have always practiced these philosophies and ensured that the teams that I have worked with knew that those on the front line and in the trenches were the most important asset of the department. They have the ability to make the team look great—or not. It was also clearly communicated that, although leadership does include management by walking around in the daily duties, the day-to-day operations and the routine interaction with others is spearheaded by those on the front lines.

Motivational Theories

The following are theories that relate to the motivation of employees and should be known and understood by members of the hospitality security leadership team.

Frederick Herzberg's hygiene theory states that the opposite of satisfaction is not dissatisfaction but, rather, no satisfaction. Hygiene factors can move someone from dissatisfaction to no satisfaction. The following are examples of hygiene factors:

- Physical work conditions
- Surroundings
- Salary
- Co-workers
- External factors
- Motivation Factors

Only motivators can move someone to satisfaction. The following are examples of motivators:

- Achievement
- Recognition
- Responsibility
- Satisfaction from work itself
- Money is not a motivator

In creating a successful and productive environment, it is important that the leaders of the hospitality security team recognize these motivators during the selection process and in the daily operation of the department.

Douglas McGregor's theory X and theory Y are based upon two types of people called "X" and "Y." The following are examples of characteristics that make up these categories.

theory X

- People are not ambitious
- Prefer to be directed
- Resist change
- Show no interest in organizational goals
- Will attempt to avoid work whenever possible

theory Y

- People are creative
- Ingenuity is common
- Show a capacity for creativity
- Work can be as natural as play
- Genuine caring/emphatic skills

Obviously, the characteristics exhibited in theory Y are those of people who would excel in the Hospitality Security Department.

The present-day hospitality security professional is expected to be knowledgeable in all areas relating to hospitality security and that the public perception of interactions with internal and external guests should be seamless. The concept of getting the "right people on the bus and, then, in the right seats" is key to the overall success of any hospitality security team that wishes to be a strong service provider, leader, and innovator in the field. The hospitality security leadership team needs to be able to recognize what motivates the members of its team and that the opposite of satisfaction is not dissatisfaction but, rather, no satisfaction. To improve the chances of having a successful team, the energies of the hospitality security team should focus on those who possess these characteristics as well as those in Mc Gregor's theory Y.

Finally, the day arrives when the security team has been selected and the continuous training of personnel should commence. Notice that the word "continuous" was used. This is a key principle and factor in determining how successful the team will be as well as to help ensure that hospitality security personnel have the proper tools and equipment to do their jobs well. This is a by-product of training, in that two-way communication occurs, and conversations are held pertaining to what is working, what could be done better, and what should stop being done. Sometimes it happens that a person, who has been in the Hospitality Security Department for five years, only has one year of experience/knowledge. That is because after his or her first year of training, his or her learning and keeping abreast of the ever-changing best practices, technologies, and laws did not occur. Remember, a well selected and trained Hospitality Security Department will ultimately help to improve profit margins by detecting suspicious activity, identifying those exhibiting unacceptable behavior, and creating a feeling a safety and security at the property.

As of the writing of this book, this is the year that the Philadelphia Eagles finally won a Super Bowl! I was born and raised in South Jersey, and as a Philadelphia Eagles fan for over half a century (oh-oh, guess I am dating myself), this was a tremendous moment. As events unfolded and more was learned about this incredible underdog team, I realized that this could be a training tool and provide reinforcement to the practice of always being passionate, believing in one another, believing in the team, and achieving departmental goals regardless of the obstacles. In a nutshell, here is the following play that was executed during the Super Bowl and a link to the speech that was delivered by Jason Kelce, center for the Eagles, at the Eagles Super Bowl champions celebration on the steps of the Philadelphia Museum of Art February 8, 2018, the very same steps where the ultimate iconic movie underdog Rocky trained for his boxing bout with Apollo Creed. See the festivities for yourself at https://www.youtube.com/watch?v=DhIFNxEz1qc.

The Philly Special play was a great example of training, practice, execution, and a management style similar to the inverted pyramid that came together when a play call was made during Super Bowl LII when the Eagles were ahead 15–12 with 38 seconds left before half-time with the ball on the one-yard line. The play call, known as the Philly Special, will be remembered by Eagles fans until the end of time. Even though backup quarterback Nick Foles mistakenly asked Coach Pederson, "You want Philly Philly?" instead of the Philly Special. Coach Pederson later stated, "We knew exactly what we were talking about, 'Philly, Philly,' 'Dilly, Dilly,' 'Philly Special'—it was all the same to us." When a team is well trained in athletics, or in the security realm, situations as previously mentioned can occur without having catastrophic results. Rather, the end result mirrors what was communicated, trained, and practiced, resulting in a sense of intuitiveness being instilled among the members of the team.

In this instance, the Philadelphia Eagles backup Super Bowl LII MVP quarterback, Nick Foles, had the confidence and freedom to suggest this play to Coach Pederson on a critical fourth and goal on the one-yard line without fear of being scoffed or ignored. A few seconds after Foles suggested the play, Coach Pederson said, "Yeah, why not", and the rest, as they say, is history. When Foles returned to the field, the Eagles team executed this intricate play, which had a significant impact on the game. The Eagles put forth tremendous effort in their training, trust development, belief in one another, and teamwork while working towards a common goal—winning the Super Bowl and, specifically, the execution of the Philly Special. Similarly, Hospitality Security Departmental leaders should motivate their team by including the previously listed principals in their training and interactions with their team.

Another area of importance is reviewing policies, procedures, and best practices with the hospitality security team. Practice makes perfect. For example, the Eagles had practiced the Philly Special play frequently, including the friday before the Super Bowl, conducting a walk-through at a hotel ballroom at the Mall of America. There were a lot of moving parts and things that had to be executed for the play to be successful. The Philly Special play was practiced, developed, and executed by the Eagles offensive unit on the biggest day and the biggest play in Philadelphia Eagle history.

It should be noted that the Patriots ran a similar play earlier in the Super Bowl, but quarterback Tom Brady could not pull in the pass. Unlike Tom Brady and the Patriots, the Philadelphia Eagles' hard work on the practice field paid off when Nick Foles and the Eagles team executed this intricate play perfectly. I believe this example illustrates the importance of teamwork, striving towards a common goal, and believing and trusting in one another. To be the best, teams and departments must focus on the training received, practice sessions, tabletop exercises, and, more importantly, demonstrating the retention of information by executing the plays or processes and procedures that were reviewed and practiced.

Many times, people do not realize the amount of work involved in being successful. For example, when I was selected to be in charge of security for the start-up of a multibillion-dollar property, I liked to tell others, tongue in cheek, that it only took me over two decades to become an overnight success. It took a lot of hard work over the years to develop the skills and knowledge needed to be successful and be recognized as one of the best. The Philly Special demonstrates the efforts that are needed to be successful. Foles admitted that when they first practiced the play he was terrible—it appears that after lots of hard work—he and the team were able to pull off one of the greatest plays in Super Bowl history by having confidence in the training received and the ability to demonstrate and execute what was practiced and planned. This is critical in any arena—especially in the security field; it could mean the difference between a situation escalating to a significant event or merely being another interaction between hospitality security team members and those guests, patrons, or others involved in a situation.

It is important for hospitality security leaders to lead by example and stress the importance of training and learning. Others cannot be expected to perform at their optimum level if they are not trained properly. After the initial on-boarding training of hospitality security personnel is completed, periodic mandatory training sessions should occur. The training should consist of material that is current; specific; and deals with the concerns, issues, and ideas of the team. For example, reoccurring errors or questions should be addressed during training sessions. If these areas are left unaddressed, it could have a negative impact on the morale of the team and, possibly, lead to the handling of an incident that puts other in harm's way.

Training is a cyclical process, which should continually be updated to meet the needs and concerns of the Hospitality Security Department. Training should be viewed as an ongoing approach to continually acquire knowledge and skills to make the team the best that it can be. Since hospitality security personnel interact and deal with people on a day-to-day basis, there are many areas that should be addressed in training. Keeping in mind that many times, when hospitality security becomes involved with a guest, it is usually addressing a situation in which a person may be exhibiting the worst behavior of his or her life.

For example, over the course of my career, I have received many letters from patrons who were evicted from a property for a variety of reasons, including breaking surveillance cameras, urinating in public, fighting, etc. These acts are committed by a full spectrum of people ranging from doctors, lawyers, construction workers, business owners, etc. Many times, after the person evicted wakes up the next day, he or she realizes the full impact of what he or she has done and understands it was out of bounds. That person will be very apologetic and send a letter stating, in effect, that the behavior exhibited was the worst he or she has ever exhibited in his or her life and requests to make full payment of any damage he or she has caused, doesn't know what came over him or her, and is truly sorry.

In my opinion, sometimes, when a patron conducts him- or herself in a manner that exceeds the boundaries of acceptable behavior at a property, he or she has the mistaken belief that it's okay to have "fun" at the expense of others. Only after the euphoric effect wears off, does a person realize that the same rules that apply inside a property apply in the rest of society, as well. This may be caused by many reasons, including alcohol, the effects of advertising campaigns, etc.

For these reasons, it is very important that hospitality security personnel are aware of the previously mentioned items and receive continual training accordingly. Training should include and range from the general to the specific. Some of the qualities that a hospitality security representative should exhibit to be successful include the ability to multitask, remain calm in stressful situations, make good decisions, and communicate with others in a clear and concise manner. Remember that the ladies and gentlemen that comprise the hospitality security team are on the front lines and in the trenches of the day-to-day interactions with guests, patrons, and employees. They are the ones who are the front lines of defense in the protection and security of the property.

Unfortunately, at times, the hospitality security personnel may be yelled at, cursed, spit on, and talked to in an aggressive manner during interactions with the patrons of the property. Sometimes, these patrons may even escalate situations to the point where they become physical with the hospitality security personnel. These are some of the reasons that initial training, on-the-job (OJT) training, and a continuous and ongoing training program is vital to the security, safety, and education of all members of the hospitality security team.

The training needed for hospitality security personnel depends upon the setting and environment. The following is a sample outline of the types of training that may be included for the hospitality security team; however, the final decision is based upon the needs of the property:

- Introduction
- Purpose and mission
- Expectations
- Organizational structure
- Policies and procedures
- Emergency procedures
- Review of job descriptions
- Responsibilities
- Open-door policy
- Customer service
- Uniforms
- Appearance
- General conduct
- Communication
- Shift change
- Post assignments
- Key control
- Temporary employee badges
- Patrol responsibilities
- Underage consumption of alcoholic beverages
- High security areas
- Firearms/dangerous weapons
- Armored car
- Duress alarms
- Property removal
- Crowd control
- Report writing
- Exclusions
- Arrest and detention
- Crime scene protection
- Counterfeit bills
- Power outages
- Heightened security alerts
- Bomb threats

- Fire evacuation
- Lost and found
- Work schedules
- Questions
- Tour of property and back-of-house areas
- Issuance of uniforms and identification

The following is a general guideline of how to present training and topics that should be included in the indoctrination of those joining the hospitality security team.

- Introduction of presenter's background, experience, and role with the hospitality security team.
- Review of the hospitality security mission statement—mission statement of the goals, objectives, expectations, and vision of the hospitality security leadership team.

This reminds me of a time when I was hired as the leader of the Hospitality Security Department and the general manager advised me that there was an "us" versus "them" type of mentality in the department that he wanted me to fix. During the first days on the job, I noticed that the door that lead to the security leadership area was always locked to prevent front line personnel from entering the area. A short time later, I called a meeting with the security leadership team and discussed the importance of an open-door policy and explained that all hospitality security team members should have direct access to all members of the leadership team, including myself, without exception. I further explained that the open-door policy aides in communicating ideas, addressing concerns, and building the morale of the Hospitality Security Department. To demonstrate my passion for this topic, I took a hammer and removed the door leading into the security leadership area off its hinges. By the looks I was receiving, I believe some of the security leaders in the room thought I might be off my own hinges.

The mission statement I developed for the department was printed out, placed on the door, and each person was asked to read it. If, after reading the mission statement, he or she agreed with it, he or she was asked to sign the door with the mission statement on it. I stressed that he or she did not have to sign—only if he or she agreed with the open-door policy and the security mission statement. Each and every leader signed.

Afterwards, the Hospitality Security Departmental meetings were conducted, and the door with the signatures and mission statement was brought to the meetings and reviewed. Each person was asked to read the mission statement and, if in agreement to sign the door with the mission statement on it. I stressed that they did not have to sign—only if they agreed with the open-door policy and the security mission statement should they place their signature on the door containing the mission statement. Every member of the security team was in agreement and signed the door.

The door with the signatures and mission statement was also placed in the security roll call area. I attended every roll call that was conducted prior to each shift and explained the open-door policy and the mission statement for those who were unable to attend the departmental meetings. The presentation of the door and mission statement was provided as previously described, and again, all were in agreement and signed the door containing the mission statement. When new members joined the security team, the initial training received included the introduction to the mission statement, open-door policy, and the opportunity to sign the door that I removed to create the actual open-door policy.

The following should be included as part of the on boarding review for members of the hospitality security team.

- Communicate clearly—understand and be understood. Repeat questions back to guests to ensure that what is being asked is being answered. Finish every conversation with words to the effect, "Is there anything else I can help you with today?"
- Review the general responsibilities of hospitality security personnel and the expectations regarding their performance.
- Review the rules of conduct of the Hospitality Security Department. Many times, when properties attempt to limit expenses, training comes under scrutiny. In an effort to be efficient, is not necessary to review the rules of conduct presented by the Human Resource Department during the candidate's property orientation program.
- The emergency procedures should be reviewed and discussed.
- The hospitality security standard operational procedures should be reviewed and discussed.
- Review the hospitality security radio procedures, codes, and the use of plain language when communicating over the two-way radio system.
- Hospitality security post assignments should be reviewed and discussed; both normal and emergency post roles and responsibilities should be reviewed. The following are some basic examples of normal hospitality security post assignments to help provide a general idea of what they are. Basically, post assignments are a specific location or assignment with an explanation of what is expected of those who are assigned to the post. When developing your post assignments, list as much detail that you feel is needed to clearly describe what is expected from those assigned to each area.
    - Hospitality Security Operations Center
        - Communication nerve center of the property located in the back-of-house area.
    - Fixed post—Usually located at property entrances, areas that provide access to the property or secured areas.
        - Remain at assigned post.
        - Provide guest service and greet guests while monitoring those who enter and exit.
        - Immediately report any suspicious persons or activity.
        - Provide directions and answer patron questions
    - Hospitality security rover
        - Remain in assigned zone.
        - Provide guest service.
        - Provide directions and answer guest questions.
        - Respond to alarms and incidents located in assigned zone.
        - Be alert for suspicious persons or activity.

One method to identify those with bad intent is to observe where they are looking if they are randomly walking around the property. Patrons of a property generally behave in a particular manner by looking straight ahead, etc., as compared to a person who constantly looks about, scans the crowd, and looks over the heads of people, possibly looking for a potential victim. I generally make a comparison to the animal kingdom when it comes to this topic. For example, predators like lions tend to look out over prey while they are grazing and target those that appear to be weak or inattentive to their surroundings. Suspicious persons behave in a similar manner. They look out over the guests of a property until they find someone who may be inattentive, left his or her jacket, purse or other personal item over a chair, or simply walked away from his or her items. Many times, crimes of opportunity can be prevented at a property if the hospitality security team is properly trained and conducts proactive patrols identifying guests with unsecured items and those on the prowl for their next unsuspecting victim.

Evictions

- Review of loitering and eviction policy—prior to establishing a list of offenses that is considered loitering or offenses that can cause eviction, the list should be reviewed with the legal department and with members of the property leadership team—including the general manager. Training to members of the hospitality security team should include what loitering is and what should be done when it occurs. A loitering policy should include the following:
  - Loitering is not permitted. Those loitering are subject to ejection and possible criminal prosecution.
  - One definition of a loiterer is anyone who exceeds the acceptable bounds of behavior and includes, but is not limited to, the following:
    - Obscene language
    - Asking people for money
    - Creating a disturbance
    - Criminal acts
- When a person is reported to be in violation of the loitering policy, his or her actions should be witnessed by a hospitality security representative or a complaint must be made by a guest or employee. A member of the hospitality security leadership team should gather all the facts and decide on the course of action. If a decision is made to eject the subject, the Hospitality Security Operations Center should be contacted and advised. After confirmation from the Security Operations Center that the transmission was received, the subject should be approached and notified of the complaint and the loitering policy. The subject should be read the eviction notice, the necessary paperwork should be completed, and subject should be escorted out of the property. Only a member of the hospitality security leadership team should have the authority to effect an eviction.

The following is an example of an eviction notice that should be communicated by a member of the hospitality security leadership team to the subject being ejected:

- I represent the landlord of ________________ property. Your conduct has exceeded the boundaries of proper behavior for a person invited or privileged to remain on the premises. You are being formally evicted. If you refuse to leave or return after being evicted, you will be arrested for trespassing.

Proper Documentation

The Hospitality Security Department is responsible for keeping records of all incidents that occur on the property. These reports are taken to accurately record any incident or complaint reported to the Hospitality Security Department. For example, when an incident involves a guest injury, it is the responsibility of the Hospitality Security Department to properly document the incident in case the report is needed at a later date to support the facts of the incident. It is important that reports are completed in an accurate, truthful, and professional manner since they may be needed for criminal court cases or liability issues.

- Written reports are basic to security work. These reports are a permanent record and give important information to others.
- Reports will state the facts of the incident and answer who, what, when, where, why, and how.
    - **Who**—Who was involved in the incident? Victims and/or witness information—name, address, date of birth, and phone number should be included.
    - **What**—What happened? Exact description of what occurred, all items missing, and their approximate values should be included.
    - **When—**When did the incident occur? Record the date and time the incident was reported to the Hospitality Security Department and the date and time the incident occurred. Both should be included.
    - **Where**—Where did the incident occur? If possible, record the exact location of the incident or where victim believes the incident occurred should be included.
    - **Why—**Why did the incident occur? Was the property misplaced, lost, or stolen should be included.
    - **How**—How did the incident occur? Were weapons or tools used? For example, did the incident involve physical force, were others involved, etc., should be included.
- Remember to write down all information as soon as possible. It is easier to write a report when all the information is fresh in your mind.
- When investigating an incident where someone slipped, tripped, or fell, ask the questions who, what, when, where, why, and how! When there are no witnesses, specify that the account given of an incident is that of the complainant. Check the floor for any water or slippery substances. Inspect the bottom of the employee's/patron's shoes. Check and see if they have a tread or if they are smooth and slippery. If complainant is wearing a dress shoe or boot with a heel, indicate your observations in your report.
- Slip and fall reports should be accompanied by two photos taken from two different vantage points of the area where the incident occurred.

- It is important when gathering information from a guest, victim, or subject involved in an incident, to show compassion. Listen to what is said, and be nice when asking for information.
- Remember the only way to get information is to ask questions.

When writing the narrative of a report, I have found the third person format to be easier for the reader to understand. The narrative portion of the report should always start with "On (date) at approximate (time) (job title, first and last name)." The following information should be contained in the narrative/details section of the report:

Key Control

- Name of the person reporting the incident.
- Name of the victim.
- Exact cause of incident and the location (if known).
- Witness names and statements.
- Description of suspect (if known).
- Description of items and value.
- When applicable, reports will include statements, CCTV coverage, and photographs.
- All reports will be reviewed by a member of the hospitality security leadership team.
- Reports will be completed on the shift the incident occurred unless approval has been given by a member of the hospitality security leadership team for the report to be turned in on the next shift after the incident occurred.

A review of the importance of key control and the protocol and procedures protecting these valuable assets should be reviewed, and the proper way to insure accountability of the keys in the care and custody of the Hospitality Security Department should be reviewed and demonstrated. The following is a description of restricted, unrestricted, and company keys that are controlled by the Hospitality Security Department.

- Restricted keys
  - All money-related keys and keys to sensitive areas.
- Unrestricted keys
  - All property-related keys.
- Company keys
  - All keys that control access to offices, storage areas, etc.
  - To ensure continuity of the keys held by the Hospitality Security Department, key control ledger books will be maintained. The key log should be kept in a bound ledger book. The information recorded in the key control log will include the following:
    - Key name
    - Date and time key is signed out
    - Signature and employee number of the receiving employee
    - Name and employee number of the issuing security officer

    - Signature and employee number of employee returning key
    - Signature and employee number of security officer receiving key
    - Date and time returned

- If an entry is made in the key control log in error, the error will be voided by drawing a single line through the entry with a red pen and making the corrected entry on the next available line. Masking the error by covering it and writing over top of the error is never to occur.
- It will be the responsibility of the incoming representative of the hospitality security leadership team to ensure that all keys are accounted for at the beginning of each shift. This verification will be completed in the presence of the outgoing representative of the hospitality security leadership team.
- In the event that a key cannot be accounted for and is missing, the leader of the Hospitality Security Department will be notified immediately.
- Keys issued by hospitality security are not to be passed from shift-to-shift or person-to-person. At the change of the department shifts, users will be required to sign the issued keys in and out at the hospitality security key issuance center.

Identification Procedures

The prevention of anyone under the legal age to consume alcoholic beverages and to enter areas that are restricted to only those who are of legal age is a very important function of the Hospitality Security Department. Failure to exhibit and document due diligence in this area can result in fines and serious repercussions. The following should be included in the training of hospitality security personnel performing their due diligence in preventing persons under the legal age to enter these areas. A review of acceptable forms of identification, unacceptable forms of identification, detecting fraudulent identification, and procedures regarding the detecting of fraudulent identification should be included in the training received by the entire Hospitality Security Department.

A predetermined age should be determined and vetted through the executive leadership team, including the general manager of the property, to determine at what age guests and patrons will be required to present a state or federal identification. When the predetermined age is established, all guests and patrons who appear to be under the predetermined age and attempt to gain access to areas restricted to the legal drinking age will be asked for a state or federal identification. The identification will be inspected to ensure that the person who possesses the identification is the actual owner and that the identification has not been altered. Identification checks are to be conducted in a polite and cordial manner to ensure minimum inconvenience to the property guests and patrons. The procedure for the inspection of identification should include the following:

- Assess the age of a guest or patron.
- If a person appears to be under the predetermined age—identification will be requested of that person.
- Inspect the state or federal identification presented and verify that the photo and physical features listed on identification, etc., match the person who is presenting the identification.
- Inspect the identification for any alterations, changes, or evidence of tampering.

Acceptable forms of identification should include a photo and date of birth. The following should be included in the list of acceptable identifications:

- State identification card
- Federal identification card
- Military identification card
- Passport
- United States Office of Immigration Naturalization card

Hospitality security representatives should include the following when identification is requested from a guest or patron:

- If the identification is contained in a wallet, purse, etc., politely request the guest or patron to remove the identification. Once the identification is handed to a hospitality security representative, the identification should be closely inspected.
- Check and inspect both sides of the identification presented.
- Match the photo with the person presenting the identification. Many times, the identification presented is a valid identification, but it belongs to someone else.
- Check the birth date, and make sure that the date indicates that the person is of the legal age to consume alcoholic beverages.
- Check the expiration date of the identification.
    - Expired identifications are not valid forms of identification.
- If necessary, request a second form of identification.
    - Many times, those with fraudulent identification do not carry another form of fraudulent identification.
- If necessary, ask the person presenting the identification basic information regarding the information contained on the identification—date of birth, middle initial, address, zip code, zodiac sign, etc.

The following should be included in the inspection of identification presented to a hospitality security representative to determine if it the identification is fraudulent:

- Inspect font and type size on the identification presented.
- The photograph on the identification should not be raised.
- Inspect the rigidity of the identification card. The identification card should not be cracked or broken. If it is, conduct a closer examination of the identification.
- Inspect the date of birth area of the identification. Font, type size, and clarity should match the other areas on the identification.
- If there are any questions or concerns, immediately contact a member of the hospitality security leadership team.

- When the word "duplicate" appears on an identification, closely examine the physical characteristics and photograph on the identification to the person presenting the identification. Someone else may have the original.
- Inspect for a smooth and even surface. A bumpy surface or an uneven surface around a photograph or date of birth are indicators of tampering. Pinholes on the surface of the identification may indicate that bleach was used to clear or blur certain aspects of the identification like the date of birth.
- Inspect the state seal or logo. A state seal or logo that appears to have been altered or is missing is an indicator that the identification may be fraudulent.
- Inspect the corners of the identification to determine if it is solid or has been peeled and resealed.
- Inspect the thickness of the identification and check for blurred lettering.

If a hospitality security representative is not positive that the identification presented is authentic, the person is not to be permitted entry into the restricted area, and a member of the hospitality security leadership team is to be contacted immediately.

Preservation of Physical Evidence

When a crime is committed at a property, an important aspect is the protection of the crime scene and physical evidence. The difference between evidence and physical evidence is that evidence is anything that can be used to determine whether a crime has been committed, whereas, physical evidence is basically any "object" that can establish that a crime has been committed or can provide a link between a crime, victim, and perpetrator(s). It is important to law enforcement and investigators to analyze and interpret physical evidence clues left behind at the crime scene; these clues could lead to the perpetrator(s) who committed the act, determine the sequence of events, or lead to the identification of those involved.

However, for this to occur, it is critical that hospitality security personnel recognize potential physical evidence, protect it, collect it, or preserve it for those conducting the investigation. If possible, it is best to leave the physical evidence in place until the arrival of law enforcement. There may be times when physical evidence must be gathered by a member of the hospitality security team. For example, if a crime scene is located outside, and it is raining, physical evidence may need to be secured by a member of the hospitality security team to prevent its contamination.

Another key element regarding physical evidence is the inability to recognize, collect, or preserve it in a timely manner. As in the previous example, failure to recognize or protect the physical evidence could result in the physical evidence being destroyed, which could seriously hamper or compromise an investigation. Remember that every crime scene has a victim, and the proper identification, preservation, and collection of evidence increases the chances of identifying the perpetrator(s) of the crime. If there is ever a doubt as to whether an item or object is physical evidence, treat it as if it is, protect the physical evidence and notify a member of the hospitality security leadership team and law enforcement if applicable.

Some types of physical evidence that may be available for recovery at a crime scene include the following:

- Biological evidence—blood, saliva, hair, semen etc.
- Tool marks
- Firearms and ammunition evidence—weapon, shell casings, etc.
- Weapons—knife, blunt object, etc.
- Fingerprints—located on weapons, paper, etc.
- Toxicology evidence—drugs, poisons, etc.
- Documentation evidence—written notes, paper, ink, etc.
- Explosives
- Drug evidence—left at scene, on person, etc.

The proper identification, collection, and establishment of a chain of custody regarding physical evidence is very important. If any one of these areas is not done properly, it could result in the physical evidence being contaminated or inadmissible in court. The basic role of a hospitality security representative is to identify, protect, and, if necessary, collect the evidence. The hospitality security representative who identifies or locates specific evidence should be listed in any reports or in any documentation regarding the incident and the evidence. The information that should be listed includes the following:

- Date physical evidence was located.
- Time physical evidence was located.
- Exactly where the physical evidence was discovered.
- If physical evidence was handled—list by whom, date, and time.
- To establish chain of custody of physical evidence—list date, time, and the person to whom the physical evidence was turned over. The following should be included regarding the person the physical evidence was turned over to:
    - Name
    - Rank
    - Identification number
    - Law enforcement department

The advantage of following the proper protocol for physical evidence to be utilized in an investigation and eventual prosecution of a case includes the following:

- Physical evidence cannot be distorted.
- Physical evidence is tangible—it can be seen and, possibly, touched by a jury.
- Physical evidence can usually be effective in rebutting statements made by a defendant.
- Many times, physical evidence helps to solve a case.
- Physical evidence can usually confirm the facts of a case and prove that a defendant's statements are false.
- It is advantageous to have physical evidence over the testimony of a witness. Over time, witness testimony is subject to memory loss, whereas, physical evidence is not.

- A person accused of a crime based upon physical evidence can have the physical evidence tested by an independent expert. This adds to the credibility of the investigation process, the physical evidence, and the judicial system.

Transfer of Monies and Assets

One of the many areas in the hospitality security environment that requires the strictest adherence and execution of policy and procedures is the transfer of monies and assets from the property. This process is a joint effort executed by the Hospitality Security Department in conjunction with an armored car company. Both are responsible for the safeguarding of company assets. Generally, the Hospitality Security Department is responsible for the monies and assets while they are being escorted to the armored car bay until they are turned over to the armored car company's representatives. Any time money is handled by members of the Hospitality Security Department, care and caution must always be exercised.

For example, a couple of decades ago, a security representative was escorting money at a property. While providing the escort, a subject attempted to grab a bag of cash from the cart that the security representative was using to transport the money. While the subject was grabbing the bag of money, the security representative, instinctively, also grabbed the bag. This resulted in the subject shooting the security representative in the face, at which point, the security representative fell to the ground, and the subject fled the premises. While exiting the property, the subject discarded his jacket into a trash can, which was retrieved. A search of the jacket revealed the driver's license of the perpetrator in the jacket pocket. A short time later, the subject was apprehended by law enforcement at his residence and was convicted of the crime based upon the evidence and CCTV coverage of the incident. After being hospitalized, the security representative who was shot during this incident eventually returned to work and continued a long career in the security field. Afterwards, procedures were implemented to ensure that any carts used to transport money and assets were locked and secured with the keys to unlock the transportation cart being located at the destination of the pick-up and drop-off points.

During my career, I have transferred money to and from armored car bays. During each money escort and transfer, sometimes in excess of millions of dollars, safety of all involved and the protection of the money and assets were paramount. I remember, early in my career, the first time I saw a bag containing millions of dollars, I asked the representatives of the armored car company if it was okay if I picked the bag up. Permission was granted, and I picked the bag up off the ground. If I recall correctly, the bag contained approximately three million dollars. It was an interesting experience, to say the least. This is one of the many reasons that I love the security field; there is always something new and exciting that happened, is going to happen, or preparations are made in anticipation of various scenarios or the unexpected that may happen. Before becoming involved in the security field, I would have never imagined coming into contact with such a large amount of money. But I did—and it was fun.

The following are steps that should be included in the transportation of assets and money to and from the armored car transfer location to ensure the safety of personnel, monies, and assets:

- The armored car company will contact the Security Operation Center via the telephone approximately five minutes prior to arriving at the property at the predetermined location.

- Security Operation Center personnel will notify the transfer area of the arrival of the armored car company.
- The Security Operations Center will observe and record all movement of monies and assets until all are secured and the transfer is completed.
- Hospitality security representatives should be posted along the money transfer escort route, ensuring that all doors are secured and the areas is clear of everyone not involved in the money transfer.
- The hospitality security representative located outside of the armored car bay will confirm that the armored car company is authorized for entry. First, the password and photo identification of the armored car occupants are confirmed with the Security Operations Center using the armored car company's authorized driver name and photograph list of all its drivers. Then, after confirmation of the driver's credentials and passwords, the armored car bay will be opened, the armored car will enter the armored car bay, and the armored car bay will be secured.
- A member of the hospitality security leadership team will report to the money transfer location and ensure that a representative of the area displays each bag to the CCTV camera prior to placing the cash bag into the hospitality security escort cart. Immediately after all cash and assets are placed into the hospitality security escort cart, the lid will be locked and secured. The key to the hospitality security escort cart will not be accessible nor will it accompany the escort team during the money transfer escort.
- A member of the hospitality security leadership team will escort the hospitality security cart out of the money transfer location to the armored car bay.
- After a member of the hospitality security leadership team enters the armored car bay with the hospitality security escort cart, the hospitality security representative in the armored car bay will unlock the cart.
- A member of the hospitality security leadership team will observe the armored car company representative inspect the money bags for rips and tears.
- The armored car company representative will transfer and deposit the cash and assets from the hospitality security escort cart and complete the deposit transfer of the money and assets.
- If money is being transferred from the armored car company to the property, it will be returned to the money transfer location using the same hospitality security personnel to escort the cart and utilizing the route that was previously used to bring the money and assets from the money transfer location to the armored car bay.

During my career, I have had the opportunity to meet many of the movers and shakers of the hospitality industry. I clearly remember one encounter I had about twenty years ago while I was on vacation in the Bahamas. During my trip, I met a person who owned a plane and was asked if I was interested in flying to Paradise Island in the Bahamas. Of course, I said yes, and when we arrived, we went to visit the Atlantis Casino Resort. While walking around the grounds, I noticed Sol Kerzner, who was instrumental in the success of the property I was working at during this time, giving an interview to a reporter. I wanted to introduce myself to him, but I did not want to interrupt his conversation, so I continued admiring the property.

Later in the day, when getting ready to leave the property, I observed Kerzner finishing a conversation with someone in the lobby, and as he turned and began to walk quickly out of the public area, I called out to him, "Hi Mr. Kerzner." He stopped dead in his tracks, turned around, and walked towards me with a smile. I shook hands with him, and introduced myself and, thanked him for giving me the opportunity to work at his property in the United States. I stated that I realized he was a busy man and did not want to take up anymore of his time—I just wanted to thank him. At this point, an amazing thing happened, Mr. Kerzner started making conversation and we talked for about ten minutes. Once again, I thanked him for taking the time to speak with me and that I knew he was probably very busy and I excused myself from the conversation.

I learned a very valuable life lesson that day. Kerzner made me feel like talking to me was the most important thing he had to do that day even though I know he was an extremely busy man. He took the time to actually listen to the words that were spoken and made conversation with me and those in my group. He did not know me personally from Adam, yet he talked with me as if he had known me all of his life. Even though he was extremely busy, he did not rush the conversation to its conclusion; I actually I ended the conversation, partially because I was feeling guilty for taking up so much of his time. From that day on, every time I have had conversations with others, I always try to emulate the way Kerzner spoke with me and made me feel.

The reason I shared this story is to demonstrate the importance of being courteous, demonstrating good manners, and the impact it has on others. Here it is approximately two decades later, and I still remember how Kerzner made me feel. The same holds true when guests or patrons interact with hospitality security representatives. It is important to train the hospitality security team to respond to others in a similar manner. Generally, people may not remember exactly what is said to them, but they do remember how they were made to feel when spoken to. If a sense of respect and courteousness is conveyed through actions and body language by members of the Hospitality Security Department, it is usually remembered more than the words that were spoken.

Courtesy is the essence of good manners. I remember when my children were about eight years old and ten years old, and they were introduced to a person who owned a business. At the end of the conversation, the owner of the business stated to both of my children, "You two are going to go far in this world." When they both looked at him in a puzzled manner, he added, "Because you have manners and are polite. It is amazing how many people do not. As long as you always have those two things, the rest is easy."

This is a good point, and the reason that I brought it up is that numerous contacts with the public may cause those in the field of hospitality security to develop a veneer of hardness, which may lead to an "us" versus "them" mentality. It must always be remembered that patrons and guests provide for the existence of any property, and they should be treated accordingly. One way to ensure that a positive image is projected is to treat others using the platinum rule, which is to treat others the way that they want to be treated. Elements that comprise the way that this can be achieved include being courteous, friendly, and treating others with dignity and respect.

It is also important to remember that hospitality security is a high profile, very visible position that is constantly observed by guest, patrons, and employees. Therefore, members of any hospitality security team must always project a sincere, friendly, outgoing, and approachable image. To many, this is a skill that may need to be fine-tuned because the trick is to be friendly without being overly familiar and to maintain your professionalism without giving the perception of being unapproachable.

Remember, any situation that hospitality security representatives respond to may seem like a major occurrence to those guest or patrons involved even though it may seem like a "routine" call to hospitality security representatives. The approach used by hospitality security representatives when addressing issues, opportunities, or situations can make all the difference in the world in regard to it being quick, easy, and routine or it being very difficult and border on the edge of a catastrophe. The difference between the two outcomes involves the following:

- How those involved are initially approached.
- An accurate evaluation of the situation.
- Providing an opportunity to those involved to voluntarily comply.
- It is always a good idea to initially suggest a course of action rather than make a demand.
- Try to cause as little disruption as possible.
- Maintain composure; do not shout or speak harshly.
- Anticipate and plan for a worst-case of scenario.

I have found that throughout my career that it was always helpful and useful to review and distribute a list of procedures that should be done to improve guest service and things that should not be done. It is a simple approach that is easy for everyone to understand. Of course, when reviewing this topic, I always like to add the caveat that the list of do's and don'ts is not an exhaustive list—rather, it is a starting point.

This is also a great ice breaker for Hospitality Security Departmental meetings and to stimulate conversation on a larger scale regarding departmental processes, policies, and procedures on what should be added, removed, things the team should be doing, and even, perhaps, things we should stop doing. It should be reiterated that next to the members of the Hospitality Security Department, patrons and guests of the property are our most valuable assets, and we want them to enjoy their time with us and keep coming back. The list of customer service do's and don'ts should include the following:

DO:

- Practice good manners.
- Acknowledge guests by greeting them or thanking them for their visit.
- Be approachable.
- Make eye contact.
- Show enthusiasm.
- Be professional.
- Smile and attempt to exceed expectations.
- Demonstrate interest and compassion when handling incidents.
- Actively listen when others are speaking.
- Be polite and courteous.
- Treat others with dignity and respect.
- Under promise and over deliver.
- Assist guests and patrons so that they want to return.
- Remain in the assigned work area.
- Ensure paperwork is accurate prior to signing.
- Keep abreast of policies, procedures, and property events.
- Be attentive and observant.
- Be a team player.

- Listen to the two-way radio and respond accordingly.
- Respond to details assigned.
- Perform duties as requested.
- Get all the facts when responding to an incident.
- Maintain a professional demeanor

DON'T:

- Act aloof or uninterested to patrons, guests, or employees.
- Ignore patrons, guests, or employees.
- Give vague or unclear directions to patrons, guests, or employees.
- Have nonwork-related conversations while on post.
- Cross arms or place hands in pockets—its projects negative body language and sends a silence signal of do not approach.
- Use profanity.
- Be rude, argumentative, discourteous, or disrespectful.
- Turn off your two-way radio.
- Discuss CCTV camera locations, etc., with patrons, guests, or anyone who does not have a need to know.
- Abuse the authority of the position of being in the Hospitality Security Department.

Another area that members of the hospitality security team should be aware of is the use of hand gestures. Being Italian, I use hand gestures frequently when speaking. People sometimes joke and tell me that if I was forced to sit on my hands, I would be unable to have a conversation. With this in mind, it is important to be aware of some hand gestures that are common in America but might have another meaning to those from other countries. For example, when a person stands with his or her hands in his or her pockets, it can be interpreted as being rude to those from Asian cultures. Making an "ok" symbol with your thumb and forefinger may seem innocent enough, however, this may be offensive to those from France who may take this symbol as meaning they are worthless, or it could be interpreted as vulgar slang to those from Turkey or Brazil.

Another real-life example occurred when I worked at a property in the southeastern United States. I would give members of my security team a thumbs up when on post, providing guest service, etc. I did this until a member of my security team told me that he knew I meant well but giving the thumbs up gesture was an offensive gesture. I apologized, of course, and upon researching, discovered that this could be considered an offensive gesture to those from other countries, including Australia, West Africa, and Russia. Needless to say, I am very careful to use the thumbs up sign when communicating approval of a job well done.

Hospitality Security Training Checklists

The following are examples of the hospitality security training checklists for various positions. These should be used as a guide as you develop a robust training program of your own.

When developing training tools, be sure to include a description of job functions and expected outcomes. If the position is a stationary post, I always like to place a photo of a hospitality security representative standing at the specific location where personnel are to be posted when assigned to the detail.

Entrance to Property

This area is usually the first and last point of contact a patron has with the Hospitality Security Department and may set the tone for the sense of safety and security the guest may have of the property and of the department. The responsibilities of the hospitality security representatives assigned at the property entrance include the following:

- Greet patrons with a warm welcome, make eye contact, acknowledge guests with a nod, and as patrons depart thank them for coming.
- Be aware of suspicious activity or unusual behavior.
- Remain at your assigned post unless directed otherwise by the Security Operations Center or a member of the hospitality security leadership team.
- Know the location of fire extinguishers and emergency exits.
- Identify and report all fire and safety hazards.
- Report unattended children to the Security Operations Center, remain with the child, and, after confirmation of identity, unite him or her with parent or guardian.

The following is an example of a training checklist that should be conducted by a leader of the Hospitality Security Department (trainer) and the hospitality security representative (trainee).

Entrance to Property

Task	Trainee	Trainer
Stand at the designated location—greet guests as they enter or leave the property.		
Be alert for suspicious packages.		
Assist guests by providing answers to questions, directions, etc.		
Always be aware of suspicious or unusual behavior.		
Identify and report all fire and safety hazards.		
Know the location of fire extinguishers.		
Immediately report unattended children to Security Operations Center.		
Know the location of AED units.		
Know the location of emergency exits.		

Property Rover

The responsibilities of the hospitality security representatives assigned as a property rover include the following:

- Patrol all areas as assigned.
- Report unattended children to the Security Operations Center, remain with child, and, after confirmation of identity, unite him or her with parent or guardian.
- Provide escorts and other details as assigned by the Security Operations Center or a member of the hospitality security leadership team.
- Be vigilant for and report the following to Security Operations Center or a member of the hospitality security leadership team: the underage consumption of alcohol, unattended minors, unusual or suspicious behavior, etc.
- Conduct frequent patrols of cash handling areas.
- Remain in the assigned patrol area unless directed otherwise by the Security Operations Center or a member of the hospitality security leadership team.
- Know the location of fire extinguishers, AED units, and emergency exits.
- Provide guest service to patrons by providing directions, answering questions, conducting proactive patrols, and reporting all fire and safety hazards.

The following is an example of a training checklist that should be conducted by a leader of the Hospitality Security Department (trainer) and the hospitality security representative (trainee).

Property Rover

Task	Trainee	Trainer
Hospitality security personnel will patrol all areas within their assigned area, including all cash handling areas, bars, food outlets, etc.		
Report all unusual or suspicious behavior and safety hazards to the Security Operations Center or a member of the hospitality security leadership team.		
Immediately report unattended children to the Security Operations Center.		
Provide escorts and other details assigned by the Security Operations Center or a member of the hospitality security leadership team.		
Conduct frequent patrols of cash handling areas.		
Demonstrate knowledge of how to address guests who need medical attention.		
Demonstrate knowledge of how to address fire emergency situations		
Demonstrate knowledge of how to address power outage emergency situations.		
Demonstrate knowledge of how to address bomb threat emergency situations.		
Demonstrate knowledge of how to implement crime scene protection procedures.		
Demonstrate knowledge of how to implement hold-up/robbery procedures.		

Hotel Rover

The responsibilities of the hospitality security representative assigned as a hotel rover include the following:

- Be aware of suspicious activity or unusual behavior.

- Remain in assigned patrol area unless directed otherwise by the Security Operations Center or a member of the hospitality security leadership team.
- Report all unusual or suspicious behavior and safety hazards to the Security Operations Center or a member of the hospitality security leadership team.
- Know the location of fire extinguishers, AED units, and emergency exits.
- Identify and report all fire and safety hazards.
- Report unattended children to the Security Operations Center, remain with the child, and, after confirmation of identity, unite him or her with parent or guardian.
- Guest room doors should be inspected for pry marks and to ensure that they are closed. Pry marks can be a result of a criminal using a large screw driver to jimmy or attempt to pry open a guest room door.
- Provide guest service to patrons by providing directions and answering questions.
- Be alert for frequent activity into guest rooms—this could indicate unacceptable behavior such as prostitution, drugs, etc.
- Proactive patrols of all areas of the hotel should be conducted and documented by recording the date and time each floor was patrolled utilizing an electronic hotel tour documentation system or, if unavailable, a manual hotel tour documentation system. Areas to be checked include guest floors, storage areas, stairwells, landings, elevators, access points to roof, and fire stairs.

The following is an example of a training checklist that should be conducted by a leader of the Hospitality Security Department (trainer) and the hospitality security representative (trainee).

Hotel Rover

Task	Trainee	Trainer
Patrol assigned hotel floors, stairwells, elevators, and areas.		
Report all unusual or suspicious behavior and safety hazards to the Security Operations Center or a member of the hospitality security leadership team.		
Immediately report unattended children to Security Operations Center.		
Demonstrate knowledge of how to address a guest locked out of their guest room.		
Demonstrate knowledge of how to address a guest locked out of the in-room safe.		
Demonstrate knowledge of how to address noise complaints.		
Demonstrate knowledge of how to address open guest room doors.		
Demonstrate knowledge of how to address guests who need medical attention.		
Demonstrate knowledge of how to address fire emergency situations		
Demonstrate knowledge of how to address power outage emergency situations.		
Demonstrate knowledge of how to address bomb threat emergency situations.		
Demonstrate knowledge of how to implement crime scene protection procedures.		
Demonstrate knowledge of how to implement unattended death procedures.		
Demonstrate knowledge of how to identify and report all fire and safety hazards.		
Know the location of fire extinguishers.		
Know the location of emergency exits.		
Know the location of AED units.		

Guest service is instrumental to the success of any Hospitality Security Department. All interactions with both the internal guests (employees) and external guests (patrons) should be performed in a professional and polite manner. Even a simple nod of the head acknowledging a guest when he or she walks by or making eye contact with a hospitality security representative can go a long way to helping a person feel appreciated. With this in mind, interactions with others should be focused on the person with the question or concern and should have the undivided attention of the hospitality security representative. The words and body language of guests should be observed, and the hospitality security representative should respond accordingly by acknowledging the guest and projecting a positive attitude through body language, eye contact, and tone of voice. Remember, guests, both internal and external, will return and enjoy their experience when they are treated with dignity and respect. Interacting with others in this manner must be constantly demonstrated; it is not something that can be done on a part-time basis but must be performed the entire time a hospitality security representative is "on stage."

The following are reasons why I believe, at times, that providing excellent guest service can be challenging for a Hospitality Security Department. During the on-boarding stage, a lot of time and energy is focused on the technical aspects of a position. Then, only after the technical training is completed, if there is any time or money left over for training, it becomes diverted and utilized for other areas such as guest service. In the past, security positions protected objects; for a person to be effective and efficient in his or her position in the Hospitality Security Department, he or she had to be well versed in the technical aspects and responsibilities of his or her position. However, modern hospitality security professionals must be well versed not only in the technical aspect responsibilities of their position but also in interacting and providing guest service, which I like to classify as people responsibilities.

In my opinion, modern hospitality security professionals who work on the property floor spend approximately 80 percent of their time on guest-based interactions and approximately 20 percent on object protection. This is one reason why it is very important when selecting hospitality security personnel that a strong profile and background in customer service should be weighted heavily. The reason for this is that the technical skills are relatively easy to teach to those who have the aptitude, ability, and desire. However, the basic building blocks—such as genuine caring skills—which are the fundamentals of providing superior guest service, can be very difficult to teach because these skills are generally from the heart and are often based in behavior and lifestyle.

For example, if a person is normally polite and always says "please" and "thank you," it is natural for that person to greet guests and be polite. Whereas, if a person has a belief that it is not important to be polite, say "please" or "thank you," that their job is secure, and that's all they really need to do, it will be difficult to change that behavior. I am not saying that it will be impossible, but that person will have to want to do these things and buy into the concept that approximately 80 percent of his or her time will be on guest-based interactions and approximately 20 percent on object protection. As mentioned, it can be difficult, but I have seen it happen. Interestingly, I have noticed that when this does occur, the person who successfully makes the transition usually becomes one of the best in regard to providing guest service and training others in this area—usually with the caveat, "If I can do it, anybody can do it. It's a matter of if you really want to."

By recognizing others, it demonstrates that you really care about your team and that you have your finger on the pulse of the Hospitality Security Department and the operation of the property. Remember, it is very important to provide recognition to the ladies and gentlemen that comprise the hospitality security team. They are on the front lines and in the trenches of the day-to-day interactions with guests, patrons, and employees. They are the ones who are the front line of defense in the protection and security of the property. Unfortunately, at times, hospitality security personnel may become involved in situations in which they are yelled at, cursed, spit on, and spoken to in an aggressive manner during interactions with others who exhibit behavior that exceeds the boundaries of proper behavior. Sometimes, the patrons of a property may even escalate situations to the point in which they become physical with hospitality security personnel. These are some of the reasons that initial training, on-the-job (OJT) training, and a continuous and ongoing training program is vital to the security, safety, and education of all hospitality security personnel.

Recognize the Work of Your Team

One final comment I would like to make is the importance of providing recognition to individuals on the hospitality security team. It is very important to always keep the morale of the Hospitality Security Department at a high level by saying and, more important, by showing that a job well done is greatly appreciated. I know a person who worked for the same company for over twenty-two years and did an exemplary job for its leader and the company—not once did this person receive recognition of any kind from his or her immediate leader, who was very high up in the company hierarchy. When this veteran retired from the industry, his or her leader did not even recognize the event; it was treated as just another day. Whether this was done on purpose or, as I believe, was done because the boss did not realize or appreciate how important recognition is from the top leadership of any organization. Again, this goes back to common courtesy. It is difficult for a person to provide excellent guest service to the internal and external guest if it is not intuitive or a normal practice for him or her.

Don't allow yourself to fall into this trap and be the type of person who does not recognize years of service or a job well done. If these behaviors do not come naturally—they can be developed. Either way, be sure to do things that recognize the hard work and commitment of those who are the first point of contact with guests and patrons. For example, to keep up the morale of the security teams that I have been involved with over the years, I have always instituted recognition programs which included individuals and the entire Hospitality Security Department. One method that I have implemented over the years is to have myself and security leadership serve the team at their seats with soda and pizza during departmental meetings.

This is done for two main reasons. First and foremost is to illustrate to the security team that is not in a leadership role that I believe in the inverted pyramid where they are at the top of the pyramid and make everyone look good. The other reason is to observe how the members of the security leadership team embrace their role of serving others. Over the years, I have, on occasion, observed a member of the security leadership team who did not follow this principle. Every time that this did occur, it involved someone who did not embrace treating others with dignity and respect, did not buy into the inverted pyramid principle, or felt it was beneath him or her to serve others. Fortunately, many times, I was able to coach, train, and change the behavior of persons who exhibited these characteristics.

Another method that I have utilized over the years was to have a security appreciation day where I would cook and serve the entire security team. For example, the following photos illustrate a barbecue that was held to demonstrate my appreciation of the team for a job well done and all they do. During this type of event, other security leaders or members may ask to help—but I always resist because this is their day and is my way of thanking everyone. At the entrance and exits of the security appreciation day, I place signage that includes the following, "Security—Thank You for All You Do!" "Security—Simply the BEST!" and "Security Appreciation Day". The synergy this creates within the Hospitality Security Department and the property is amazing. Employees from other departments have come over to talk with me while I would be cooking on a grill and ask how they can become part of the security team.

During the event, arrangements are made to have random photos taken, on which the team is given the opportunity to place captions on the photos. During the next departmental training meeting, I present a slide show with the photos and captions. It is a good time had by all and really helps to build a sense of team.

Other things that can be done to maintain the morale of the security team are potluck events. A potluck event is when a day is picked during which anyone on the security team who wishes to bring food in voluntarily may. I usually set this up in the Roll Call Room, and it is available to all members of the team throughout the shift during their breaks.

Another form of recognition that I found to be effective in maintaining the morale and energy of the Hospitality Security Department was recognition of individuals for a job well done. Some of the ways to recognize members of the security team include the following: announcements at roll call, nomination for security employee of the month, presentation of recognition certificates—signed by myself, leaders of the security team, and the general manager. The methods that can be used to recognize security team members are endless. It is important to develop a program, if one is not in place, and maintain and continuously seek ways to improve the ones that are.

In conclusion, it is always important to create, communicate, and encourage an environment that continuously implements a cycle of improvement in all areas of the Hospitality Security Department and in life. This helps to prevent stagnation, complacency, and routine from settling into the actions, performance, and mind-set of the Hospitality Security Department and its members. Constructive communication, teamwork, and treating others with dignity and respect should not only be encouraged but should be the heart of the core values of any Hospitality Security Department.

I would like to thank you for taking the time to read the ideas, procedures, processes, and information presented in this book. My hope is that you found it to be informative, helpful, and useful not only for today but also as a resource tool to be utilized in the future. Perhaps, some of the ideas presented were already known and familiar to you; if that is the case, I hope it provided confirmation of the criteria and expectations to be met in these areas. My other wish is that this book has acted as a conduit to provoke thought which has allowed your mind to go on a tangent and produce a "Eureka!" moment—or moments. The nuts and bolts of starting, operating, and maintaining a Hospitality Security Department is relatively easier than maintaining and nourishing an environment that embraces, encourages, and demonstrates continuous appreciation of all of its members on a daily and significant basis. When executed properly, it can have tremendous results for all involved—the person, the team, and the property.

Discussion Questions

1. What are the characteristics that make up categories of Douglas McGregor's theory X and theory Y?
2. Explain and give examples of the hygiene factors and motivators of Frederick Herzberg's hygiene theory.

3. Which questions should be answered when completing an incident report?
4. What does the acronym OJT stand for, and when should other types of training that are vital to the security, safety, and education of all hospitality security personnel occur?
5. Explain the difference between the internal and external guest. How should members of the hospitality security team interact with each? Provide examples.
6. Explain the importance of the selection and training of members of the Hospitality Security Department.
7. Explain the open-door policy and why it is important.

APPENDIX

ANSWERS TO DISCUSSION QUESTIONS

Chapter One

1. Technology can act as a workforce multiplier by providing the ability to do more with less and by allowing the roles of many to be completed by a few.
2. Return on investment is used to explain the benefit and profit that a project or equipment will bring to the property. It answers the question of, "What are we getting for our money?"
3. Deterrence occurs when people will not commit an act, such as criminal activity, because they are afraid of being caught and of the punishment associated with the act.
4. The most valuable asset of a Hospitality Security Department is the hospitality security personnel.
5. Displacement relocates, or displaces, undesirable acts—such as criminal activities—to another location away from the property.
6. Besides providing for the safety and security of the guests, employees, and company assets, the goals and purpose of the Hospitality Security Department also include the following:

   - **Superior customer service—**This has become an integral part of the functions of a professional Hospitality Security Department. So much so, that when selecting hospitality security personnel, persons who have the aptitude and ability to perform their duties in this manner is essential. The focus on blending the two have made customer service synonymous with hospitality security.

- **Safety committee—**Many times, the leader of the Hospitality Security Department will be responsible for being the champion of the safety committee. These duties include conducting monthly meetings, tracking accidents and incidents, documenting safety inspections, implementing safety programs, etc. An effective and robust safety program will have a positive impact on the education of employees on how to safely perform their job duties—which should result in a reduction in employee accidents and associated costs.
- **Risk management—**When responsible for this area, the Hospitality Security Department leader will address calls from guests and patrons who have claims of illness, injury, or some other mishap that has occurred. The importance of a fact-written hospitality security incident report that answers who, what, when, where, why, and how in conjunction with CCTV coverage are most useful when addressing matters in this area.
- **Valet—**Being responsible for this area involves setting the tone for the guest experience by greeting the guest, providing a fond farewell, and the acquisition and return of guest vehicle keys and the vehicles associated with them.
- **Transportation—**Being responsible for the Transportation Department of a property involves setting the tone for both the internal and external guest by greeting the guests, providing a fond farewell, and overseeing the maintenance of vehicles. Responsibilities for this area also include regulating the traffic flow into and out of the property roadways, parking garages, and overflow parking areas.

7. Some of the most important aspects of the Hospitality Security Department include the guest's experience regarding his or her feeling of safety and security. This is of paramount importance to the Hospitality Security Department, and everything possible should be done to ensure that the security team is well trained to enhance the guests' and patrons' perception that the security team provides a safe and secure environment to all patrons, guests, employees, and assets. This is demonstrated by providing protection from situations that could jeopardize the welfare and security of the patrons, guests, and employees of a property. Remember that even though hospitality security representatives are not members of law enforcement, they do have the authority and right to protect the property and its occupants. To provide for this feeling of safety and security, hospitality security representatives need be vigilant in their observations, accurate in their reporting, and respond accordingly to situations in a professional, courteous manner while abiding by all policies, procedures, rules, regulations, ordinances, and the law.

   Another key aspect that is essential for the positive perception of any Hospitality Security Department is the ability of members of the hospitality security team to be able to effectively communicate with patrons, guests, and employees in a professional, courteous manner while exhibiting good manners and following the rules of etiquette. This may be difficult, at times, when a hospitality security representative has numerous contacts with the public and is asked the same question over and over again, for example, "Where is the nearest restroom?" Each time any question is asked, it should be responded to with enthusiasm while being mindful of body language and tone of voice. The response should include a smile, eye contact, an upbeat inflection of speech spoken in a clear audible manner. The response should not include eye rolling, sighing, mumbling, looking down at the ground, ignoring the person asking the question, etc. When discourteous treatment of patrons, guests, and employees occurs, it automatically lowers the perception of professionalism of the Hospitality Security Department.

It is important that the hospitality security team is trained and remembers to practice basic courteousness at all times. This can be especially effective when handling or addressing situations involving patrons, guests, or employees. Handling and addressing situations may be a major difficulty, or it can be routine. The is determined by how effectively a hospitality security representative evaluates a situation, addresses the people involved, anticipates potential situations that may arise from any action taken—or not taken—and to has a plan to address them should they develop.

Chapter Two

1. Hospitality Security Department policies and procedures should be reviewed or updated at least every 12 months. This is important to determine if modifications are needed, if additional procedures need to be added, or if they have become obsolete and need to be removed.
2. They provide instructions on how to perform a certain operation within the Hospitality Security Department while applying a consistent standard and are helpful for retraining or disciplinary purposes when addressing situations if a mistake does occur.
3. Calibrated thinking is an essential element in ensuring the consistency of the performance of the hospitality security team regarding standard operational procedures and policies. Calibrated thinking basically gets everyone on the same page. For example, if a dress code policy or procedure needs clarification, photos should be exhibited, and "acceptable" or "unacceptable" replies should be presented after each photo, after which, the answer would be provided with an explanation.
4. Hospitality security standard operational policies and procedures should be kept as simple as possible, written in a manner that is clear and easy to understand.
5. If the importance and significance of the security standard operational procedures, processes, and training are not stressed by the leaders of the property and the Hospitality Security Department, they will be less likely to be adhered to. This could result in chaos in the form of inconsistent enforcement, training, and the abandonment of specific standard operational procedures. This could have a negative impact on the perception of, or the actual protection and safety of, the properties guests, employees, and assets. This could also result in civil or legal action against the property for failure to safeguard, protect, etc., the occupants, guest valuables, and assets of the property.
6. To demonstrate and reinforce the importance of hospitality security standard operational procedures, processes, and training, the highest-ranking members of the property and the Hospitality Security Department should place an emphasis on them, their importance, and the significant role they play in the successful operation of the property and department. When this is done, the importance and significance of these documents trickles down and is absorbed by the members of the property and the Hospitality Security Department. On the other hand, if the importance and significance of the security standard operational procedures, processes, and training are not stressed by the leaders of the property and Hospitality Security Department, they will be less likely be adhered to. This could result in chaos in the form of inconsistent enforcement, training, and the abandonment of specific

standard operational procedures. This could have a negative impact on the perception of, or the actual protection and safety of, the property's guests, employees, and assets. This could also result in civil or legal action against the property for failure to safeguard, protect, etc., the occupants, guest valuables, and assets of the property.

Chapter Three

1. Standard operational procedures should be crafted to meet the specific needs of your operation, as issues and concerns dictate, and should be reviewed by the executive committee, general manager, and the legal branch of your organization.
2. When revised, it is important to put the date of revision on the procedure and to keep the old copy of procedure that was revised.
3. Each procedure should consist of a header—which states the subject, procedure number, implementation date, revision date, approval, and page number.
4. Standard operational procedures should be crafted to meet the specific needs of your operation, as issues and concerns dictate, and should be reviewed by the legal branch of your organization.
5. This is useful when it comes to the operation of the team because it indicates what policy and procedure was in place on a given date and time. This can be critical when responding to guest complaints, performance issues, and lawsuits, as well as the proper protection of guests, employees. and company assets.
6. Remember that procedures are living documents and should be reviewed and updated at least every twelve months. When revised, it is important to put in the date of revision on the procedure and to keep the old copy of procedure that was revised. This is useful for legal, criminal, civil, and performance issues to determine what procedure was in effect at the time that an incident, event, emergency, or crisis occurred.
7. The hospitality security standard operational procedures are important to the operation of the Hospitality Security Department because there is a direct correlation between the quality, thoroughness, and absorption of the standard operational procedures and how effectively and efficiently the Hospitality Security Department should operate and respond to situations. The standard operational procedures should specify the Hospitality Security Department's mission, objectives, and the processes that should be utilized to attain them. Hospitality security personnel need to know what is required so that their performance can reflect meeting or exceeding the expected outcome of any incident, event, emergency, or crisis. The life, safety, and security of the organization and the internal and external guests depend upon the knowledge that is exhibited by security personnel in the handling of ordinary day-to-day situations and emergency situations. A well trained Hospitality Security Department along with a good understanding of the polices and standard operational procedures are key elements for results of the best possible outcome being produced in any situation.

Chapter Four

1. The postcrisis/emergency meeting should be conducted as soon as possible after the crisis.
2. The meeting should be timely so that everyone can clearly remember the facts regarding the emergency. The purposes of the postcrisis/emergency incident meeting include the following:

   - Review how and why it happened.
   - What measures have been implemented to discourage or prevent this from happening again?
   - If the preventive measures have been put into place or if the measures have not been instituted, a timeline should be established with clear lines of responsibility and a definitive timetable of when each phase and project is to be completed.
   - What worked well.
   - What could have been done better.

3. It is always advisable to make preparations regarding responses to emergency-related situations with all internal and external departments that may be involved. It is important that these procedures and responses be reviewed with fire, law enforcement, and other agencies that would respond to your property regarding these events. It is always a good practice to have periodic meetings and conduct tabletop exercises to walk through the procedures and plans. If possible, it is always beneficial for everyone to conduct training on-site where emergency responders, fire fighters, law enforcement, etc., can practice scenarios with the Hospitality Security Department. These practice sessions aid in the communication, execution, and confirmation that all responding agencies and departments are on the same page or provide an opportunity to resolve any discrepancies prior to an actual event. Areas to review include emergency situations, triage areas, communications, and "what if" scenarios. Reviewing the hospitality security emergency procedures with all agencies that will be responding to the property when emergency situations occur should result in the optimum performance, communication, and execution of these emergency procedures by all involved to provide for the safety of guests, employees, and occupants of the property.

Chapter Five

1. A single-stage system means that when a device is activated, it is designed to immediately transmit an alarm signal throughout the property to warn occupants that a fire emergency exists. For example, in most jurisdictions, a pull station is categorized as a single-stage device.
2. The three elements needed for fire are oxygen, heat, and fuel, which make up what is known as the fire triangle. If one of these elements is missing in the fire triangle, a fire cannot exist.
3. The four phases of fire are:

   - **First phase—incipient phase:** There is no noticeable smoke, heat, or flame. During this phase, flammable gases and/or combustion products are emitted.

- **Second phase—smoldering phase:** There is no substantial amount of flame or heat, but smoke is visible.
- **Third phase—flame phase:** Usually involves less smoke, but flames break out and generate substantial heat.
- **Fourth phase—high-heat phase:** Fire spreads rapidly, producing extensive flames and extreme heat.

4. The following are classifications of fire:

    - **Class A**—Involves cloth, rubber, wood, paper, or other solids containing carbon. Water is used to the stop the fire and cool the material.
    - **Class B**—Fueled by flammable or combustible liquids which include oil, gasoline, or other similar materials. The oxygen supply of the fire triangle can be smothered by the use of dry powder, foam, or carbon dioxide.
    - **Class C**—Involves energized electrical equipment. Always de-energize the equipment and use a nonconductive extinguishing agent such as carbon dioxide or dry powder.
    - **Class D**—Involves combustible metals such as magnesium and titanium. Dry powder extinguishing agents work by heat absorption and smothering the fire.
    - **Class K**—Involves cooking oils and greases such as vegetable oils and animal fats. Fire extinguishers rated for this type of fire contain a wet chemical agent that turns the cooking oil and fat that is serving as fuel to soap.

5. When using a fire extinguisher, the acronym PASS stands for the following:

    - **P**—Pull the pin of the fire extinguisher located at the top by the handle.
    - **A**—Aim the fire extinguisher at the base of the fire.
    - **S**—Squeeze the handle of the fire extinguisher.
    - **S**—Sweep the fire extinguisher from side-to-side at the base of the fire.

6. The basic components of a fire alarm system include the following;

    - **Annunciator status panel:** The annunciator status panel identifies the following:
        - Condition status of an alarm
        - Alarm type
        - Alarm location
        - Location of trouble

    When there is an alarm, an indicator light flashes on the annunciator status panel identifying the location of the alarm. Depending on the type of alarm, providing it has been verified as being a nonevent, an authorized representative of the Hospitality Security Department can control the alarm system by using a reset switch, silence the alarm, or reset the system.

    - **Control Panel**: The control panel has many functions; basically, it is the brains of the system. The control panel processes its information from field devices such as pull stations and water flow sensors. When the system recognizes that there is an alarm condition, it triggers the preset audio-visual devices. The control panel also monitors and supervises the integrity of the power supply and circuitry.

- **Field devices**: Field devices are used in the initiating zone and include the following:
  - Heat detectors
  - Smoke detectors
  - Pull stations
  - Audiovisual devices

7. A fire watch is the action of a hospitality security representative whose sole responsibility is to watch for the signs of any of the stages of fire and. if any are observed, report it immediately to the Hospitality Security Operations Center/Fire Command Center.

   The requirements of a fire watch include the following:

- When a required fire protection system is out of service for four hours or more in a twenty-four-hour period, the authority having jurisdiction will be notified, and the property will be evacuated **OR** an approved fire watch will be implemented for all areas left unprotected until the fire protection system has been returned to service.
- A fire watch will involve some special action beyond normal staffing. Additional hospitality security personnel, who are specially trained in fire prevention, will be assigned to conduct documented patrols in the areas requiring a fire watch.
- The duties of those involved in a fire watch include the following:
  - Periodic documented patrols of the affected areas and property will be conducted by those assigned to a fire watch detail.
  - The Fire Command Center will communicate with the fire department.
  - Those assigned to a fire watch detail will be able to recognize and identify any life, fire, or property hazards.
  - If an emergency is discovered, the Fire Command Center will notify 911 with the exact address and specific type of emergency.
  - If the property needs to be evacuated, emergency evacuation procedures will commence.
  - Hospitality security personnel assigned to a fire watch detail and the Fire Command Center will maintain a log of fire watch activities available for inspection by the fire department.
  - Hospitality security personnel assigned to a fire watch detail and the Fire Command Center will have knowledge of the location and use of fire protection equipment, fire extinguishers, etc.
  - Hospitality security personnel assigned to a fire detail cannot be assigned to any other duties.
  - Hospitality security personnel assigned to a fire watch detail will not perform firefighting duties beyond the scope of an ordinary citizen.

Chapter Six

1. The Hospitality Security Operations Center.
2. The steps that should be implemented to ensure that the hospitality security team has the tools and equipment needed to perform its job include the following:

    - At every roll call and preshift meeting, ask if any tools or equipment are needed. Part two of this inquiry is, are there any tools, equipment, etc., needed to perform the job better?
    - When tools or equipment are needed, members of the hospitality security leadership team should ensure that it is clearly communicated to those who control the purse strings and establish a timeline of expected delivery of the items.
    - A repair, maintenance, and replacement schedule for items should be established, budgeted, and executed.

    This is critical for the morale and synergy of the Hospitality Security Department. Nothing can be more frustrating than having a team that really wants to be the best but is not allocated the proper tools and equipment to perform at its highest level. It is the responsibility of the leader of the Hospitality Security Department to ensure that all tools, equipment, and any other items that are needed are acquired, maintained, and replenished, as needed, to ensure the top performance of the team.

3. The following are some of the circumstance and steps that should be included when conducting a review of policies, procedures, and best practices:

    - Periodic reviews of these areas should occur at least every 12 months. However, sometimes a situation will occur, something may come to light, or an idea may be so good that it may require the immediate revision or creation of a policy, process, or best practice.
    - During a normal periodic review, one of the first things that should be done is to observe current practices and conduct one-on-one meetings with members of the hospitality security team. The topics of discussion should include the following:
        - What are we doing well?
        - What can we improve upon?
        - What should we start doing?
        - What should we stop doing?

    When completed, and the responses to these questions are composed, group meetings with the members of the hospitality security leadership team should be conducted to review and discuss the department's policies, processes, and best practices. After all areas have been vetted, action should be taken to create; modify; start; or discontinue specific policies, processes, or best practices of the Hospitality Security Department. When the polices, processes, and best practices have been updated, Hospitality Security Departmental meetings should be conducted, focusing on a review and discussion of the polices, processes, and best practices that are currently in place. At these meetings, the information should be communicated, reviewed, and acknowledged by the hospitality security team.

Chapter Seven

1. It is important to deescalate these situations before they attract a crowd and have others become involved which could morph from a verbal altercation between two people into the worst-case scenario evolving into mob violence.
2. The proper identification, collection, and establishment of a chain of custody regarding physical evidence is very important. If any one of these areas is not done properly, it could result in the physical evidence being contaminated or inadmissible in a court.
3. Crime scene protection—The protection of an area varies depending on the crime and its location. The following are the elements regarding the protection of a crime scene:

   - Do not touch anything at the crime scene.
   - If crime occurred in a room, do not use the telephone in the room.
   - Create a log of all persons arriving and entering the crime scene until law enforcement arrives and takes control of the crime scene.
   - Protect evidence from physical elements, i.e., rain, wind, traffic, etc.

4. Some types of physical evidence that may be available for recovery at a crime scene include the following:

   - Biological evidence—blood, saliva, hair, semen, etc.
   - Tool marks
   - Firearms and ammunition evidence—weapon, shell casings, etc.
   - Weapons—knife, blunt object, etc.
   - Fingerprints—located on weapons, paper, etc.
   - Toxicology evidence—drugs, poisons, etc.
   - Documentation evidence—written notes, paper, ink, etc.
   - Explosives
   - Drug evidence—left at scene, on person, etc.

5. The responsibilities of hospitality security personnel when responding to an incident should include the following:

   - The protection of the crime scene.
   - Gathering information.
   - Separating witnesses.

- Keeping the parties involved separated; they should not be within speaking distance of each other (providing it is safe to do so and it does not place the responding security representatives in danger).
- Notify the Security Operations Center, and provide all of the pertinent information regarding the incident.

6. Regardless of the type of investigation, CCTV coverage should be reviewed, and any pertinent coverage should be saved immediately. This is very important because after a certain amount of time, usually a couple of weeks, the CCTV coverage may not be available due to storage limitations. Failure to secure CCTV coverage of an incident or event could prove detrimental to the investigation, identification of those involved, the sequence of events, or the prosecution of a case.
7. The proper identification, collection, and establishment of a chain of custody regarding physical evidence is very important. If any one of these areas is not done properly, it could result in the physical evidence being contaminated or inadmissible in a court. The basic role of a hospitality security representative is to identify, protect, and, if necessary, collect the evidence. The hospitality security representative who identifies or locates specific evidence should be listed in any reports or in any documentation regarding the incident and the evidence. The information that should be listed includes the following:

- Date physical evidence was located.
- Time physical evidence was located.
- Exactly where the physical evidence was discovered.
- If physical evidence was handled—list by whom, date, and time.
- To establish chain of custody of physical evidence—list date, time, and the person the physical evidence was turned over to. The following should be included regarding the person the physical evidence was turned over to:
  - Name
  - Rank
  - Identification number
  - Name of department

The advantages of following the proper protocol for the handling of physical evidence that is to be utilized in an investigation and eventual prosecution of a case includes the following:

- Physical evidence cannot be distorted.
- Physical evidence is tangible—it can be seen and possibly touched by a jury.
- Physical evidence can usually be effective in rebutting statements made by a defendant.
- Many times, physical evidence can help to solve a case.
- Physical evidence can usually confirm the facts of a case and prove that a defendant's statements are false.
- It is advantageous to have physical evidence over the testimony of a witness. Over time, witness testimony is subject to memory loss, whereas physical evidence is not.

- A person accused of a crime based upon physical evidence can have the physical evidence tested by an independent expert. This adds to the credibility of the investigation process, the physical evidence, and the judicial system.

Chapter Eight

1. Ethics are moral standards and how they affect conduct. The Greek root for ethics is *ethos*, which stresses the perfection of the individual and the community to which he or she belongs. There are many aspects of ethics, which include the following:

    - Ethics is about what is right and what is wrong
    - Ethics is about vice and virtue.
    - Ethics is about benefit and harm.
    - Ethics describes what should be.
    - Ethics is the way morals are practiced.

2. Morality originates from the Latin word *moralis*, which means "traditional customs or proper behavior." Basically, morals refer to a set of rules defining what is considered to be right or wrong and accepted by everyone in a group or society.
3. Values can be described as beliefs or ideas shared by members of a culture, which include the following:

    - Values provide direction in determining right from wrong or good from bad.
    - Values are what a person believes to be valuable, have worth, or importance.
    - Values influence a person's behavior.

4. *Merriam-Webster* defines the root word of professionalism in the following manner:

    - A profession is a "calling requiring specialized knowledge and often long academic preparation."
    - A professional is one that is "participating for gain in an activity often engaged in by amateurs" or one that "engages in an activity professionally."
    - Professionalism is exhibited by "the conduct, aims, or qualities that mark a profession or a professional person."

    Certifications are an important way to establish professionalism. The following are some of the key elements of professionalism:

    - Ethics
    - Philosophy
    - Knowledge

- Guidelines
- Standardization of job performance

5. Crime displacement theory

   Ronald V. Clarke developed the crime displacement theory, arguing that crimes are displaced by removing opportunity for crime or by changing the situation of the crime. When this occurs, it does not actually prevent crime but merely moves or shifts the crime to another location. Putting these types of measures in place creates an awareness to those who may wish to cause harm to others that the property implementing these measures has become a hardened target with capable guardians. This should have an impact on those who have intentions of doing bad things at a property by displacing criminal activity from the property to other properties that do not have these proactive preventive measures in place. When this occurs, it does not mean that similar types of crime stop happening everywhere, it merely means that the crimes may continue to occur but not at the property that instituted measures designed to make it difficult to commit a crime without being detected. This is known as the displacement theory and is a valuable tool for Hospitality Security Departments that wish to proactively deter criminal behavior at their property.
6. It is important that the Hospitality Security Department performs its duties in a professional, ethical, and moral manner This is important for many reasons; first and foremost, not performing and executing duties in this manner could impact the safety and security of the guests, occupants, and employees of the property and their overall perception of the Hospitality Security Department. Additional negative consequences include possible civil, criminal, or legal action resulting from a Hospitality Security Department performing its duties in an unprofessional, unethical, and immoral manner.
7. Hospitality Security Departments must exhibit reasonable care and be vigilant in protecting guests from foreseeable risks. Reasonable care is the degree of caution and concern an ordinary, prudent, and rational person would use regarding similar circumstances or events. It is a standard used to determine a legal duty and whether such duty was fulfilled. The responsibilities of a Hospitality Security Department exhibiting reasonable care include protecting guests from other guests and negligent acts committed by the employees of the property. One method of accomplishing this is proactive patrols of the property by the Hospitality Security Department. These patrols should be documented, and any hazardous conditions or safety hazards should be immediately reported and corrected. Areas that hospitality security personnel should address immediately include noncompliance with fire regulations and keeping hallways, passageways, stairways, entrances, and exits clear of obstructions and hazards. Additional areas include proper lighting levels and the repair, maintenance, and inspection of elevators.

Chapter Nine

1. Douglas McGregor's theory X and theory Y are based upon two types of people called X and Y. The following are examples of characteristics that make up these categories.

   <u>theory X</u>

- People are not ambitious
- Prefer to be directed
- Resist change
- No interest in organizational goals
- Will attempt to avoid work whenever possible

<u>theory Y</u>

- People are creative
- Ingenuity is common
- Capacity for creativity
- Work can be as natural as play
- Genuine caring/emphatic skills

2. Frederick Herzberg's hygiene theory states that the opposite of satisfaction is not dissatisfaction but, rather, no satisfaction. Hygiene factors can move someone from dissatisfaction to no satisfaction. The following are examples of hygiene factors:

   - Physical work conditions
   - Surroundings
   - Salary
   - Co-workers
   - External factors
   - Motivation Factors

   Only motivators can move someone to satisfaction. The following are examples of motivators:

   - Achievement
   - Recognition
   - Responsibility
   - Satisfaction from work itself
   - Money is not a motivator

3. The following questions should be answered when completing an incident report—who, what, when, where, why, and how.
4. Initial training, on-the-job (OJT) training, and continuous and ongoing training programs are vital to the security, safety, and education of all hospitality security personnel.
5. Guest service is instrumental to the success of any Hospitality Security Department. All interactions with both the internal guests (employees) and external guests (patrons) should be performed in a professional and polite manner. Even a simple nod of the head acknowledging a guest when he or she walks by or makes eye contact with a hospitality security representative can go a long way to making a person feel appreciated. With this in mind,

interactions with others should be focused on the person with the question or concern and should have the undivided attention of the hospitality security representative. The words and body language of guests should be observed, and the hospitality security representative should respond accordingly by acknowledging the guest and projecting a positive attitude through body language, eye contact, and tone of voice. Remember, guests, both internal and external, will return and enjoy their experience when they are treated with dignity and respect. Interacting with others in this manner must be constantly demonstrated; it is not something that can be done on a part-time basis but must be performed the entire time a hospitality security representative is "on stage."

6. The selection and training of members of the Hospitality Security Department is of paramount importance. Before any training program can begin, the focus of selecting people to be part of the hospitality security team must occur. The selection of candidates and the training of hospitality security personnel are among the most important aspects of setting the foundation of the department. A mind-set should be created that being a member of the Hospitality Security Department should be a coveted position where one does not simply apply for a job but, rather, is invited to have the opportunity to be part of a team. It is important to invest the time, money, and resources into the training of members of the hospitality security team. These reasons include the safety of patrons, guests, visitors, employees, and the protection of company assets.

   Candidates who wish to become part of the hospitality security team should have the ability to interact, communicate well with others, and have the aptitude to develop the skills needed for the position. In today's hospitality security world, it is important to select candidates who have the innate ability to interact and communicate with others in a genuine manner while providing guest service to both the external and internal customer. Of equal importance is the ability of a hospitality security candidate to possess the aptitude and the desire to learn the skills needed to perform the essential duties required of his or her position.

7. The open-door policy is an important concept that should be utilized by the leadership of a Hospitality Security Department. The execution of an open-door policy allows hospitality security team members direct access to all members of the leadership team, without exception. I further explained that the open-door policy aides in communicating ideas, addressing concerns, and building the morale of the Hospitality Security Department.

APPENDIX A

GLOSSARY OF TERMS AND DEFINITIONS

A

Access control Implementing security measures to protect an area by restricting the access and movements of vehicles, materials, and persons.

Active listening Fully concentrating on what is being said by the speaker. Actively engaging the speaker by demonstrating understanding, comprehending, and responding back to the topic of discussion.

Admission A statement provided by a person in which admission of fact or facts that would tend to prove guilt of a crime but does not entail full acknowledgment of guilt of a crime.

AED Acronym for automatic external deliberator. A portable defibrillator used for responding to a cardiac emergency.

Affidavit A written declaration or statement of facts given before an officer having authority to administer oaths.

Assault Intentional unlawful use of force.

Alarm A warning from a sensor that it has been activated. Usually signaled by light or sound, it may indicate a valid alarm, nuisance alarm, or alarm malfunction.

Alarm initiating device Any audible or visual signal used to indicate a fire condition.

Alarm malfunction An alarm signal that is received without the presence of an alarm condition.

Annunciator An audible or visual device that indicates an active alarm or other conditions.

ASIS Founded in 1955—acronym for American Society for Industrial Security. In 2002, officially changed its name to ASIS International and is the leading organization for security professionals worldwide.

Asset Anything of value that needs to be protected.

Attempted battery a physical act or threat by a person with the intention of causing harm.

Audit A formal verification of accounts, records, operational activities, or performance.

Authorization Permission, approval, or clearance granted to an individual or group to enter an area or perform a function.

B

Bill of Rights The first ten amendments of the US Constitution.

Biometrics Biometrics is the technology and science of authenticating individuals by measuring their physiological or behavioral features.

Blank An uncut, unfinished key before any cuts have been made.

Brainstorming An idea generation process that encourages all alternatives without being critical of any of the ideas or alternatives presented.

Breaker A member of the hospitality security team who provides breaks to members of the hospitality security team. This person is generally well versed in all post assignments, duties, and responsibilities.

Budget Plan for allocating resources; an estimate of revenues and expenses over a specific period of time.

C

CCTV Acronym for closed-circuit television. Captures a scene image and converts it to a display or recording device.

Central station An alarm system's control center in a subscriber's premises are connected, circuits are supervised, and where personnel are maintained continuously to record and investigate alarms or trouble signals. Facilities are provided for the reporting of alarms to police, fire departments, or other outside agencies.

Central station alarm system An alarm system that transmits the alarm signal to the central station. This differs from a proprietary alarm in that the central station is owned and operated independently of the subscriber.

Certification A document which provides proof that a person completed and meets knowledge, skills, and eligibility requirements for a specific designation.

CFE Acronym for Certified Fraud Examiner. Credential issued by the Association of Certified Fraud Examiners for the demonstration of expertise in fraud prevention, detection, and investigation.

Command Center Is established when an event or incident requires multiple departments and agencies to be in one place to receive, share, and communicate information

Company keys Are generally office and storage room keys.

Confession A statement, usually written, in which a person admits or acknowledges guilt of a crime.

Contingency plan A plan designed to take possible future events or circumstances into account and respond accordingly to provide for the safety, protection, and assistance to guests, employees, and occupants of a property.

Corpus delicti The body of the crime; it consists of the following: *mens rea*—criminal intent, *actus reus*—wrongful conduct and the combination of criminal intent and the criminal act.

Counterfeit An imitation of currency, chips, or other items of value with the intention to deceive or defraud the property.

CPTED Acronym for crime prevention through environmental design. A method for reducing the opportunities for crime to occur by creating defensible space through environmental factors such building design, lighting, and landscaping.

CPP Acronym for Certified Protection Professional. Credential issued by ASIS for the demonstration of knowledge, experience, and management skills in seven key domains of security.

D

Deterrent Something that discourages a person from committing an unwanted or criminal act. For example, if the deterrent is a punishment, it must be swift, certain, and severe to be effective.

Displacement The relocation of crime and criminals resulting from crime prevention efforts of hospitality security. When motivated offenders are deterred, they will commit crimes elsewhere at another property.

Door alarms Also known as intrusion alarms. Activated when alarmed doors have been opened. Examples include perimeter doors or entrance doors.

Duress alarm A device used to notify hospitality security that assistance is needed without arousing suspicion. Usually placed in areas that have items of high value or where money is exchanged.

E

Effectiveness A measurement used to determine if goals were achieved.

Embezzlement The conversion of personal property by a person to whom the property was entrusted.

Emergency lighting An automatic lighting system that is activated and maintained when primary power fails in a property. Provides adequate light for occupants to safely move about the property.

F

Fail-safe A feature of a system or device that initiates an alarm or trouble signal when the system or device either malfunctions of loses power. For example, doors that are normally locked will unlock in the event of a fail-safe condition.

Fail secure A feature of a system or device that initiates an alarm or trouble signal when the system or device either malfunctions of loses power. For example, doors will lock in the event of a fail secure condition. A setting where this would occur is in a prison environment.

False alarm An alarm signal that is received without the presence of an alarm condition. This can be caused by many factors, including mischief, rain, fog, wind, animals, insects, etc.

False imprisonment The unlawful restraint of a person or holding someone against his or her will without legal authority or justification.

FCC Acronym for Fire Control Center. Location where appropriate switches, indicators, controls, alarms, etc., are located for the operation and monitoring of life-safety and fire protection systems.

Fire alarm single-stage system Any alarm activation will cause all the signals in the property to sound. For example, in most jurisdictions, a pull station is categorized as a single-stage device.

Fire alarm two-stage system Transmits a distinct alert signal to the Fire Command Center. The source of the alarm is immediately investigated to determine if an evacuation process is to begin. Two-stage alarm systems are used to reduce the possibility of risk and injury when evacuating a property due to an alarm malfunction which could result in jeopardizing the safety of the occupants due to a nonevent.

Fire stair Enclosed stairway that is part of a fire-resistant egress.

Fire triangle Heat, oxygen, and fuel

Fixed post A post assignment which requires a hospitality security representative to remain at a specific post location. Generally, it is located at the entry or exit of an area; duties include assisting and directing guests and observing and reporting suspicious activity.

Flow alarm When water begins to flow through the fire sprinkler system, a priority one water flow alarm signal is sent to the FCC alarm panel, which activates the fire alarm system.

Forecast A prediction of future outcomes.

Foreseeability Element of proximate cause in a tort claim—should have been able to see that an event could happen.

Fraud Theft by deception.

Fraud triangle The components of why people commit fraud: opportunity, pressure, and rationalization.

FTE Acronym for full time equivalent. Hours × Days / 40 is the formula utilized for budgeting purposes. Formula - 24 hours × 7 days = 168 hours / 40 hours work week = 4.2 FTEs. However, this does not take into account vacation days and other paid time off.

G

General alarm Is a priority one alarm. For example, when a pull station or water flow alarm is activated, an annunciation notification of an evacuation throughout the property will occur.

Grand master key A key designed to open all locks under several master keys in a system. The use of a grand master key is not recommended.

H

Hazard Conditions that may produce a risk of injury.

Holdup button A manually activated mechanical switch used to initiate a duress alarm signal. Locations include areas that contain cash or items of high value. Should be installed in a manner to prevent accidental activation.

Hotel rover A post assignment that requires a hospitality security representative to remain in an assigned area. Duties include responding to alarms and observing and reporting suspicious activity.

Hotline A hospitality security hotline allows employees to report suspicious activity, criminal activity, or supply security-related information anonymously.

Hygiene theory Frederick Herzberg states that the opposite of satisfaction is not dissatisfaction but, rather, no satisfaction. Hygiene factors such as salary, co-workers, and surroundings can move someone from dissatisfaction to no satisfaction. Motivators such as recognition, responsibility, achievement, and satisfaction with work itself can move someone satisfaction.

HVAC Acronym for heating, ventilating, and air-conditioning.

I

Incident report A report written by hospitality security personnel after information is gathered pertaining to an event involving the property. Who, what, when, where, why, and how should be answered during the investigative stage, and the findings of the investigation should be compiled into an incident report.

Intentional tort When a person acts with specific intent to perform an action that can cause injury or harm to another. A person who performs an action intentionally does not have to know that injuries would occur because of the action, only that the action would have consequences.

Interviewee Person who is interviewed.

Interview A method of gathering information, facts, and truth by conversation.

Interviewer Person who conducts interviews.

J

Jamming An intruder's attempt to prevent radio communications through destruction of communications equipment or by inserting unwanted signals into the frequency channel of the communications system.

L

Log book Used to track the issuance and return of items such as keys, badges, etc., from the Hospitality Security Department. A log book should document when the item was issued and returned to hospitality security. The following information should be included in the log book: name, signature, identification number, date, time of the requester, and issuer.

Likelihood The chance of something happening.

Local alarm When activated, produces audible or visual signal in the immediate location of the protected area or object.

M

Mantrap A room where a door can only be opened only when the other door(s) are closed and only after the access level of those requesting entry has been confirmed and verified. Often used in sally ports and other access control systems.

MOU Acronym for memo of understanding. A memo of understanding is a formal agreement between two or more parties to establish a partnership.

N

Norms Accepted and recognized rules of social behavior.

Negligence Failure to use proper care resulting in the damage or injury to another. Consists of four elements: a standard of care, breach of this standard, proximate cause, and harm or injury was produced.

Nuisance alarm Any alarm that is not caused by an intrusion. Also referred to as a false alarm or alarm malfunction.

P

Package Pass A form that is completed and signed by an authorized member of the leadership team for items that are being removed from the property. Rule of thumb: If a person did not bring an item into the property, then, he or she must have a package pass to leave with it.

Pass Acronym used for use of fire extinguisher. P—Pull pin of the fire extinguisher. A—Aim the fire extinguisher at the base of the fire. S—Squeeze the handle of fire extinguisher. S—Sweep the fire extinguisher from side-to-side at the base of the fire.

PCI Acronym for Professional Certified Investigator. Credential issued by ASIS for the demonstration of knowledge and experience in areas of investigations, including case management, investigative techniques, investigative procedures, and case presentation.

Photoelectric alarm system Uses a light beam and a photoelectric sensor to provide a line of protection. Any interruption to the light beam will be detected by the photoelectric sensor. Mirrors may be used in this system to change the direction of the beam.

Post orders Written instructions for each hospitality security post assignment that lists the duties and responsibilities of the personnel assigned to post.

Piggybacking When one or more people attempt to enter an access controlled area by following an individual who has the proper access level. When the subject is granted permission to enter, those attempting unauthorized entry follow the subject closely by tailgating the subject through the control point.

Plain language Is the term used for using regular language when communicating on two-way radios. The Department of Homeland Security encourages plain language in its National Incident Management System.

Proprietary alarm system An alarm system like a central station alarm system except that the annunciator is owned and operated by the facility. The facility ensures that it is constantly maintained and monitored, that all alarm signals and alerts are responded to, and notification is made to the proper authorities.

Prosecutor Prosecutes another for a crime in the name of the government.

PTT Acronym for push to talk. All two-way radios have a PTT button which must be depressed to open a channel for transmission.

PSP Acronym for Physical Security Professional. Credential issued by ASIS for the demonstration of knowledge and experience, including in-threat assessment, risk analysis, physical security systems, and physical security measures.

R

Reasonable care The degree of caution and concern an ordinarily prudent and rational person would use regarding a similar circumstance or event. It is a standard used to determine a legal duty and whether such duty was fulfilled.

Recruitment A very important part of building and maintaining the Hospitality Security Department by identifying, locating, and attracting talented people to the team.

Reset When an alarm system is returned to its normal operating condition.

Response A hospitality security reaction to an observation or threat that requires action.

Restore Return to normal.

Restricted keys Are generally money-related keys that should be retained under the strictest conditions. Usually requires two or more persons from different departments to sign out the key.

Robbery Taking something of value from a person using force, fear, or threat of force.

ROI Acronym for return on investment.

Roll call Occurs at the start of every hospitality security shift where important information is passed on, and training and a roll call is conducted to determine who is present.

Rubbernecking The method criminals use to constantly look around to detect if anyone is watching them or is aware of their activities.

S

Safety committee A committee usually championed by the leader of the Hospitality Security Department that takes a proactive approach to reducing accidents, ensuring safety standards are practiced by employees, and that safety hazards are identified and corrected.

Security Operations Center Hospitality security operational area where dispatchers receive calls; monitor radios; monitor emergency alarm systems; and coordinate, orchestrate, and prioritize hospitality security detail assignments.

SoD Acronym for separation of duties—also referred to as segregation of duties. It is a security principle utilized to prevent fraud, errors. or theft by one individual. An example is when key reconciliation is conducted at the change of shift by two separate members of the hospitality security team.

Silent alarm A remote alarm activated without bells, horns, etc.

Smoke detector A detector that responds to invisible or visible particles of combustion.

Spoofing Any technique that allows for an intruder to pass through a sensor's detection zone without generating an alarm by tricking or fooling its detection system.

Stages of Fire Incipient, smoldering, flame and heat.

Subpoena A request for a person to appear in court or other legal proceedings.

Supervisory alarm system Monitors conditions and signals any deviation from an established norm.

Surveillance The observation of person(s), activities, places, or things, to answering who, what, when, where, why, and how.

T

Tabletop exercise A narrative discussion pertaining to a simulated emergency or crisis scenario where responses, procedures, and policies are discussed.

Ten-codes Brevity codes used by hospitality security to represent phrases, incidents, etc. For example, 10-4 is usually translated to mean the following: message received, affirmative, ok, understood.

Theory X Theory put forth by McGregor with assumptions that employees dislike work, avoid work, have little ambition, and must be coerced to get work done.

Theory Y Theory put forth by McGregor with assumptions that employees find work to be a source of satisfaction, seek responsibility, are creative, and self-motivating.

Tort An act, or failure to act, that wrongly causes harm to someone.

Trouble signal A visual or audible indication of equipment failure, fault condition, or operational malfunction. Indicates trouble of any nature, including opening or breaking of an electrical circuit and possible system failure.

Two-way radio A radio that can transmit and receive. Type of radio used by the Hospitality Security Department.

U

Unrestricted key Are generally non-money-related keys. Usually only requires one person to sign for key.

UPS acronym for uninterruptible power supply. A secondary power source which supplies power to a generator or system for the continued operation of a property during a power failure.

Uttering When a person knowingly passes a check that has insufficient funds to cover the check.

V

Vicariously liable An employer is liable for actions committed by an employee when the employee is acting within the scope of employment.

W

Water flow alarm An electronic sensor that detects water flow in a sprinkler piping system and causes an alarm condition.

Z

Zero-based budgeting Budget starts at a zero base. All items added to the budget must be analyzed for its needs and costs.

APPENDIX B

GLOSSARY OF FORMS

HOSPITALITY SECURITY DEPARTMENT RADIO LOG

RADIO #	ISSUED/RETURNED BY	OUT	IN	RADIO #	ISSUED/RETURNED BY	OUT	IN
1				41			
2				42			
3				43			
4				44			
5				45			
6				46			
7				47			
8				48			
9				49			
10				50			
11				51			
12				52			
13				53			
14				54			
15				55			
16				56			
17				57			
18				58			
19				59			
20				60			
21				61			
22				62			
23				63			
24				64			
25				65			
26				66			
27				67			
28				68			
29				69			
30				70			
31				71			
32				72			
33				73			
34				74			
35				75			
36				76			
37				77			
38				78			
39				79			
40				80			

SHIFT: ____________________ DATE: ____________________

HOSPITALITY - SECURITY LEADER - PRINT NAME / ID #: ______________________________

HOSPITALITY - SECURITY LEADER - SIGNATURE: ______________________________

HOSPITALITY SECURITY DEPARTMENT RADIO REPAIR LOG

RADIO #	REASON	DELIVERED BY	RECEIVED BY	DATE OUT	DATE IN

HOSPITALITY SECURITY DEPARTMENT
Vendor / Visitor Log

Date Out	Time Out	Badge # Issued to Vendor/Visitor	Issuing Hospitality Security Representative	ID #	Visitor/Vendor (Print Name)	Visitor/Vendor (Signature)	Vendor Company	Property Contact Person	Date In	Time In	Receiving Hospitality Security Representative	ID #

HOSPITALITY SECURITY DEPARTMENT EARLY OUT LOG

Circle one: (DAY SWING GRAVE)

______ / ______ /20______ thru ______ / ______ /20______

NAME	MON	TUES	WED	THURS	FRI	SAT	SUN	TOTAL

TOTAL HOURS								

HOSPITALITY SECURITY DEPARTMENT SHIFT ACTIVITY LOG

DATE:______________ SHIFT: DAY SWING GRAVE (*CIRCLE ONE*)

TIME	DESCRIPTION OF ACTIVITIES	INITIALS

HOSPITALITY SECURITY REPRESENTATIVE: ______________________________

(Print Name and ID #)

HOSPITALITY SECURITY REPRESENTIVE SIGNATURE: ______________________

HOSPITALITY SECURITY LEADER: ______________________________________

(Print Name and ID #)

HOSPITALITY SECURITY LEADER SIGNATURE: ___________________________

HOSPITALITY SECURITY DEPARTMENT KEY INVENTORY

Date: ___________________________

Circle Shift: DAY SWING GRAVE

Key #		# of Keys	Start	End	Comments	
1						
2						
3						
4						
5						
6						
7						
8						
9						
10						
11						
12						
13						
14						
15						
16						
17						
18						
19						
20						
21						
22						
23						
24						
25						
26						
27						
28						
29						
30						
31						
32						
33						
34						
35						
36						
37						
38						
39						

____

Out-going Hospitality Security Leader Signature / Identification Number:

____

In-coming Hospitality Security Leader Signature / Identification Number:

HOSPITALITY SECURITY DEPARTMENT KEY LOG

All keys must be issued and received by a member of the Hospitality Security Department

Date	Time	Key issued - Print name	Signature	ID#	Issued by - Signature	ID #	Date	Time	Key returned - Print name	Signature	ID #	Key received - Signature	ID #

HOSPITALITY SECURITY DEPARTMENT - KEY REQUEST / TRACKING FORM

HR USE ONLY
Name
Signature
Employee # Date
HR places copy of this document in employee's personnel file.

Date: ____________

Person Requesting Key(s): ______________________ **Identification #:** ________

Number Keys Needed: _____ **Job Title:** ______________

Reason Key(s) Needed: ______________ **Is the Key for Personal Use? YES ____ NO ____**

Does the Key need to be placed in the Electronic Key System? YES ____ NO ____

______________________ ______________________

Department Leader or designee – Signature and ID # **Hospitality Security Department Leader – Signature and ID #**

Upon approval, return this form to a member of the Hospitality Security leadership team. A Hospitality Security leader will contact you when the key(s) is ready. If new keys are made the following must be completed:

Date request received by Hospitality Security Department: ________ **Received By:** ______________

A member of the Hospitality Security leadership team must complete the following.

Key Stamp Number: ________ **Key Name:** ____________ **Access Level:** (CIRCLE ONE) **Single Double Triple**

Key Ring Number: ________ **Date Entered:** ____________

Hospitality Security Leader Signature: ______________________________

If key(s) are to be made - attach the above requested key information with appropriate number of blank keys.

Date: ________ **Received Blanks:** ________

Employee Signature and Identification #: ______________________________

Keys made by: Employee Name and Identification #: ______________________________

Date returned to Hospitality Security Department: ____________

Hospitality Security Leader: ______________________________

PRINT NAME – PROVIDE SIGNATURE AND IDENTIFICATION NUMBER

The following is to be completed by a member of the Hospitality Security leadership team when keys are issued:
Date Key(s) Issued: ________

Hospitality Security Leader: ______________________________

PRINT NAME – PROVIDE SIGNATURE AND IDENTIFICATION NUMBER

Key Issuer: ______________________________

PRINT NAME – PROVIDE SIGNATURE AND IDENTIFICATION NUMBER

The following must be completed by a member of the Hospitality Security leadership team when keys are returned: (Circle one)

Reason key(s) returned: Broken Promotion Replacement Termination Other ______________

Key(s) returned by: ______________ **Date key(s) returned to Hospitality Security Leader:** ________

Key(s) received by Hospitality Security Leader: ______________________________

PRINT NAME – PROVIDE SIGNATURE AND IDENTIFICATION NUMBER

PROPERTY CLEARANCE FORM

NAME / ID #: ______________________ **POSITION:** ______________ **DATE:** __________

QUANITITY AND DESCRIPTION OF ITEMS:

____

____

____

____

DEPARTMENT LEADER - NAME SIGNATURE AND IDENTIFICATION NUMBER

____

HOSPITALITY SECURITY REPRESENTATIVE - NAME SIGNATURE AND IDENTIFICATION NUMBER

---------- *(COPY 1 – HOSPITALITY SECURITY)* ----------

NAME / ID #: ______________________ **POSITION:** ______________ **DATE:** __________

QUANITITY AND DESCRIPTION OF ITEMS:

____

____

____

____

DEPARTMENT LEADER - NAME SIGNATURE AND IDENTIFICATION NUMBER

____

HOSPITALITY SECURITY REPRESENTATIVE - NAME SIGNATURE AND IDENTIFICATION NUMBER

---------- *(COPY 2 – EMPLOYEE)* ----------

NAME / ID #: ______________________ **POSITION:** ______________ **DATE:** __________

QUANITITY AND DESCRIPTION OF ITEMS:

____

____

____

____

DEPARTMENT LEADER - NAME SIGNATURE AND IDENTIFICATION NUMBER

____

HOSPITALITY SECURITY REPRESENTATIVE - NAME SIGNATURE AND IDENTIFICATION NUMBER

---------- *(COPY 3 – DEPARTMENTAL LEADER)* ----------

TEMPORARY IDENTIFICATION BADGE REQUEST FORM

DATE: ______________________ TIME: ______________________

FOR HOSPITALITY SECURITY USE ONLY:	
TEMPORARY I.D. BADGE NUMBER:	ISSUED TO:

NAME: ______________________ IDENTIFICATION #: ______________________

POSITION: ______________________ DEPARTMENT: ______________________

____

LEADER SIGNATURE AND ID # OF EMPLOYEE RECEIVING TEMPORARY BADGE:

DEPARTMENT: ____

DAY SWING GRAVE

______________________ ____________ ______________________

ISSUED BY HOSPITALITY SECURITY REPRESENTATIVE (PRINT NAME) | DATE | SHIFT (circle one)

TOTAL BADGES ISSUED: ______________________

____

HOSPITALITY SECURITY REPRESENTATIVE SIGNATURE AND IDENTIFICATION #

Hospitality Security Department Pass-On of Information

Date: ______________________

To: **Hospitality Security Leaders**

From: ______________________

Subject: ______________________________

Information:

____

____

____

____

____

____

Comments:

____

____

____

ID Number	Initial	Date

SECURITY LOST AND FOUND FORM

Lost ______ Found______ Date/Time Occurred: ______________ Date/Time Reported: _______________

PERSON WHO LOST ITEM(S)

Name: ____

Home Address: ____

Cell Phone Number: ________________________ Alternate Telephone Number: ________________________

Location Item Last Seen: ____

DETAILED DESCRIPTION OF ITEM(S)

____

____

Reporting Security Personnel Signature ________________________________

PERSON WHO FOUND ITEM(S)

Name: ____

Home Address: ____

Cell Phone Number: __________________________ Alternate Telephone Number: _______________________

Recovery Location of Item(s) _______________________________________

Reporting Security Personnel Signature ________________________________

DETAILED DESCRIPTION OF ITEM(S)

____

____

Reporting Security Personnel Signature ________________________________

PERSON CLAIMING LOST/ FOUND ITEM(S)

Name: ____

Date/Time: ____

Home Address: ____

Person Claiming Item(s) ____

Photo ID Type: Driver's License Number _____________________________________ State__________

Other Type of Photo ID: Description: _______________ ID # ______________________________________

Reporting Security Personnel Signature ________________________________

SHIFT (Circle one) DAY SWING GRAVE **HOSPITALITY SECURITY SAFETY TOUR CHECKLIST Date ______**

Location	Checkpoint #	Remarks
	1	
	2	
	3	
	4	
	5	
	6	
	7	
	8	
	9	
	10	
	11	
	12	
	13	
	14	
	15	
	16	
	17	
	18	
	19	
	20	
	21	
	22	
	23	
	24	
	25	
	26	
	27	
	28	
	29	
	30	
	31	
	32	
	33	

NOTIFY THE SECURITY OPERATIONS CENTER OF ALL DISCREPANCIES

Include checks of the following: Torn carpeting, unsecured doors, wet floor surfaces, egress obstructions.
Include inspections of the following: Exit signage, high volume areas, fire extinguisher gauge levels.

______________________________ ______________________________

Print name and ID # - Hospitality Security Representative Signature

______________________________ ______________________________

Print name and ID# - Hospitality Security Leader Representative Signature

HOSPITALITY SECURITY - VEHICLE RELOCATION LOG

DATE	TIME	MAKE	MODEL	COLOR	LICENSE PLATE	LOCATION	RELOCATED TO	REASON	AUTHORIZED BY

HOSPITALITY SECURITY - VEHICLE TOW LOG

DATE	TIME	MAKE	MODEL	COLOR	LICENSE PLATE	LOCATION	TOWED TO	REASON	AUTHORIZED BY

HOSPITALITY SECURITY DEPARTMENT ALARM CHECKLIST

LOCATION	DATE	TIME	ALARM WORKING YES/ NO	HOSPITALITY SECURITY REPRESENTATIVE	COMMENTS	TIME ALARM ACTIVATED	TIME ALARM RESET

Print name and ID # of Hospitality Security Representative

Signature

Print name and ID# of Hospitality Security Leadership Repersentative

Signature

HOSPITALITY SECURITY DEPARMENT

FIRE DRILL EVALUATION FORM

Department: ______________________________ Location: ____________________

Date: ____________ Time Started: __________ Time Ended: ________________

Details and Results:

____
____
____
____
____
____
____
____
____
____
____

Participants complete the following:

Print Name	**Identification #**	**Signature**

___________________________________ ___________________________________

Hospitality Security Department Evaluator (Print Name and Identification Number)

Hospitality Security Department Evaluator (Signature)

HOSPITALITY SECURITY DEPARTMENT FIRE EXTINGUISHER INSPECTION FORM

INSPECTION DATE	LOCATION	EXTINGUISHER IDENTIFICATION	INSPECTED YES or NO	USED YES or NO	REPLACED YES or NO	HOSPITALITY SECURITY ID #

HOSPITALITY SECURITY REPRESENTATIVE PRINT NAME AND IDENTIFICATION NUMBER

HOSPITALITY SECURITY REPRESENTATIVE SIGNATURE

HOSPITALITY SECURITY DEPARTMENT – FIRE COMMAND INCIDENT REPORT

Incident Report Number:	**Date:**
	Time:

Fire Department Involvement: Circle – Yes or No **Ambulance:** Circle – Yes or No

TYPE of INCIDENT: Circle one – Fire Alarm Malfunction Other

If Other – please explain: ______________________________

LOCATION: ______________________________

TYPE of ALARM: Circle one – Smoke detector Pull station Heat detector Water flow

Duct detector Other **If Other - please explain:** ______________________________

Summary Report:

____
____
____
____
____
____
____
____
____
____
____
____
____
____
____
____

HOSPITALITY SECURITY REPRESENTATIVE (PRINT NAME)	IDENTIFICATION #	DATE	HOSPITALITY SECURITY REPRESENTATIVE: (SIGNATURE)

REVIEWED BY: HOSPITALITY SECURITY LEADER: (PRINT NAME)	IDENTIFICATION #	HOSPITALITY SECURITY LEADER (SIGNATURE)

HOSPITALITY SECURITY DEPARTMENT
LIFE SAFETY SYSTEMS
IMPAIRMENT NOTIFICATION FORM

This form must be submitted to the Security Operations Center any time that the function of any Life Safety System component will be disabled. At the end of shift, the life safety system must be restored to full operation; and this impairment notice must be closed-out by a member of the hospitality security leadership team.

DATE: ______________________________

NAME:______________________________

COMPANY:______________________________

EMERGENCY CONTACT NUMBER: ______________________________

TYPE OF IMPAIRMENT: (Please circle the type of impairment)
Fire Alarm System
Fire Protection System
Other (describe) ______________________________

SYSTEMS TO BE TAKEN OUT OF SERVICE: (Please circle type of impairment listed below)

Central Station Dialer   Fire Alarm Initiation   Fire Alarm Evacuation Signals   Smoke Exhaust

Fire Pump   Sprinkler Zone__________   Generator   Other (describe) ____________________

DURATION:

Estimated Time Out: ______________________________

Estimated Restoration Time: ______________________________

REASON: ______________________________

____

____

____

LIFE SAFETY SYSTEM OUT OF SERVICE

____
Hospitality Security Representatvie - Print Name & ID #

____
Hospitality Security Representatvie Signature

LIFE SAFETY SYSTEM RESTORED

____
Hospitality Security Representatvie - Print Name & ID #

____
Hospitality Security Representatvie Signature

FIRE WATCH

A fire watch is the action of an on-site person whose sole responsibility is to watch for the occurrence of fire.

FIRE WATCH REQUIREMENTS

When a required fire protection system is out of service for more than 4 hours in a 24-hour period, the authority having jurisdiction will be notified, and the building will be evacuated **OR** an approved fire watch will be implemented for all areas left unprotected until the fire protection system has been returned to service.

A fire watch should involve some special action beyond normal staffing, additional personnel who are specially trained in fire prevention should be assigned to walk the affected areas.

FIRE WATCH DUTIES

Periodic patrols of the affected areas and facility should be conducted.

Direct communication with the Fire Department, i.e., telephone.

Identify any life, fire or property hazards.

If an emergency situation is discovered, notify 9-1-1 with the exact address and type of emergency.

If facility needs to be evacuated, notify the occupants.

Maintain a log of fire watch activities.

Knowledge of location and use of fire protection equipment, i.e., fire extinguishers.

Fire watch personnel cannot have other duties.

Fire watch personnel will not perform fire-fighting duties beyond the scope of an ordinary citizen.

RECORD KEEPING

A fire watch log will be maintained at the facility. The log must be available to the Fire Department at all-times during the fire watch. The fire watch log should contain the following:

- Address of facility, name of the person conducting the fire watch, times that each patrol was completed.
- Communications to the Fire Department and monitoring company.
- Any other information as directed by the Fire Department.

CANCELLATION OF FIRE WATCH

Once the fire protection system has been fully restored, it is the responsibility of a member of the Hospitality Security leadership team to ensure that the fire watch is cancelled and that all of the proper notifications, including notification to the Fire Department and monitoring company has occurred.

HOSPITALITY SECURITY DEPARTMENT - FIRE WATCH LOG

DATE:		ADDRESS:
Time Patrol Completed	**Person on Watch**	**Comments**

______________________________________ ____________________

Print name & ID # of Hospitality Security Representative — Signature

______________________________________ ____________________

Print name & ID # of Hospitality Security Leadership Representative — Signature

Page ___ of ___

DATE: __________ TIME: __________

HOSPITALITY SECURITY DEPARTMENT
EMERGENCY NOTIFICATION FORM

INCIDENT #: __________

BRIEF DESCRIPTION OF EMERGENCY: ______________________________

EMERGENCY NOTIFICATIONS WILL BE MADE FOR THE FOLLOWING INCIDENTS:

- BIO, CHEMICAL, SUSPICIOUS SUBSTANCE INCIDENT
- BOMB THREATS, EVACUATIONS, GENERAL FIRE ALARM
- CRITICAL MEDICAL RESPONSE INCIDENTS, (CPR, AED USAGE, FIRST AID, ETC.)
- MAJOR CRIMES, (ROBBERIES, AGGRAVATED ASSAULTS, CRIMES COMMITTED WITH WEAPONS, ETC.)
- CRIMES RESULTING IN THE INJURY OF PATRONS OR EMPLOYEES
- POLICE OR FIRE PERSONNEL ON SITE RESPONDING TO INCIDENTS SERIOUS IN NATURE
- SEVERE PROPERTY DAMAGE/FLOODING/HAZARDOUS CONDITIONS/ETC.
- DEATHS, SUICIDE, HOMICIDE, HOSTAGE SITUATION, JUMPER INCIDENT, SERIOUS INJURY SUSTAINED BY PATRON OR EMPLOYEE, ETC.
- INFORMATION RECEIVED FROM LAW ENFORCEMENT INDICATING THERE IS A CREDIBLE, SPECIFIC OR IMPENDING THREAT.

THE INDIVIDUALS LISTED BELOW MUST BE CONTACTED FOR ANY OF THE ABOVE EMERGENCY SITUATIONS

NAME	EXT.	CELL	CONTACTED BY (INTIAL & ID #)	TIME
SECURITY LEADER	______	______________	______________	__________
GENERAL MANAGER	______	______________	______________	__________
MANAGER ON DUTY	______	______________	______________	__________
FIRE COMMAND CENTER	______	______________	______________	__________
SECURITY OPS CENTER	______	______________	______________	__________
FACILITIES LEADER	______	______________	______________	__________
OPERATIONS LEADER	______	______________	______________	__________
POLICE DEPARTMENT	______	______________	______________	__________
FIRE DEPARTMENT	______	______________	______________	__________

A MEMBER OF THE HOSPITALITY SECURITY LEADERSHIP TEAM WILL DETERMINE IF ANY OF THE FOLLOWING NEED TO BE NOTIFIED:

DEPARTMENT	EXTENSION	CELL PHONE NUMBER	NOTIFIED BY (INTIALS AND ID #)	TIME
IT LEADER	______	______________	______________	__________
RISK MGT.LEADER	______	______________	______________	__________
HUMAN RESOURCE LEADER	______	______________	______________	__________

HOSPITALITY SECURITY REPRESENTATIVE (PRINT) ______________________________

SIGNATURE: ______________________________ ID#__________

REVIEWED BY MEMBER OF HOSPITALITY SECURITY LEADERSHIP TEAM: (PRINT)______________

SIGNATURE: ______________________________ ID #__________

HOSPITALITY SECURITY SHIFT SUMMARY REPORT

Shift: (Please circle one) Day Shift Swing Shift Grave Shift

Date:

HOSPITALITY SECURITY LEADERS:

-
-
-
-
-

INCIDENTS:

-
-
-
-

PASS ON INFORMATION FOR UPCOMING SHIFTS:

-
-
-

ROLL CALL NOTES:

-
-

ATTENDANCE: (Absent / Late)

-
-

HOSPITALITY SECURITY DEPARTMENT STAFFING LEVELS

Staffing Levels	Day Shift		Swing Shift		Grave Shift		
Post Assignment	Mon-Fri **1**	Sat-Sun **2**	Sun-Thur **1**	Fri-Sat **2**	Sun-Thur **1**	Fri-Sat **2**	

	Day Shift		Swing Shift		Grave Shift		TOTAL
TOTAL							
Hours per day							
Hours per week							
FTE Total per week							
FTE = Total hours / 40							
TOTAL							
Hours per day							
Hours per week							
FTE Total per week							

Hospitality Security Department - Earthquake Documentation of Event Form

Section I

	Date	Time
• When did the earthquake impact the property?	______	______
• When were property operations stopped as a result of the earthquake?	______	______
• When did the property lose power?	______	______
• When did the property commence the use of backup power/generator power?	______	______
• When was electrical power restored?	______	______
• When was the use of back up/generator power discontinued?	______	______
• When did the property return back to normal operations after the Earthquake?	______	______

Section II

Please attach information regarding any of the following to this form.

- Restricted access to the property and the cause. Causes may include power line, trees, road blocks, etc.
- Damage sustained to property caused by event and the estimated repair or replacement costs.
- Expenses that were incurred to reopen the property.
- List all earthquake related spoiled food losses with documentation.
- Payroll that was incurred as a result of all team members who worked as a result of the earthquake. List function performed by those who worked i.e., Security of property, maintenance of property, repairs to property, reopening duties, etc.
- Provide documentation of any significant activities or events not listed above.
- When possible, please include photos, receipts, time slips etc., to substantiate claims.
- Return completed form, attach items listed above including any other pertinent information that may aid in explaining any damages or losses that the property sustained to a member of the Finance leadership team.

Prepared by:	Received by:
______________________________	______________________________
Print Name and ID #	Print Name and ID #
______________________________	______________________________
Signature	Signature
______________________________	______________________________
Date	Date

Hospitality Security Department -Tornado Documentation of Event Form

Section I

	Date	Time
• When did the tornado impact the property?	_______	______
• When were property operations stopped as a result of the tornado?	_______	______
• When did the property lose power?	_______	______
• When did the property commence the use of backup power/generator power?	_______	______
• When was electrical power restored?	_______	______
• When was the use of backup/generator power discontinued?	_______	______
• When did the property return back to normal operations after the tornado made land fall?	_______	______

Section II

Please attach information regarding any of the following to this form.

- Restricted access to the property and the cause. Causes may include power line, trees, road blocks, etc.
- Damage sustained to the property caused by event and the estimated repair or replacement costs.
- Expenses that were incurred to reopen the property.
- List all tornado related spoiled food losses with documentation.
- Payroll that was incurred as a result of all team members who worked during the tornado. List function performed by those who worked, i.e., Security of property, maintenance of property, repairs to property, reopening duties, etc.
- Provide documentation of any significant activities or events not listed above.
- When possible, please include photos, receipts, time slips etc., to substantiate claims.
- Return completed form, attach items listed above including any other pertinent information that may aid in explaining any damages or losses that the property sustained to a member of the Finance leadership team.

Prepared by:	Received by:
______________________________	______________________________
Print Name	Print Name
______________________________	______________________________
Signature	Signature
______________________________	______________________________
Date	Date

Hospitality Security Department - Hurricane/Tropical Documentation of Event Form

Section I

	Date	Time
• When did the hurricane/tropical cyclone impact the property?	_______	______
• When were property operations stopped as a result of the hurricane/tropical cyclone?	_______	______
• When did the property lose power?	_______	______
• When did the property commence the use of backup power/generator power?	_______	______
• When was electrical power restored?	_______	______
• When was the use of backup/generator power discontinued?	_______	______
• When did the property return back to normal operations after the hurricane/tropical cyclone made land fall?	_______	______

Section II

Please attach information regarding any of the following to this form:

- Restricted access to the property and the cause. Causes may include power line, trees, road blocks, etc.
- Damage sustained to property caused by event and the estimated repair or replacement costs.
- Expenses that were incurred to reopen the property.
- List all hurricane/tropical cyclone related spoiled food losses with documentation.
- Payroll that was incurred as a result of all team members who worked during the hurricane/tropical cyclone. List function performed by those who worked, i.e., Security of property, maintenance of property, repairs to property, reopening duties, etc.
- Provide documentation of any significant activities or events not listed above.
- When possible, please include photos, receipts, time slips etc., to substantiate claims.
- Return completed form, attach items listed above including any other pertinent information that may aid in explaining any damages or losses that the property sustained to a member of the Finance leadership team.

Prepared by:	Received by:
______________________	______________________
Print Name	Print Name
______________________	______________________
Signature	Signature
______________________	______________________
Date	Date

HOSPITALITY SECURITY DEPARTMENT EMPLOYEE REFERRAL

Do you wish to remain anonymous? Please place an "x" in the appropriate area. ( ) Yes ( ) No.
If yes, please do not provide any of the following employee information.
If no, please provide the following employee information.

EMPLOYEE providing referral: ______________________________
(PRINT NAME)

Position: ______________________________ **Department:** ______________________

Identification number: __________________ **Phone (____)** ______________________________

PERSON OF INTEREST: ______________________________
(PRINT NAME)

Position: ______________________________ **Department:** ______________________

Location: ______________________________ **( ) Observed ( ) Rumor ( ) Admitted**

INFORMATION RELATING TO CONCERN

Please describe exactly what you observed, information you were told or rumors you heard relating to this referral. When possible, please include the following: who, what, when, where, why, and how.

____

____

____

____

____

____

____

____

____

____

____

______________________	______________________	________	________
Signature of Employee Providing Information	Print Name	Date	Time

Page ____ of ____

HOSPITALITY SECURITY DEPARTMENT
EMPLOYEE REFERRAL - CONTINUATION PAGE

____

____

____

____

____

____

____

____

____

____

____

____

____

____

____

____

____

____

____

____

____

____

____

____

Signature of Person Providing Statement	Print Name	Date	Time

Page ____ of ____

HOSPITALITY SECURITY DEPARTMENT
EMPLOYEE WITNESS STATEMENT

This is the statement of: ______________________________
(PRINT NAME)

Address ______________________________ **City:** ____________________

State: ______________ **Zip Code:** ______________ **Phone (____)** ____________________

Identification Number: ____________ **Date of Hire:** ____________ **Department:** ______________

Date of Incident: __________ **Time of Incident:** ________ **Location of Incident:** ______________

STATEMENT

Please describe exactly what you observed relating to the incident. When possible, please answer the following: who, what, when, where, why and how.

____

____

____

____

____

____

____

____

____

____

____

____

____

____

____

____

Signature of Person Providing Statement	Print Name	Date	Time

Page ____ of ____

HOSPITALITY SECURITY DEPARTMENT EMPLOYEE WITNESS STATEMENT - CONTINUATION PAGE

____

____

____

____

____

____

____

____

____

____

____

____

____

____

____

____

____

____

____

____

____

____

____

____

Signature of Person Providing Statement	Print Name	Date	Time

Page 1 of ____

HOSPITALITY SECURITY DEPARTMENT
VOLUNTARY STATEMENT

This is the statement of: ____
(PRINT NAME)

Business Address ________________________________ **Phone (____)** ______________

Home Address __________________________________ **Phone (____)** ______________

1) I, ____, voluntarily make the

2) following statement to __________________________________, who has been identified

3) as a Hospitality Security Representative for ________________________________.

4) No threats or promises have been made to induce me to make this voluntary declaration, which I acknowledge

5) is made of my free will.

6) ____

7) ____

8) ____

9) ____

10) ____

11) ____

12) ____

13) ____

14) ____

15) ____

16) ____

17) ____

18) ____

19) ____

20) ____

21) ____

Signature of Person Giving Statement	Print Name	Date	Time
Signature of Person Taking Statement	Print Name	Date	Time

Page ____ of ____

HOSPITALITY SECURITY DEPARTMENT
VOLUNTARY STATEMENT

Statement of ____
(PRINT NAME)

1) ____
2) ____
3) ____
4) ____
5) ____
6) ____
7) ____
8) ____
9) ____
10) ____
11) ____
12) ____
13) ____
14) ____
15) ____
16) ____
17) ____
18) ____
19) ____
20) ____
21) ____
22) ____
23) ____
24) ____
25) ____

______________________	______________________	________	________
Signature of Person Giving Statement	Print Name	Date	Time
______________________	______________________	________	________
Signature of Person Taking Statement	Print Name	Date	Time

Page ____ of ____

HOSPITALITY SECURITY DEPARTMENT
VOLUNTARY STATEMENT

Statement of ____
(PRINT NAME)

1) ____

2) ____

3) ____

4) ____

5) ____

6) ____

7) ____

8) ____

9) ____

10) ____

11) ____

12) ____

I have written, read and understand the above ______ lines and declare, under knowing the penalty of perjury, that they are true and correct. I (have) (have not) requested representation.
(Circle one of the above)

Signed at	____________	____________	____________
	City	County	State
Date:	____________	____________	____________
	Day	Month	Year

____________	____________	______	______
Signature of Person Giving Statement	Print Name	Date	Time
____________	____________	______	______
Signature of Person Taking Statement	Print Name	Date	Time
____________	____________	______	______
Signature of Witness (if applicable)	Print Name	Date	Time

HOSPITALITY SECURITY DEPARTMENT
LOCKER INSPECTION FORM

LOCKER #: ____________

DATE & TIME LOCK REMOVED ______________________________

DETAILED DESCRIPTION OF ITEMS REMOVED:

1. ____
2. ____
3. ____
4. ____
5. ____
6. ____
7. ____
8. ____
9. ____
10. ____
11. ____
12. ____

HOSPITALITY SECURITY REPRESENTATIVE

PRINT NAME AND ID #: ______________________________________

SIGNATURE: ____

WITNESS PRINT NAME AND ID #: ______________________________

SIGNATURE: ____

DEPARTMENT AND TITLE: ____________________________________

IT IS REQUIRED THAT A MEMBER OF THE HOSPITALITY SECURITY LEADERSHIP TEAM AND ANOTHER TEAM MEMBER FROM HUMAN RESOURCES—OR SECURITY—WITNESS THE REMOVAL OF ANY LOCK AND THE RECORDING OF CONTENTS REMOVED FROM THE LOCKER.

~ATTACH THIS FORM TO THE INCIDENT REPORT~

HOSPITALITY SECURITY DEPARTMENT EVIDENCE CHAIN OF CUSTODY FORM

____________	____________	____________	____________
Report #	Date and Time of Incident	Type of Incident	Date and Time of Recovery
____________	____________	____________	____________
Suspect	Victim	Location of Recovery	Item Recovered By

List Quantity and Description of Each Item:

1.____

2.____

3.____

4.____

5.____

6.____

7.____

I acknowledge that the above represents all items taken from my possession and that I have received a copy of this receipt.

____________________	____________________
Print Name and Identification Number	Signature

I acknowledge that the above represents all items received by me as Hospitality Security Department representative and that these items have been retained as evidence.

____________________	____________________
Print Name and Identification Number	Signature

Received By	*Reason*	*Date/Time Received*	*Date/Time Returned*
____________	____________	____________	____________
Received By	*Reason*	*Date/Time Received*	*Date/Time Returned*
____________	____________	____________	____________
Received By	*Reason*	*Date/Time Received*	*Date/Time Returned*
____________	____________	____________	____________
Received By	*Reason*	*Date/Time Received*	*Date/Time Returned*
____________	____________	____________	____________

DEPARTMENTAL BOMB THREAT CHECKLIST

Immediately notify the Hospitality Security Operations Center by telephone (**DIAL** ____________) when receiving any sort of bomb threat. If possible, utilize and complete the following:

Date and Time Reported: ______________________________

(Note telephone digital displays if applicable, for call origin)

Exact words of caller/informer: ______________________________

____

____

Ask the caller the following questions:

- When is the bomb going to explode? ______________________________
- Where is the bomb located? ______________________________
- What type of bomb is it? ______________________________
- What does the bomb look like? ______________________________
- What will cause the bomb to explode? ______________________________
- What is your address? ______________________________
- What is your name? ______________________________
- What phone number are you calling from? ______________________________
- Why did you plant the bomb? ______________________________

Description of caller's voice:

Male: __________ Female: __________ Young: __________ Middle Age: __________Older: __________

Accent:____________________Tone of Voice: ______________________________

Background Noise: ______________________________

Remarks: (familiar voice characteristics, etc.) ______________________________

Did the caller provide any special instructions? ______________________________

____

Time caller hung up: ________________ Time Security Department Notified: ________________

HOSPITALITY SECURITY DEPARTMENT BOMB SEARCH ASSIGNMENTS

ZONE	LOCATION	ASSIGNED TO	SEARCH RESULTS
1			
2			
3			
4			
5			
6			
7			

Hospitality Security Leader: ______________________________

Name and ID #

Hospitality Security Leader: ______________________________

Signature

HOSPITALITY SECURITY DEPARTMENT
ATTEMPTED ROBBERY / ROBBERY – SUSPECT DESCRIPTION

Time of Incident: __________ Location of Incident: ____________________________

Number Involved: Male: ____ Female: _____ Route of Escape: ____________________

Approximate Height: _____ Approximate Weight: _______ Approximate Age: _______

Vehicle Description: Year: _______ Make: ______________ Model: _____________

Plate #: ______________ Color: __________ Damage: ________ Other: __________

General Information and Description of Suspect

(Please Circle)

Method of Escape: Foot Car Truck Bicycle Motorcycle Other _______________

Weapon Used: No / Yes – Handgun Rifle Shotgun Knife Club Other _______

Male / Female: White Black Spanish Oriental Other ______________________

Body Type: Small Average Large Distinguishing Features: __________________

Glasses: No / Yes – Wire Frame Plastic Frame Other: __________ Color: ________

Eyes: Blue Brown Hazel Green Black Gray Other: ___________________

Hair Color: Brown Black Blonde Red Gray Other: ____________________

Hair Length: Short Medium Long Shoulder-Length Other: ________________

Hair Type: Straight Curly Bald Other: ______________________________

Facial Features: Beard Mustache Goatee Acne Clean Shaven Other: ________

Identifiers: Accent Scars Tattoos Deformities Other: _______________

Please explain and provide description of any identifiers:

____

____

____

____

Description of property stolen: ______________________________

____

____

____

______________________________ ______________________________

Print Name Signature and Identification #

HOSPITALITY SECURITY DEPARTMENT INCIDENT REPORT

TYPE OF INCIDENT	DATE	TIME	CASE #
LOCATION OF INCIDENT			
CIRCLE ONE - VICTIM COMPLAINANT SUSPECT	SEX	HT.	WT.	D.O.B.
NAME	PHONE NUMBER		
ADDRESS			
(1) WITNESS NAME:	(2) WITNESS NAME:		
ADDRESS	ADDRESS		
NARRATIVE (ANSWER WHO, WHAT, WHEN, WHERE, WHY & HOW)			

HOSPITALITY SECURITY REPRESENTATIVE: (PRINT NAME)	IDENTIFICATION #	DATE	HOSPITALITY SECURITY REPRESENTATIVE (SIGNATURE)

REVIEWED BY: HOSPITALITY SECURITY LEADER (PRINT NAME)	IDENTIFICATION #	HOSPITALITY SECURITY LEADER SIGNATURE

Hospitality Security - Guest Room Noise Complaint Log

Date	Room #	1st Complaint Time	2nd Complaint Time	3rd Complaint Time	Removal Time	Hospitality Security Leader Involved

INDEX

K

L

M

N

O

P

R

CPSIA information can be obtained
at www.ICGtesting.com
Printed in the USA
LVHW061907090820
662765LV00025B/730

9 781793 512543